UNDER
THE
HENFLUENCE

UNDER THE HENFLUENCE:

INSIDE THE WORLD OF
BACKYARD CHICKENS
AND THE PEOPLE
WHO LOVE THEM

TOVE DANOVICH

A SURREY BOOK

AGATE

CHICAGO

First printed in March 2023

Printed in the United States of America

10 9 8 7 6 5 4 3 2 1   23 24 25 26 27

Library of Congress Cataloging-in-Publication Data

Names: Danovich, Tove, author.
Title: Under the henfluence : inside the world of backyard chickens and the
  people who love them / Tove Danovich.
Description: Chicago : Surrey Books, an imprint of Agate Publishing, [2023]
  | Includes index. | Summary: "An immersive blend of chicken-keeping
  memoir and animal welfare reporting by a journalist who accidentally
  became obsessed with her flock"-- Provided by publisher.
Identifiers: LCCN 2022043491 (print) | LCCN 2022043492 (ebook) | ISBN
  9781572843219 (hardcover) | ISBN 1572843217 (hardcover) | ISBN
  9781572848726 (ebook)
Subjects: LCSH: Chickens.
Classification: LCC SF487.3 .D36 2023 (print) | LCC SF487.3 (ebook) | DDC
  636.5--dc23/eng/20220923
LC record available at https://lccn.loc.gov/2022043491
LC ebook record available at https://lccn.loc.gov/2022043492

Cover design and illustrations by Morgan Krehbiel

Author photo by Jamie Bosworth

Surrey Books is an imprint of Agate Publishing. Agate books are available in bulk at discount prices. For more information, visit agatepublishing.com.

For my flock

TABLE OF CONTENTS

INTRODUCTION

WHEN I TOLD MY GRANDMA I WAS GETTING CHICKENS, THE FIRST thing she did was ask me how many.

"Three," I said proudly.

"Three?!" she repeated.

"Three!" I was sure that she was shocked by how amazing it was that I was adding so many chickens to my family.

Grandma laughed. "You can't just get three chickens," she finally said. "You have to get twenty-five—at *least*."

I tried to explain that things had changed since she last had chickens, that most people in cities often only had three to six because of local laws.

She scoffed, "I'll believe it when I see it."

"They're coming next week! I'll show you. Three is plenty."

Before my grandma was born, my great-grandma Gyda got a wedding present from her new husband. They lived on a farm in North Dakota where farm wives worked just as hard as the men, though they usually had no control of the household income besides what the "man of the house" deigned to give

1

them. Instead of an allowance, my great-grandfather and his brother, another newlywed with a farm nearby, cooked up the idea of building henhouses for their wives. The husbands would provide money for feed and chicks so the women could "raise as many chickens as they wanted," as my grandma recalls, and avoid one wife getting jealous of the other for having a bigger income. (It's unclear whether the women would have wanted to raise any chickens at all if given the option. But I digress.) My great-grandma kept white ducks and White Leghorn chickens that she sold to people in town. "She'd get orders and butcher them, and I would have to stand there holding them while they were bleeding to death," Grandma remembered almost fondly, a childhood memory that's slightly less common today.

This chicken money paid for my grandma's and great-uncle's piano and music lessons. Gyda, like other farm women in the early 1900s, sold chickens and eggs to city folk for cash or in exchange for credit at the local grocery store. In farm households, women's income was often called "egg money" because it so commonly came from raising chickens. It was treated as separate from *real* farm income even though it kept the family fed, clothed, and educated and paid for memorable items like musical instruments or class rings.[1]

That all started to change after World War II. Extension programs began to suggest men get involved in the chicken industry and modernize it.[2] Chicken farming had been looked down on as women's work but now was advertised to men as a good way to make a living. New production breeds were developed that gained weight faster or laid more eggs. Extension programs recommended chickens be raised in modern warehouses, where they were confined 24/7, rather than backyard coops like the one my great-grandmother used. Outside truly rural areas, a flock of chickens in the backyard became an oddity.

My family was proud enough of their farming roots and the old dairy they used to own that I always felt comfortable around farm animals and the realities of farming—at least the realities of how farming used to be. My grandma remembered her role in her mother's chicken business. A generation later, my mom and her sisters all told the same story about visiting the family dairy and having to hold the cows' tails during milking ("or else," their uncle warned them, miming a chopping motion to make the girls scream). I knew from a young age that everything on a farm had to have a purpose, whether it was the draft horses pulling heavy wagons or the chickens laying eggs. But we've lost touch with the bargain early farmers made with their animals—that these creatures would have easy, safe lives free from predators except for us humans.

Today, there's never been a worse time to be a chicken. Since 1992, Americans have eaten more chicken than any other meat (chicken became more popular than pork in 1985 and went on to wrest beef out of the number one spot a few years later).[3] In 2020, over nine billion of these birds were raised for eggs or meat on industrial farms in America alone.[4] (Globally the number is sixty-five billion.) More chickens are killed for food every year than there are people on the planet. By weight, 70 percent of all birds on the planet are the poultry that humans raise for food.[5] We've bred chickens to produce more eggs and grow faster. Some scientists have even dabbled with the idea of creating a meat chicken that never develops feathers just so we can save a step between slaughter and the grocery store. Broiler chickens, raised to gain weight quickly, are slaughtered before they're even two months old. If allowed to live a "natural" life, these birds' genetics are so unnatural that they often die from heart failure or become lame because their skeleton can't support their weight.

Chickens on industrial farms live their lives in cramped cages or perhaps in cage-free facilities, stuffed together on a dusty floor where at least they can spread their wings. The Humane Methods of Slaughter Act, passed in 1958, requires all animals be "rendered insensible to pain" before being shackled or killed—all animals except for poultry.

I was in middle school when I read about the realities of the meat industry for the first time. It was so different from Old MacDonald and the family farms that I'd heard stories of growing up. There were no childhood hijinks with the animals. No roosters chasing kids across the yard. In industrial farms, the only people who interact with these animals tend to them like machines—giving food and water or shoveling waste.

I was horrified by the information. I stayed up all night on the internet, watching undercover videos and reading every article I could find. I made a plan with a few of my other animal-loving friends to sneak into school an hour before classes started. We taped fliers about meat and farming to everyone's blue lockers. I wanted them to know what I knew. Why wasn't everyone outraged? I was only thirteen and I knew, immediately and without question, that what was happening to animals on these farms was wrong.

As I got older, it shocked me how little people knew about farm animals. People knew that cats liked to rub themselves on human legs and that dogs' paws twitched when they ran in their dreams. Kids learned that snakes shed their skin and that iguanas used camouflage to hide. Yet most of us would be hard-pressed to come up with facts about pigs, cows, chickens, or turkeys outside of what to do with their meat in the kitchen.

A few years ago, I was at a wedding, discussing with the table what animals we'd like to have as a pet when my own husband said he'd always wanted a pet cow. "Because then you could have milk whenever you wanted!" Everyone agreed this was a great idea. "Milk from your own backyard. Delicious."

"You can't just *have milk* from a cow," I interrupted. "They need to have a calf to produce milk."

The table was quiet for a moment before bursting out in a flurry of disagreement. They were positive that this wasn't the case, that cows were—due to a quirk of nature—endless milk-producing machines.

"Think about the biology of it," I protested. "Human women have to have a baby to produce milk. So do cows. The cows are kept pregnant, and the male calves often become veal."

Finally, someone got out their phone and searched, "Do cows have to be pregnant to produce milk?" After Google also agreed with me, they were forced to acquiesce. A pet cow, it turned out, was not such a great thing after all.

There are countless books about the behavior of cats and dogs. Parrots and other birds got a boost after a gray parrot named Alex proved that certain avian species were capable of using language. There are even a few books about living with pet pigs or cows.

The chicken has not been so lucky. Most people don't even know basic facts about chicken biology. I regularly get questions like:

Don't you need a rooster if you want eggs? While a rooster is required to make a chick, the eggs we eat are just a product of ovulation, which hens do naturally.

How many eggs do you get a week? We get more in the spring and summer, slowing as the days get shorter until the chickens go on winter break.

How long can chickens live? Some exceptionally healthy chickens have lived to be twenty, though most have a lifespan of five to ten years.

People are usually surprised to find out that chickens can fly—though often poorly and for short distances since most breeds are bred to be too fat to get much lift. But people are starting to pay more attention to chickens for one simple reason: they're back in backyards! As the new millennium started, people decided to raise small flocks of happy hens. Homesteaders and people in rural areas never stopped keeping chickens, even as prices of eggs and meat started falling in the 1950s. But it had been decades since chickens were a regular fixture of cities and suburbs. Some people trace the rise of the backyard chicken to Martha Stewart, whose first book, *Entertaining*, published in 1982, contained numerous pictures of her decidedly glamorous chickens and their colorful eggs. They've been popping up in her magazines, TV shows, and social media ever since.

Stewart undoubtedly introduced people who were already keeping chickens to breeds they may not have considered—the Polish breed, with their floppy feather hat, or the Americana hen, who lays teal blue eggs. But two books about food helped drive people straight into the fluffy embrace of backyard chickens: Eric Schlosser's 2001 book, *Fast Food Nation*, with its descriptions of the industrial meat industry and the way the chicken nugget changed poultry farming, and Michael Pollan's *The Omnivore's Dilemma*, released in 2006, which showed a vision of what the meat industry could be if we did things on a smaller, more humane scale. "Know your farmer, know your food" became a popular bumper sticker. What better way to know where your food came from than to grow it yourself?

But because many of these new urban homesteaders had small backyards, zoning regulations limited the size of their flocks to just a few birds (if chickens were allowed at all). This made people get closer to their birds than even my grandma and other farm wives with their flocks of a few hundred. Now the first thing people do after picking up their chicks is name them. This would have been unthinkable when my grandma was a little girl.

Today people pamper their pets—still most often dogs and cats—like never before. Pets sleep on the bed with their owners and snuggle on the sofa during a television binge. People might drop off a dog at daycare on the way to work like they're any parent in the carpool lane. Luxury products, like treat dispensers equipped with a nanny cam so anxious owners can keep an eye on their pets have become normal. In this context, it's no surprise that chickens today don't get just names but also lavish backyard coops, landscaped gardens with safe-to-peck plants, and special-ordered mealworms to snack on.

When lockdowns for COVID-19 closed schools and businesses, forcing families to stay home for months on end in 2020, many people's first impulse was to order baby chicks. When times get tough, as one hatchery employee told me, people turn to chickens.[6] Hatcheries were overwhelmed by the demand and many breeds sold out for the remainder of the year. Chicken coops became all but impossible to come by, and even feed was in low supply. Desperately seeking chickens, families turned to local farmers as a source of hatching eggs or chicks.

These new flocks were an eventual source of eggs and entertainment for people stuck at home. In many families, these Corona-chickens (as some people referred to them on social media) were a teaching tool for kids. Homeschool lessons might involve using math to figure out how much feed the birds needed or to measure the diameter of the coop, reading and writing about their new flocks, and even creating art inspired by the growing hens.

Chickens were domesticated over three thousand years ago and have been living in our yards—more or less—ever since. They've been pets, a valuable source of household income, the expensive subjects of adoration, and a calming influence on the sick or elderly.

Walking around Brooklyn in the late aughts, I never heard chickens over the noise of the city but often did a double take when I spotted a coop tucked into the front yard of a stately brownstone. The birds are trendy enough that it has become hard to find a profile of the many celebrity chicken keepers, like the Duke and Duchess of Sussex, Kate Hudson, Jennifer Garner, Ang Lee, or Isabella Rossellini, that fails to mention their pet chickens and fancy backyard coops. Chicken leashes, diapers (so your chicken can live indoors), and even tutus have all become popular accessories. There are companies dedicated to chicken sitting like you might find for dogs or cats, and, if you're watchful, you can spot a nervous owner holding a bundled-up chicken in some veterinary waiting rooms.

Looking at my hens, all distant relatives of the *Tyrannosaurus rex*, it's easy to see the predator's gaze in their eyes. They move differently from mammals. So much about their bodies marks them as decidedly "other," from their feather-covered bodies to their scaly reptilian legs. But when they waddle-run up to me for treats or allow me to pick them up and stroke their silky feathers, it's impossible not to feel like I'm part of the flock.

I was touched and surprised when I found out that my grandma, who scoffed at my flock of three chickens, had been printing out photos I'd posted of the birds on social media. When I went to visit for her eighty-fifth birthday party, I watched as she showed them to her longtime friends and neighbors. I wasn't the granddaughter who was a journalist; I was the granddaughter who raised chickens. In fairness, I talk about my flock all the time. Over the years, my girls have helped me make friends with people all over the world. When we connect with the chickens in our backyards or neighborhoods, we often connect with members of our own species too.

This is a book about chickens, yes, but it's also about how they can change your life if you let them.

CHICKENS

AT

HOME

CHAPTER ONE:
MAKE WAY FOR CHICKENS

F ROM THE MOMENT I SAW SOMEONE RAISING CHICKENS IN THEIR SMALL front yard in Brooklyn, I knew I had to have them. There was something so delightfully incongruous about farm animals in the city. I was painfully aware that I was stuck in a concrete jungle, but as far as these hens were concerned, this was how every chicken everywhere lived. There was something freeing in that. They seemed to live happily wherever people placed them. But I knew I'd never be able to afford a yard worthy of chickens until I left New York City.

After eight years there, I was ready for a change. Mesa, the puppy my then-fiancé, Lyle, and I adopted together, had grown to hate the city so much, she pulled to go back into the apartment every time we tried to take her outside. I knew how she felt. Every day was an endless cycle of subways and crowds and obligations. I worked from home, and the commute from the bed to my small desk was claustrophobic. I found myself spending more and more time sitting next to Mesa, both of us staring at the birds and squirrels outside the window. It was time.

Lyle and I both had jobs we could do from just about anywhere, and it was hard to narrow down where we wanted to live other than the qualification "anywhere but here." Over time, a few must-haves rose to the top of the list. We wanted to live in a place where it didn't get too cold in the winter. Somewhere with a lot of good food. A place where we could afford a house with a yard, so we never had to deal with a terrible landlord or neighbor again. (Our first New York apartment came with a downstairs neighbor who banged on our floor if we walked or sneezed. The second flooded after the pipes in the shoddily built apartment burst—then the landlord kept our security deposit.) We eliminated one city after another until just one place was left—Portland, Oregon. I once read that it had more dog parks per capita than anywhere else in the United States. Later I would learn that it was a hotspot for backyard chickens too.

We found and bought an old house on half an acre, and I giddily made plans to paint and garden and buy new light fixtures—all the things that never made sense to do in a rental. There would be more than enough space for our dog to get a friend while leaving room for another important addition. In our final months in New York, the first thing that came out of my mouth after I told people we were moving was, "We're going to get chickens!" I wanted to name them Dolly, Loretta, and Patsy, after the country music legends.

I imagined getting three classic chickens—a buff colored one, a red one, and a barred black-and-white one, all with shiny red combs. I'd grown up in the dream-board, "manifest your desires" 1990s but had never taken it seriously until now. If I just kept talking about the chickens, I knew they'd happen. Eventually.

As it turns out, moving across the country, fixing up a new home, finding new furniture because almost everything we'd planned to take with us had been ruined in the aforementioned flood, and getting married two months later is a lot of work. Maybe we'd just gotten too used to chaos at this point because we also decided to get a second dog a month after we moved in.

I don't know what we were thinking. But in my last few years in New York, it had felt like life was on hold. I'd been mentally making a list of things that I would do as soon as I left; now I had. I wanted to start my new life right away. So I did—despite the chaos.

"Once we get settled, I'll get chickens," I'd tell my friends (even though it was more of a promise to myself that this day was just over the next hill of painting or dog-proofing the yard). I didn't really know what it would mean to "be settled," only that I'd know it when we got there. The endless to-do list would feel manageable; the two dogs would stop finding new ways to escape into our neighbors' yards; I'd start feeling like I knew what to do with guests who came to town instead of being as much of a tourist as they were. Chickens felt like the cherry on top of a perfect life—a way to mark that our house had become a home.

>

Nearly two years after we moved to Portland, we'd repainted every room in the house and taken out most of the ivy choking the yard. I'd become familiar with my local plant stores, creating gardens where there had once just been lawn. The dogs had stopped escaping—more or less. I had at least ten restaurants on my list of favorite places to go. I'd even made a few friends. One day, I looked at our house to-do list and realized that it wasn't nearly as long as it once had been. I could go outside and sit in the sun instead of donning work clothes and garden gloves. Portland felt more like home than anywhere else I'd ever lived. It was time. We were ready for chickens.

I started researching chicken coops and eyeing the yard whenever I was outside, thinking of the best place to put my hens. I spent hours reading about chickens on the internet and checked out nearly every book I could find at the local library. (And in Portland, the library had a lot of books on chickens.) My laptop slowed to a crawl from all the tabs I opened on different chicken breeds. I'd never known there were so many to choose from.

There are 120 breeds recognized by the American Poultry Association, the oldest poultry organization in North America, and closer to 450 variations to choose from once you take recognized sizes (either full-size or pint-sized bantams), colors, and patterns for each breed into consideration. Most of those are rare breeds that are impossible to find at a hatchery or local farm store, but that doesn't make the choice less staggering. Those numbers don't even account for the numerous mutt breeds of chickens developed to have certain qualities customers like in their pets or egg layers. The site that I ordered my birds from had eighty-seven types of day-old chicks to choose from.[7] Some breeds had beards or giant floppy combs on their heads. Certain breeds were larger than a toddler while others were so small they could fit in the palm of my hand. There were chickens that laid blue eggs or chocolate eggs or pink-tinted eggs. Some eggs even came out splashed with spots! The classic chickens with their white and brown eggs no longer seemed as exciting as they had a few years before. Now that I knew what was out there, I didn't know what I wanted anymore. Still, if I wanted chickens, I knew I had to make a decision.

Slowly, I closed one tab after another until only three were left. I decided on a classic black-and-white barred Dominique, the oldest chicken breed in America; an Olive Egger, a mutt that would lay a large egg the warm green of a Spanish olive; and a Frost White Legbar, a blue-egg layer with a mohawk of feathers on her head.

They would arrive in three weeks. After so many months of planning, it felt like the blink of an eye. But the timing was poetic—a chicken egg, I'd learned from the many books I'd read, has to incubate for twenty-one days before it hatches. Within hours of my order, the fertilized eggs that contained my chicks were popped into the incubator with thousands of others.

Like those moms who post throughout their pregnancies about how their babies are the size of a peach or a watermelon, I'd check a chick development chart as my girls developed inside their eggs. On day three, I proudly informed my husband, "The chicks have a heartbeat!"

Lyle nodded and said something wise like, "Huh," before going back to his breakfast.

Two days later I exclaimed, "The chicks have knees! Isn't that funny? Knees!" They weren't even a week in their shell, and they already had knees. It boggled my mind.

On day eleven, I looked at the chart and grinned. "Wow! The chicks should have toes and their first feathers. They look like aliens," I said, peering at an image of my favorite development chart. Day twelve of incubation is when a chick embryo begins to hear. Mother hens cluck to their eggs constantly, probably singing them chicken Mozart and Beethoven songs so they grow up to be the smartest chicks in preschool.

There are a lot of chick embryo charts, but few of them are quite so, let's say, *informative* as the one I'd stumbled across. Often these charts have pleasant cartoon drawings of squiggly bodies that become bigger and more chick-like each day. For this one, some intrepid researcher had clearly broken open an incubating chicken egg and photographed its contents once a day throughout the twenty-one days. Day sixteen, described in the poster as "feathers cover entire body, albumen [the egg white] nearly gone," looked more like something a person might cough up during a bout of pneumonia than a bird-in-waiting.

Apparently showing a photo of this to your spouse while he's trying to eat a breakfast bagel is "gross" and "not really what I want to look at first thing in the morning" and "Tove, seriously, I'm glad you're excited about the chickens, but I really don't need to keep seeing this chart."

On Monday, April 16, my chicks hatched somewhere in Ohio.

I opened up my email to a message saying, "Your chicks are on their way!" They were scheduled, in fact, to arrive the very next morning. I scurried around getting accommodations ready for my new houseguests. Chicks, covered with that adorable downy fluff, can't regulate their temperature until their feathers come in. That's why hatcheries have a minimum number of chicks in every order, so their accumulated body heat in the box can keep everyone warm. In a natural setting, they'd hatch underneath their mother hen, who would warm them against her 106-degree body. My chicks just had me. So they'd be spending their first weeks in a brooder made from a large blue plastic storage tote in the upstairs bathroom. I covered the bottom of the bin with pine shavings, then carefully laid paper towels on top of it so their developing legs would have an easier time learning to walk. I filled the chick-sized food and water dispensers. I was nervous. I was excited. I was ready.

The message came at about 7:30 a.m. "Good morning," said a woman with a sing-song voice. "This is the post office. Just calling to let you know your baby chicks are here for pickup."

I was already dressed but woke up my husband just in case he wanted to come with me to meet the newest members of our flock. "Lyle," I whispered. "The chicks are here! Are you sure you don't want to come?"

"What time is it?"

When I told him, he groaned. "It's so early. I need to sleep." He'd been up working until nearly two the night before.

"You're going to miss out," I tried one more time.

"It's so bright. Close the door on your way out," he said, then added, just as I was about to leave the room, "And can you try not to wake me up when you get back?"

There was one person ahead of me in line at the post office, and I danced from one foot to the other like I had to pee while I waited. I wondered where the chicks were hiding and whether anyone else had their own chick orders coming to Portland through the USPS today.

When I got to the front and told the woman what I was there for, her face lit up with a smile. "They're just over on my desk. I'll go get them for you."

She walked into the back. I heard her coming toward me a few seconds before I saw her. "Peep! Peep! Peep! Peep!" the chicks yelled furiously from their cardboard box. It had air holes in the side that the little ones were using to their full advantage. For three small birds, they sure could make a lot of noise.

I signed for the package. "Do you get a lot of chicks at the post office?" I asked her.

"Oh, all the time," she said. "I just love it."

She looked at the sealed box longingly. I was about to whisk the box off the counter when she suggested I "check to make sure they're okay," then handed me a box cutter. I carefully opened the lid as the two of us crowded around the box like we were unveiling a lost treasure. The chicks had all made it and stopped peeping for a moment to look up at this disturbance to their dark cardboard world of the past twenty-four hours. Their toes made rustling sounds as they moved around in the nesting materials and scratched the cardboard with their fuzzy wings. The box felt warm from the heat of their bodies. I closed the box and carried it to the car. They peeped the whole way home, pausing briefly as they heard the opening chords of Dolly Parton's "Jolene." (Chickens probably like country music, I reasoned.)

I hurried to get them from the box into the brooder where the heater had been warming up since I left. I took each of their fuzzy heads in my hand and gently dipped their beaks into the water dish since I'd read that sometimes they had trouble finding it on their own. Then I sat next to them and watched. Time slipped away. It was easy to tell the chicks apart—they were gray (the Olive Egger), yellow (the Legbar), and black with yellow spots (the Dominique). When they walked on their thin, wormlike feet, they stumbled around like drunken sailors. The first time I saw them take a sip of water on their own I giggled. They'd scoop water into their beaks, then tilt their heads back, nibbling their beaks to help the water get down their throats. It was like watching a baby sip like a French sommelier. It was just a drink of water, but to me it was unbelievably adorable. This must be how moms feel watching their babies, I thought.

"They're shaped like little eggs with legs!" I told Lyle when he came upstairs to see the chicks for the first time. It was so obvious that this would be the case (after all, each *had* just hatched from an egg), but I couldn't get over it. I took pictures of an egg next to the chicks for comparison. They were just over a day old and looked like they could almost pop right back inside the shells if the world got to be too much for them.

The chicks soon made their names obvious. It was clear that Patsy, Dolly, and Loretta weren't good fits for the chicks I'd picked out. I needed names that felt less country homestead and more modern. I tried to brainstorm new ideas. Female poets? Mystery writers? I was still waffling when Lyle started rewatching the TV show *Mad Men* and I was reminded of how much I liked the female characters. There was tough Peggy, who'd broken out of the secretarial pool to become an advertising creative; beautiful Joan, who was smart and driven but often felt she had no choice but to use her femininity to get what she wanted; and Betty, a perfect suburban mother who'd struggled with her desire for something more than what society told her she should be happy with.

The gray chick was the bravest in the bunch. She was the first to drink and eat, the first to realize she could flutter her baby wings to hop on top of the heat plate. "This one's Peggy for sure," I said.

The yellow chick was shy and preferred comfort over exploration. She'd come out to eat and quickly retreat under the heater, a square radiant heat plate that sat over the chicks on adjustable legs, which Lyle and I soon took to calling "plate mother." If she was forced to leave her hatchmates for a minute, she'd peep wildly until we put her back down. (The other two would at least peck around for a little before wanting to go back.) "She's such a Betty," I decreed, which left Joan, a funny-looking chick who I knew would grow up to be a stunning hen someday. "They're the Mad Hens!" I squealed once I named them. I'd rarely met a pun I didn't like.

~~

In the mornings, I woke up to the sound of chicks peeping upstairs. They'd start a little after the sun came up and then chatter away until it got dark again. I tried to work in my office across the hall from the bathroom but kept finding that my "breaks" from work stretched into hours. I sat on the toilet lid and stared down at the chicks in their brooder. Sometimes when they hid under plate mother, I'd hold my phone next to it and take photos of them sleeping. Often they splayed out, faces squished against the shavings. Betty slept primly, settled down onto her legs, eyes closed. Once, I invited some people over to meet the chicks, and one of the babies fell asleep cupped in a friend's hand. It's been years and she still talks about it, eyes glowing.

Our only other resident pets, Bandit and Mesa, had different feelings toward our growing flock. Bandit, a merle mutt, seemed to join me in thinking that the chicks were the most fascinating thing that had ever happened to our household. He'd come into the room with me and stare at them with a slack-jawed expression. He seemed bewildered by the birds. When the week-old chicks started fluttering onto the top of plate mother, he jumped back in shock and looked at me as if saying, "Are they allowed to do that?" Meanwhile, our black Golden Retriever mix, Mesa, might walk into the bathroom to get a few pets from me but spared little more than a passing glance for the chicks, whom she seemed to think were beneath her.

I had dreams of walking into the yard to find the dogs and chickens taking a nap in the sun together. Perhaps a chicken might decide that a dog was a better way to get around than walking, and fly up to perch on Mesa's back. Unfortunately, it seems that for every photo of a dog lovingly protecting his flock of chickens, there's a story about a dog-on-chicken massacre. I searched for information on "chicken training" a dog and found suggestions ranging from reasonable to cruel. (One method people still frequently suggest is to take a dead chicken and tie it around the dog's collar until it rots off. Considering how much my dogs love rolling in smelly things and how often they snuggle on our couches and beds, I quickly put this one into the No pile.) Overall, the idea seems to be to teach the dog that the chickens are part of the household, which involves allowing the two species to spend a lot of (supervised) time together. So when I went to sit with the chicks, the dogs did a polite sit next to me while we both watched them. After a few weeks, when the chicks were big enough to go outside, I let one dog at a time come outside with us. Once, Mesa let the chicks crawl all over her as she lay on her side in the sun. We were all in heaven.

My days were filled with chicks and thoughts of chickens. I counted chickens before falling asleep at night. Literally. I'd peek under plate mother to make sure they were fast asleep. "Good night, birds," I'd say. "Sleep well, cheeps." We had quickly stopped calling these little balls of fluff chickens or chicks. They were "the cheeps," named for the noise that they made every minute they were awake.

➤—

Whenever I talked about the chickens, I couldn't help but mention that they'd come in a cardboard box from the post office. The whole thing was so extraordinary. Though the post office employees in Portland are, on the whole, much nicer to deal with than the ones I used to meet when I lived in New York City, "USPS" and "magic" aren't two words that I'd usually put together. But there was something undeniably enchanting about the idea that my new chicks had travelled half of the country in a cardboard box within a day of hatching. How was it that the same post office clerks who handled my Amazon packages and electric bills were also flying and trucking the majority of the day-old chicks in the country to their new homes? Until I started researching where to get chickens of my own, I hadn't been aware that the USPS sent chicks—or any live animals—through the mail. But, as it turns out, the Postal Service will send day-old chicks, bees, snails, scorpions, goldfish, and other "small, harmless, cold-blooded animals" throughout the country.[8]

And it isn't a new phenomenon either. My own great-grandmother used to place mail orders for her Leghorn chickens, shipped every spring to North Dakota. The practice started in the late 1800s, when a man named "Chicky" Joe Wilson opened a small hatchery in his backyard in Stockton, New Jersey. He was aware of the fact that chicks didn't need to eat or drink for forty-eight hours after hatching because they get so many nutrients from their first meal—the yolk of their egg. Though chicks generally hatch in twenty-one days, some are slower or faster to break out of their shells. In a natural setting, the hen has to keep sitting on the eggs until the brood has hatched out before she can show them to food and water. The yolk meal provides some extra time for the chicks who are still breaking out of their eggs, by keeping those already hatched from starving.

Wilson wondered whether this natural behavior might be good for business. Why bother ordering fertilized hatching eggs and waiting to incubate them—sometimes with poor results—or buying more expensive pullets (the term for a hen under a year old) when you could just buy some day-old chicks and have them delivered right to your town? In the 1890s, Wilson's first order travelled sixty miles to East Orange. It was a test run just to be sure that the idea really worked. The following year, he hatched five hundred chicks, tucked them into boxes, and sent them by rail to a Chicago suburb. The birds arrived safely. "One half of one percent of the chicks that Pine Tree Chicken Hatchery shipped died in transit," Keith Strunk writes in a history of the Delaware River Valley, though Wilson also started what became a common practice: adding a few chicks to each large order to compensate for losses.[9] In the days before urban chickens or suburban zoning laws, having extra chickens was never a problem.

Soon other hatcheries started sending chicks by rail through private companies. But it was relatively expensive and inconvenient for anyone who lived far away from a rail station. When the USPS started their parcel post service in 1913, it was an overnight success. Over three hundred million packages were sent in the first six months alone.[10] There was even a Farm to Table program that allowed farmers to mail produce, cheeses, and other items to urban customers. So it came as little surprise when, in 1918, the USPS accepted its first shipments of day-old chicks. In the few decades since Chicky Joe started his New Jersey business, 250 new hatcheries had sprung up in the United States. But the addition of the USPS to the new industry was like pouring kerosene on a fire. Less than a decade later, there were over ten thousand hatcheries in the country.

How was it possible that millions of chicks had been flying across the United States throughout my lifetime without me knowing, much less ever once seeing someone pick up a peeping box at the post office? I knew I wasn't the only one who didn't know about it. So I wrote an article about the history and mind-boggling logistics of hatching and shipping all these chicks for a publication I often contributed to.[11] Most people enjoyed it, sharing the piece on social media with comments about how the post office was delivering cuteness right to your door.

A week later I started seeing messages from someone at a nonprofit called United Poultry Concerns, an organization that "promotes the compassionate and respectful treatment of domestic fowl," according to the email footer. Karen Davis, the organization's founder, wrote that the whole process was inhumane. "Chicks are shipped like luggage," she detailed, adding that while chicks often went twenty-four to forty-eight hours without food or water after hatching, the seventy-two hours allowed by the USPS was neither natural nor good for them. Not to mention, Davis wrote, that half of the chicks hatched were roosters. They were often killed at the hatchery if there weren't orders for them or, perhaps worse, were sent as "packers" to keep the other chicks warm before being abandoned by their owners once they developed large combs and started crowing. Her email—and the feeling that what once felt like a glorious form of progress was actually just another way that we make animals suffer—began to feel like a rock in my shoe.

My chicks had arrived healthy and thrived after shipping, but I knew this wasn't always the case. It was tempting to believe that if we've been shipping chicks by mail for one hundred years, surely there couldn't be anything wrong with it. But until recently, people regularly gave fragile chicks as Easter presents to small children without giving much thought to keeping the birds warm enough or fed. You can still find colored Easter chicks for sale in some places, pre-dyed in their shells so they hatch in bright shades of yellow, red, pink, purple, green, or blue. We love babies and puppies and kittens, but chicks are still seen as somewhat disposable. These thoughts crept into my mind every time I sat with my small flock.

I had to find out more about what my chicks had gone through. One night, I sent an email to one of the hatcheries I'd spoken with for the article. "Would it be possible for me to fly to Iowa and visit the hatchery?" I asked.

Murray McMurray Hatchery has been in business since 1917, even before the Postal Service got involved. Not only is it one of the oldest hatcheries in the United States still in operation, but the company also specializes in heritage breeds for backyard poultry keepers.

Founder Murray McMurray was an Iowa banker who got serious about the poultry business when incubators became widely available—ending the reliance on broody hens to hatch out chicks. In 1919, he sent out a price list and "catalog," which consisted of little more than a few pieces of paper. The chicken business, as it turned out, was more reliable than banking in those days. (Even today, hatchery orders for chickens go up when the economy goes down.) His bank closed during the Depression, and McMurray decided to put everything he had left into the hatchery business.

Over its century in business, Murray McMurray Hatchery has sent chicks by rail, truck, and airplane. They've seen chicken keeping go from something local women did for egg money, to a closed-loop system on big farms, all the way to today's urban flocks.

Many agricultural companies worry about bringing in outsiders because of concerns over bad press and animal welfare complaints. I wasn't sure if they'd go for it. But less than twenty-four hours later, I had a response. As long as I hadn't been around chickens for a few days prior, I was welcome to come. Summer was their busiest time.

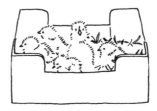

CHAPTER TWO:
UNITED STATES POULTRY SERVICE

YOU'RE HERE EARLY," TOM WATKINS SAYS IN LIEU OF HELLO. IT IS early, 5:15 on a Monday morning and still dark outside, though I feel like I'm already late. Watkins takes a sip from his large Murray McMurray mug with a nearly life-size picture of a chick on it. He's the company vice president and I can't help but wonder if he could use a different mug even if he wanted to. Watkins asks if I need a cup of coffee. I can tell he's trying valiantly to wake up. He only arrived fifteen minutes before me.

"I'll have some in a bit," I say. "I don't want to miss the chicks." The hatchery managers have already been here for two hours pulling freshly hatched chicks out of the incubators.

Watkins nods and grabs his mug, and we walk toward the back of the building. We pass a wall of celebrity photos and letters, all people who have ordered chicks over the years. There are photos of Martha Stewart, Bruce Springsteen, Isabella Rossellini, and Loretta Lynn, among others. Even George Foreman has a photo on the wall, though it's unclear whether his birds were pets or eventually wound up on one of his namesake grills.

We pass an office full of cubicles, where people will begin fielding questions about chickens and orders at a more reasonable hour. There's a room full of merchandise that Watkins says they don't sell much of anymore, adding, "People buy so many things on Amazon now. It used to be a much bigger part of our business." Today, Murray McMurray is all about what's behind the door we're now standing in front of. It's the kind of door I might think led to a closet if it weren't for the large sign reading "biological security area."

"Come on in," Watkins says, and we leave the sleepy front office to enter a whirlwind of activity, hot air, and thousands of baby chicks. Together, they sound like a swarm of insects—nothing like the gentle noises I was used to hearing from my bathroom brooder.

"Oh, wow, that's a lot of smell," I say as it hits me like a slap in the face. I try to think of how I'll describe the smell in my notes—a combination of heat and dust and something almost sulfurous and rotten.

"The chicks themselves don't smell bad," Watkins explains as we get closer to the source. "It's the other eggs. The ones that didn't hatch. You just cooked an infertile egg for three weeks."

Just imagine the scent of an overcooked hard-boiled egg, then keep it at one hundred degrees for three weeks and multiply that by tens of thousands in a room that has to stay warm enough for the chicks to thrive. Ah, the smell of incubation in the morning.

Kurt and Ken, the hatchery managers, have their hands full of chicks. They're sorting the hatched from the hatched-not in a process they call "pulling." They grab two fuzzy chicks in each hand and move them onto a white hatching tray. The egg trays, just out of the incubator, are full of still-whole eggs, eggshells, and chicks toddling among the wreckage of their former homes. These particular chicks are the yellow of a Golden Retriever, so fuzzy and new to the world that they almost look fake. The fuzz travels all the way down their legs. It's the telltale sign of a booted breed chicken that will grow up to have feathers that splay over their feet like snowshoes.

"These are Cochins," Watkins says. "I love the full-size. When a kid has one in his arms, it's almost as big as he is." He smiles. Watkins has four kids at home, all under six years old. A Cochin rooster might very well be taller than Watkins's youngest. But right now, these chicks can fit two to a hand. They're small and vulnerable. Even in the best conditions, hatching doesn't always go according to plan.

A few of the chicks have something visibly wrong with them. One has a leg that's out of place; another's eye didn't develop right. A few sit at the edge of the tray, not bothering to huddle with the others for warmth. Some of them are strong enough to get halfway out of their shells, then stop trying. Even in nature, chicks don't all survive.

When artificially incubating eggs, humans might get none, some, or all of the chicks to hatch. Hens aren't much more reliable. Though some chickens make excellent mothers, many modern breeds never "go broody," a state that makes a hen want to sit on and hatch a clutch of eggs. Other hens might start sitting on eggs only to get distracted and walk away, stopping incubation before the chick can develop and hatch. Even when chicks make it out of their shells, there's no guarantee they will survive to adulthood. On a recent trip to Hawaii (which, like many tropical locations, has been overrun by feral chickens, as you'll read about later), I regularly saw chicks trailing after a clucking mother hen. But I also saw dead chicks. Once, I found one left abandoned in the grass, weakly peeping, without siblings or a mother anywhere in sight. With a flight to catch and no brooder in my hotel, there was nothing I could do but leave him and let nature take its course.

❧

The hatching room floor is full of broken eggshells that crunch underfoot. "We have about 110 chicken breeds that we do," Watkins says. They sell a few other types of fowl, but those come from other facilities. This year, they've been having trouble with their smaller bantam breeds. "We're having to push back customers' orders because we're not getting enough from the bantams to fill them," Watkins says. "People get upset, but . . ." He trails off with a shrug.

Watkins absently picks up a couple eggshell halves and tries to piece them back together again as though it's a puzzle. He sighs. "For all I know, this one doesn't go together at all," he says. The chicks trek over the shells to huddle close to their hatchmates. Watkins spots one with a bit of shell still stuck to her back and gently uses his nail to pick it off.

I ask him how many chicks they'll be sending out today. Watkins walks over to the computer, which has a spreadsheet that Ken and Kurt have been using to input numbers of live chicks by breed all morning. About thirty thousand of them will be leaving the hatchery today to fill four hundred orders. While some of the orders will be for this hatchery's minimum of six chicks (in the first cold months of the year, the minimum is twenty-five), many are for a few hundred—mostly to people with small farms or homesteads where they raise chickens for food or have small egg businesses.

I remember when I first moved my own chicks from the shipping box into the brooder. How they peeped and peeped until I used my hand to nudge them underneath their plate mother. Warm at last, they fell silent.

These chicks never stop yelling. They peep because they are chilly. They peep because they're looking for a mother hen who isn't there. They peep because it's their first day in the Big World and, know it or not, they still have a big journey ahead of them.

Watkins shows me on a spreadsheet that out of forty-three thousand eggs put into the incubator, they expect a little over half of them to hatch. I'm surprised by the low rate until Watkins tells me that it's easier for them to hatch out all the eggs from their breeding stock than to separate and only use ones that are fertilized. Roughly half of the chicks will be sent off unsexed (which is cheaper than buying only females but more expensive than buying roosters). "We maybe have five hundred requests for males," Watkins says.

Watkins points to some of the pulling boxes in the hallway and tells me that those are all getting ready to go to the sexers in the next room. "It's, uh, not something I can do," he admits.

While these unsexed chicks will go directly from the hatching room to the shipping area, many make this odd stop to the sexing room along their journey. Here, four people in face masks, hairnets, and coveralls peer painstakingly at chick bottoms for hours at a time to determine whether a chick is male or female. The only light comes from bright lamps that hang close to the sexers, giving the room the air of a back-alley doctor's office. I sniff, trying to zero in on the source of a new smell. It doesn't take long to guess where it's coming from. Each station has a receptacle (in one case, it's a plastic milk jug that's been sliced at an angle) filled with chunky green material. Chick poop.

It's not hard to figure out why the reality TV show *Dirty Jobs* came to Murray McMurray to showcase chick sexing in its first season. Like most birds, chickens don't have external genitalia. Instead, chickens have a posterior orifice known as the vent, or cloaca, that releases digestive waste and serves a reproductive function.* In other words, poop and eggs come from the same place. This makes it difficult to tell whether a chick is male or female until secondary sex characteristics like larger combs and wattles, fancy tail and hackle feathers, or a distinctive cock-a-doodle-doo develop. (Some chicken breeds are color sexable because the males and females are bred to look notably different right out of the egg. There are also feather sexable chicks, whose wing feathers will be a slightly different shape on females than males. Both of these methods only work on certain breeds.) "Vent sexing," the only way to reliably sex all chicken breeds, is still so difficult to do that Murray McMurray only guarantees 90 percent accuracy on their chicks—fairly standard for the industry.

Watkins walks over to the closest man in the sexing room. "Roberto, this is Tove," he says. "You want to show her how to sex a chicken?"

"Yeah," Roberto says, with a shrug in his voice as though I'm not the first person to come to his workstation asking for a lesson in how to look up a chicken's butt. He picks up a previously sexed chick from the blue bin (blue for boys, yellow for girls) and turns him over, squishing the bird's posterior and pulling lightly to reveal the inside of the vent.

"The male has, how you say, 'bump'?" Roberto explains. "The female would have nothing."

"It's, uh, yeah. Good luck," Watkins laughs.

I peer closely at the chick, who is clearly ready for this experience to be over. I'm not looking forward to it either, to be honest. But I gamely squint my eyes at the baby bird's fuzzy, round behind.

"Right there, you see?" Roberto says.

Finally, after what feels like a very long time with both Watkins and Roberto lurking over my shoulders, I think I see what he's pointing out—a

---

* The word "cloaca" comes from the Latin word for "sewer." Delightful!

small circle of white sticking out from the rest. That's it. For all I know it's just skin that's been pushed to one side.

I furrow my brow. I nod. I look at the chick then back at the tiny bump.

"No, not really," I admit with a sigh.

Roberto smiles and moves his finger to help me out.

"That thing in the middle?" I ask.

"So that's the penis . . . well, what a chicken has."

Chickens have sex through a process known as a "cloacal kiss." The hen squats for the rooster, who balances himself on top of her so that their vents can touch. It's, um, very romantic.*

Chicken sexing is not easy and can only be done on hatch day, while the vent is still pliable. Roberto picks up a chick to give me another chance to play "spot the papilla," the proper name for a rooster's sex organ. But first, he points the chick's bottom toward the goo bucket and gives the chick a quick squeeze. A bit of goopy material comes flying out of him as though the chick has just hawked a gob of tobacco into a spittoon.

"This one should be easier," he says, peering at the now-cleared bottom.

It's not. My eyes and brain are already tired from trying to identify tiny bits on a tiny chicken that seem like they'd be just as easy to imagine as to correctly observe. I'm in awe of these sexers, who somehow manage to do this for hours every day.

Until the 1930s, the only way to tell the sex of a chicken was to wait and see if they crowed or laid an egg. That all changed when Japan's Zen-Nippon Chick Sexing School began offering two-year courses in the art of sexing, training over 1,400 people by 1934.[13] The best of them could sex over a thousand chicks in an hour with a 98 percent accuracy rate. When sexers began displaying their prowess to chicken people in other countries, audiences were amazed.

Watkins has great respect for his sexers. Without them, the hatchery would have a hard time staying in business since so many customers want assurances that they're ordering female chicks. It takes two years for someone

---

* Fun fact: a hen who isn't all that fond of the rooster who has just mounted her can rid herself of most of his genetic material and only hatch chicks from a more desirable sire.[12] You may or may not want to bring any of this up as an icebreaker on your next date.

to become proficient at sexing. It's a hard job to hire for these days. I imagine the help wanted ad: "Must have years of experience telling bird orifices apart and eyesight that never tires! Not afraid to get your hands dirty."

Between the vagaries of customer demand and Mother Nature's insistence on producing roughly as many males as females, this feels like an impossible business to plan for. How can they tell how many Silver Spangled Hamburgs people will want versus the chocolate-egg-laying Copper Marans when they're planning the size of next year's breeding flock?

"It's better to have more birds than less birds," Watkins says. "It's one reason why we offer assortments—that's our wiggle room." It might ensure that the hatchery can fill its orders, but it also means more chicks are incubated and hatched than ordered.

Chicks are fragile even under the best of circumstances, and Murray McMurray, like every other hatchery, only sends the strongest off to new homes. No one wants to receive a cardboard box of chicks that's gone silent, to open it up and find dead chicks inside. Many hatchery websites go so far as to recommend that parents not tell their children how many chicks have been ordered and to open the box before the children are around to avoid them seeing a dead chick. Customers want their chicks to be alive and healthy. So all the dying happens ahead of time.

❧

We come back to the hatching room as Ken and Kurt are finishing up. One chick has fallen onto the floor, and Watkins stoops down to gently pick her up and set her back in the middle of her hatchmates to warm up again. It's a sweet moment.

I look up from this to see Kurt and Ken tipping trays full of black-and-yellow chicks into large black trash cans lined with plastic bags. The birds go rolling out like a waterfall. One, two, three trays of chicks tumble down into the bottom of the bin. I feel my breath catch in my throat. I make myself take the few steps toward the barrel and look down. There's a foot-high stack of chicks sitting at the bottom, making the same peeping noise they've been making all morning.

"What—what about these ones?" I ask Watkins, trying to keep my voice steady. These chicks, I already know, are not going to be sent to their new homes today.

He rubs the back of his neck. "Not all the chicks are viable, so they're going to be gassed," Watkins says. "We do gas them."

"Is this a hatch deformity issue?" I ask.

"Um," he pauses. I can tell he hates what he's about to say next. "We probably had too many."

I don't know what to say to that. "That's too bad," I settle on lamely. This is the part of the story where the room full of chicks being whisked off to backyard coops and dust baths and green pastures no longer feels fit for a children's book.

The birds, had they lived, would have grown up to be Light Brahmas—one of the largest chicken breeds in the world. A few years ago, a video of a rooster bursting out of a small coop in Thailand went viral. The Brahma dwarfed his surroundings and seemed too big to be real. "Demand skyrocketed after that," Watkins says, and the hatchery sold out. "We doubled the flock, then nobody wanted them."

It's not that there are more chicks than there are orders—there are just too many of the ones that look like this. Meanwhile, other people's orders are getting postponed because the bantams and Polish, both types that tend to wind up in the pet market, didn't hatch well.

It reminds me of all the fast fashion that sends tons of clothing into the landfills every year. Trends don't last forever. Sometimes that means trash cans full of wide-leg jeans, but when living animals become part of the trend cycle, it means death. "Efficiency," that ideal that always goes hand in hand with "progress," isn't much better. Efficiency has given us hens that can lay over three hundred eggs per year but also male chicks with nowhere to go; they can't lay an egg but are "too expensive" to raise for meat compared to broiler breeds. Efficiency is good for the wallet, but it can be cruel.

Compared to the number of male chicks that industrial agriculture kills every year, I know the loss of life I'm looking at is a metaphorical drop in the literal barrels of dead chicks. It's nothing. But standing there in person, it feels like too much.

"Do you know how many chicks are . . . binned every order?" I ask, using the euphemism I heard him give earlier.

"It's probably about half."

The number feels so high. I realize that if thirty thousand chicks are being sent to their new homes today, that means that another thirty thousand will be killed before they even leave the hatchery.

Watkins explains that while they sell the majority of their hens and a good number of roosters, that's how it tends to work out. "It's not great PR to say half our birds are dead. The industry doesn't want to talk about it, but that's the truth, and if you hide it, it only makes people mad." As we've been walking through the hatchery, I've watched him help struggling chicks get the last bit of the way out of their shells, or coax one on the fringes of the hatching tray to get closer to the others for warmth. While some people pick the birds up quickly by a wing or toss them back into the trays when they're done counting, Watkins scoops them into his cupped hands like he's making a nest and waits to let go of the chicks until they can stand on their wobbly legs.

When he describes himself as "an animal person," I'm not surprised. Though I do ask him if it makes it better or worse to be one in this business, overseeing so many deaths every week.

"You have to be," he says, noting that the example he sets will affect how the employees treat the birds.

"One of the positive notes is that a lot of our chicks will go to a raptor rehab center," Watkins says. A woman comes to pick up the gassed chicks, which are kept frozen and then fed to hawks and eagles and other animals that need to eat small birds and mammals to stay alive.

"It's not pleasant and it's something a lot of people don't want to talk about, but I'd rather not hide it because it makes it seem even worse," Watkins says of gassing the unordered chicks. At the end of the day, I'll walk around the hatchery and hear peeping coming from small buckets near the sexing tables, in the hatching room, in the hallway. But as I keep walking, I see some of the barrels wheeled off to a room where a long hose pumps carbon dioxide into them. The rooms get quieter. The peeping stops.

This is why Watkins says he "doesn't particularly care for the online retail people who don't have actual chickens." Some companies that sell day-old chicks are drop-shippers, middlemen who accept orders and provide the customer service but don't actually raise or send the chicks themselves. (Murray

McMurray's waterfowl and some of the broilers are drop-shipped, though the company breeds, hatches, and sends every other bird themselves.) "It's not something they have to see and touch and gas," Watkins says. "It's just a number to them." Every time he sees something like the Light Brahmas that didn't get ordered or the occasional chick that hatches too late or too weak to be shipped, it's clear that it distresses him. He never set out to be in the chicken business (his wife's father, Bud Wood, now runs Murray McMurray). In the rural community in Nebraska where he grew up, it wasn't popular to have backyard chickens. "But now I've been here since 2013, and I love it," he says.

~

Of course, what the first hours of a hatchery chick's life looked like was only one of the questions I'd come here to answer. I wanted to know what kind of life these chicks' parents had too. Because of biosecurity concerns, I had to come back two days after seeing the chicks to avoid inadvertently spreading diseases from the hatchery to the breeding barns. Many of the birds are raised by five contract growers, who raise the birds and give the fertilized eggs back to Murray McMurray to be incubated. But the hatchery also keeps a few of their own barns.

Watkins sighs a lot when he talks about the upcoming visit. "It makes me really nervous," he admits. "There is—there's a transition between the life of a backyard chicken and those nice-looking birds," Watkins begins and then trails off. "For better or worse, we are industrial." The roosters are sometimes rough on the hens, who lose feathers from being mounted too many times. The birds live inside big barns, which each have a capacity of five thousand to six thousand birds.

I'd seen this nervousness from other farmers, notably at the large Wisconsin dairy I once visited. They made me watch an informational video about how everything I was about to see was completely state of the art and humane before I could visit the cows and walk closer to the manure lagoon, which was so overpoweringly putrid that I forgot how to breathe. The smell stuck to my clothing long after I'd driven home. Watkins has the energy of an anxious host, suddenly seeing the mess and clutter in his home from an outside perspective.

Journalists aren't invited inside many industrial animal farms anymore—regardless of size. In some states, so-called "Ag-Gag" laws have made it illegal for whistleblowers, activists, or anyone else to film the conditions inside agricultural facilities and release it to the public without the owner's permission. Undercover footage from industrial animal farms has led to public outcry against typical industry practices—ranging from housing chickens in small wire battery cages stacked on top of each other in long rows to placing pigs in restrictive gestation or farrowing crates that prevent them from moving or turning around. This footage, not government oversight, has also resulted in citations against people and companies for outright animal abuse. Many animal farmers, worried about what the public might think of how their animals are raised (even in the best circumstances, industrial animal agriculture is a far cry from sunny pastures and big red barns filled with straw), are wary of close media attention. So I understand Watkins's worry and am also thankful for his willingness to be upfront about every side of the hatchery business—not just the part with cute chicks going to their homes.

When we get to the barns, three unassuming concrete sheds in the middle of a cornfield, I can smell the chickens as soon as I get out of the truck. We stop just inside the door and put blue boot covers over our shoes before getting closer to the birds. Despite the industrial fans constantly trying to freshen the chicken poop–scented air, there's no forgetting that I'm in an enclosed space with thousands of birds. My eyes don't water. My breath isn't taken away. But I do stop and consider the relative benefits of breathing through my nose versus my mouth.

The barn itself is surprisingly clean. It's divided into two long rows of pens with a concrete walkway down the middle. The doors and trim are all painted white. The room is brightly lit. Surprisingly, it feels like a lot of farmhouse coops I've seen on the internet but on a much bigger scale. Each pen has a different breed of chicken inside of it, and as we pass by each group, they move away from us in unison like a wave.

"Their faces are so white," I note. Instead of the red or pink combs and wattles my chickens have, these birds look washed out.

"We're at the end of our year," Watkins says. "That's hard." He sighs and smiles nervously. Laying an egg is hard work for hens who need calcium to make each eggshell in addition to what goes into the white albumen and yolk. It can take a toll during the laying season, making even the healthiest free-range flock look a bit ragged by the time winter comes.

When the barn is at maximum capacity, the bigger birds get a minimum of 2.5 square feet of space, while bantams get less. "Obviously we're not anywhere near that," Watkins tells me. The hatchery sizes the flocks to meet demand and hasn't needed to use all the space in the new(ish) barns since building them. In the meantime, the birds seem to enjoy the extra legroom. Some of the birds sit on the ground dust bathing, while others sleep on the A-frame perches installed in each pen.

I've seen birds rehomed after living in cages for their first year of life—these birds are nothing like those. But compared to my healthy, shiny-feathered flock at home, the breeding flocks look tired and drained. I ask Watkins if living indoors is part of why their combs are so pale. The barn is fully enclosed without windows (so they can control when "sunrise" happens with artificial light), which means the chickens never see the real sun. Though there is natural fluctuation in color, if I saw a face this pale on one of my chickens, I'd be taking her inside to monitor her or maybe scheduling a trip to the veterinarian.

"They're using all their energy to lay eggs," Watkins says, explaining that they lose color like this as it gets later into the year. "They have all the formulated feed they can eat, but it's no comparison to spending time outside." He wishes they could free-range, but if they caught a disease and the hatchery sent those diseased chicks to customers, they could be infecting flocks throughout the United States. "It's a hard little world. That's the truth of it," Watkins says. "In order to do the best for our customers, this is the best we can do for them," he says, referring to the flocks in front of us. He seems genuinely bothered that he can't do more.

The sound of so many birds bouncing off the cement and metal walls is sometimes overwhelming. I hear hens clucking and belting out egg songs, the call that hens make after laying an egg. Roosters echo each other's crows until I wonder whether chickens ever wear out their voices from crowing too much.

"Hi, friends," I say to a few of the chickens who come up to the door of the pen, curious about their visitors. Though it's funny to see so many of one breed together, versus my tiny flock where every chicken is completely different, there are still a few that stand out. Some are particularly gorgeous with glossy feathers and faces that are light red despite the conditions. They are friendly or shy or even a little aggressive. Some of the chickens lay in the nest boxes, while others find a different spot on the floor to lay each egg every day, as though they're trying to cause as much trouble for their keepers as they're able to. Civil chicken disobedience. Even in the short amount of time I spend with them, I can see their distinct personalities. But I doubt many employees are developing close relationships with the birds—this time next year, these barns will be filled with an entirely new set of chickens.

Every chicken in these buildings is less than a year old, and in just a few months, the barn will be silent. Every year, the birds are sold either to a buyer who uses them for his own laying flock or to someone who takes the birds to be sold in Minneapolis's live markets. The hens' first season of laying is their most prolific, and they slow every year afterward. When chickens molt, they can also stop laying for up to three months, using their spare energy to regrow feathers instead of laying eggs. It's not good business to keep them. The chickens might live longer than industrial broiler chickens, who are slaughtered for meat at just six weeks old, but they're about on par with industrial laying hens, who are often "retired" after eighteen to twenty-four months.

The two barns I see aren't anywhere close to as bad as caged or even cage-free facilities. It's also nothing like the life a pastured chicken, much less my backyard flock, gets to have. The noise is so loud that sometimes it sounds like the chickens are wailing. The smell is strong enough that I'm glad I didn't have a large breakfast before coming in. I can't help but think about everything I've read about birds and their delicate respiratory systems. Backyard chicken books often advise chicken owners that by the time you smell any ammonia, your coop is already too dirty. Despite the big fans, this barn is far past that point. The day-old chicks Murray McMurray sells will leave this building as eggs, but the parent birds live their lives here before being sent off for slaughter. The thought crosses my mind that maybe it's better that their lives are short when this is how they're living it.

It's not ideal or good, but what the hatchery's barn is helping to replace is objectively worse. The fact that thousands of chickens live like this every year means that hundreds of thousands get better lives. The people who own them are eating eggs and meat from those chickens instead of ones raised on industrial farms. It's the few suffering for the good of the many.

Of course, for the individuals that don't get good lives, it's not much of a trade-off at all. It's tempting to be utilitarian about animal agriculture, but

I know I wouldn't be willing to sacrifice my hen Peggy to save three of these birds' lives, even when I'm looking at them through the grates of their breeding pens. It's like the famous trolley problem that's been vexing ethicists since the 1960s—would you pull a lever that killed one person if doing so saved five?

While there are plenty of people out there who think we should do away with raising chickens for eggs and meat entirely, I doubt it will happen on a large scale until we become better acquainted with chickens as a species. It's easy for people to have sympathy for a baby cow sent off to become veal at just a few days old, but it's less so for what most people consider a "dumb bird" with a reptilian predator's stare. It's no coincidence that pastured poultry and eggs have become more common since the backyard chicken movement began again. A rising tide lifts all boats, as the saying goes.

But raising chicken breeds that are bought based on their looks or the color of their eggs, and the simple fact that a healthy flock has to balance the rooster-to-hen ratio (if roosters are allowed at all), means that some chickens will never be wanted. And for every batch of cute, fuzzy chicks—no matter where you order them from—there were some that didn't hatch or hatched too late for the order timing or "failed to thrive" in a way that made it obvious to the hatchery that they'd die on their way to their new homes or shortly after arriving. There are the too-numerous roosters and the others that don't match the orders for the day. They all get left behind and killed. Some of them will go to feed birds of prey, while others will go to a landfill. Then there's the parent stock, those hens and roosters that live indoors their entire lives, pumping out as many fertilized eggs as they can before being slaughtered for meat.

They're all part of the story that you're a part of when you get a flock of backyard chickens, either from a feed store or in the mail. It isn't pretty. It isn't what you want to think about when you're busy loving on your first small flock of chickens. But it's true.

Overall, the chickens that do get sent to homes throughout the country will have a better life than they'd get in the meat and egg industry. By raising chickens in your yard, you're taking money out of the pocket of a cruel system; that doesn't mean it's cruelty-free.

As I learned how the hatchery worked and saw the pale breeding stock in the pens, I kept returning to the thought that for most people, chickens don't matter. They're dumb birds that taste good and lay eggs that help make items as varied as gin fizzes, omelettes, or cakes. As long as chickens are tucked away in sheds on big industrial farms, nothing will change. The ones that go from Murray McMurray and other hatcheries to people's backyards become ambassadors for a species that no one cared about very much until recently. They're spokes-hens.

I knew plenty about the chicken industry before getting my birds, yet I needed a spokes-hen of my own to show me that chickens could be more than funny animals that laid eggs.

Now it's time for an admission: when I planned to get my chicks, the first thing I did was look up places that would "process" them for me. I knew that hens were only good layers for a few years, and I doubted I'd want to keep them past that point. If they weren't supplying fresh eggs, what were chickens good for? I didn't think I'd be able to eat the meat myself but figured I'd give it away to a friend when it was all done. Many people who don't want to keep their chickens, often roosters or older hens, try to send them to a sanctuary rather than dispatching the chickens themselves. I didn't want to outsource my guilt onto an overburdened organization. It didn't seem much better than someone who keeps buying puppies just to give the older dogs away to a shelter.

Part of me still thought they were "just chickens," even as I watched my chicks grow into gawky pullets who liked to fly up and perch on my shoulder. I was so set on the thought that chickens weren't real pets—like my beloved dogs, who snuggled up to me on the couch and sometimes were allowed to sleep in the bed—that it took a tragedy for me to realize raising chickens had already made me see them as something more.

CHAPTER THREE:
THE LOST CHICK CALL

T HE CHICKS WERE GROWING UP FAST. THEY LOST THEIR EGG shapes within the first few days as their necks grew longer and feathers began appearing on the tips of their wings. My sweet, fuzzy chicks looked more like fledgling hawks—a mess of down and tiny feathers coming out at all angles. Their beaks seemed too big for their faces. I often caught them looking at me with sideways glances, trying to decide whether I might be good to eat. They'd gone from cute chicks to awkward (and often angry-looking) teens. It was hard to look at them and not reminisce on my own human adolescence: the angsty music and questionable fashion choices, the pimples and frizzy hair that never quite got tamed, no matter how long I spent trying to straighten it. (Chickens: they're just like us!)

The girls began going on outdoor excursions as soon as the weather allowed it, bounding into grass blades that were taller than they were. Their first set of baby feathers were growing in, giving them a protective layer that meant they could finally regulate their temperature on their own. Betty was the least friendly of all the chickens, and I could rarely coax her into my hands, but she was an excellent forager. It took just a few minutes outside for her to find and hunt her first bug—an earwig that was twice as big as her beak. Rather than gobbling it down right away, Betty started cheeping with excitement. Joan and Peggy looked up from what they were doing and began to chase Betty—earwig still tucked firmly in her beak—looking for all the world like they were playing a rousing game of chicken football.

Betty had a few tufts of feathers on top of her head, which I thought were just strangely askew until I looked up some more photos of her breed, a White Legbar, and realized that they all had little mohawks. Often they were brushed back into a shape resembling a poorly fitted toupee, which is why I hadn't noticed it before. But when Betty was hot or annoyed, her head feathers would stick straight up like an elaborate punk hairdo. It was a delightful surprise.

The chicks were rarely silent during the day. They chirped softly to each other as they ran around in the brooder or stopped for a snack break. There were no soloists in the group, just a pleasant musical hum, a way to say, "I'm here and I'm okay." The longer I spent with them, the more I understood their repertoire of sounds. If I gave the chicks a special treat, they'd look at it and trill with alarm before deigning to get closer. They circled the food and craned their necks to get as close as possible while still leaving room for a hasty exit if the item I placed down was not a tasty snack but, instead, something like a snake in disguise. It took a few minutes for them to try new things, switching back and forth between the contented burble and their alarm trill as they took a step forward then two steps back. I imagined little exclamation points appearing over their heads with every alert.

When they spilled their water or felt like complaining, the usually contented chick sounds got louder until Lyle and I could hear the cheeping from our bedroom downstairs. They often cheeped loudly to greet the morning, so I took to waking up at six and checking in on them for a few minutes until they quieted back down.

Sometimes I'd take one chick out of the brooder and let her sit in my lap or on my shoulder while I worked in my office next door. Unfortunately, the novelty of new things to jump on and peck wore off quickly as the lone chick realized her flockmates had been left behind. This was my introduction to a particularly piercing sound I called the "lost chick call." It's an endless, volume-at-eleven, two-note sequence (the higher note is always the louder one) that they'll repeat until returned to their flock. In the wild, a chick would use this if they were separated from their mother since the lack of warmth and protection would quickly lead to death. The quick rhythm of the call and the fact that it always hits the same notes (unlike their complaints, which are more musical though almost equally shrill) made it an easy call to remember. The noise made me feel bad, so even though I wanted to spend more time with the chicks, I contented myself with watching the three of them play together.

At two weeks, their fluttering hops turned into attempts at flight. I came into the bathroom where the chicks had safely been contained in their brooder to find them perched menacingly on the rim of the box—daring me to try putting them back again. I found a grate and began placing it on top of the brooder just to keep them enclosed. But they were getting too big to stay inside their small world much longer. I started closing the bathroom door and allowing the chicks to fly around the small room and perch and preen on top of their brooder when I was around to supervise. We were sitting like that one day when Peggy made the extra jump from the brooder onto my shoulder and then my head. I walked around the upstairs with her settled happily onto her new taller perch. I imagined myself a pirate with a parrot first mate.

But the bathroom brooder felt smaller every week. I started letting them into their outdoor coop for a few hours at a time on warm days. They were so small that the steps on the ramp up to the nest box were taller than they were. They had to hop-fly their way up the stairs. Sometimes I'd find them fluffing their feathers in the silty dirt or taking a dust bath. Along with preening themselves with oil from the uropygial gland located near the base of their tails, this was how they kept their feathers clean and free of things like mites and lice. The first time I saw them taking a nap in the sun, I worried something had gone terribly awry. They were lying in a small pile on the ground. Peggy's head was twisted at an angle that didn't seem possible, while her wing splayed away from her body. Betty lay next to her with her legs fully outstretched. Joan buried herself in the middle. The shapes they made reminded me of TV-show chalk outlines of bodies that have fallen from great heights. It went against everything I knew about bodies and how they were supposed to bend. There were no signs of movement.

As I rushed closer to the coop, the chickens sleepily opened their eyes and rolled back onto their feet. They half-heartedly rose as though I'd interrupted them in the middle of a very nice dream, which, I suppose, was exactly what I'd done.

Most chicken wisdom says that chicks will be ready to move outside full time at between six and eight weeks old, when they're fully feathered. Of course, each chicken feathers at a slightly different rate, and depending on whether the chicks have hatched in February or July, you might want to relocate them faster or slower than that.

But there's another factor in deciding when to move them outside that chicken books often neglect to tell people about: by the time your chicks are about a month old, you will want very much to have them out of your house. It's not that they aren't cute anymore—they are, in their gangly teenage way—but the cleaning all gets to be a bit much. Bigger bodies mean bigger waste. No matter how often I cleaned the brooder, I walked in a few hours later to find the sides daubed with bird poop. Then there was their habit of jumping on top of the waterer and spilling it into their clean shavings. Now when friends came to visit, they didn't want to stay nearly so long in the chicken bathroom. They'd come in and coo over the funny little birds, but I'd watch as their eyes quickly started to dart between the chickens and the closed window.

"I think we could use a little fresh air," they'd say.

But even with the window open, it was hard to keep from coughing after a few minutes. Because while the poop and the food and water spillage are a hassle, it's really the chick dust that gets you. The once navy-blue walls were coated in it. When a feather is formed, it pokes out of the skin encased in a firm quill made of keratin. As the feather gets bigger, this keratin sheath breaks off (I've often caught the birds preening off the last bits of this sheath themselves) and apparently turns into fine dust particles that are next to impossible to get rid of. I've wiped down the wall of the bathroom multiple times since the chicks have been in there using dry towels, wet towels, even a vacuum cleaner, and it still has a light white film of chicken dust that just won't go away.

In other words, the chicks were wearing out their welcome. On May 28, nearly six weeks after they'd shown up at the post office, I brought them to their coop and let them spend the night. It was nerve-racking. While Betty and Peggy were covered in feathers, Joan still looked patchy. She was a bit of an ugly duckling as a teenage chicken. Tufts of black-and-white down frizzed out between her feathers. Her tail feathers were strangely short. All three of the chickens were so small.

But the weather was long past the point of freezing. Even in the coldest part of the night, it had been staying above fifty degrees, and the chickens, I knew, would have each other for warmth. I'd turned off their heat plate a week or two before, though they still liked to use it like a loft to get extra space in the brooder. I'd catch them going to sleep beneath it or happily preening on top. Chickens naturally like to roost when they sleep, and I guess the plate was the closest thing to a perch.

The coop was a strong one, built with thick cedar wood and hardware cloth. I'd even buried a three-foot strip of hardware cloth all along the perimeter to make it harder for burrowing animals to get inside. I double-checked the latch. I stole out after the sun went down to make sure the hens had made it inside the nest area and then closed the door so they'd stay as cozy as possible inside.

I didn't sleep well. When the dogs ran out barking in the night, I wondered if they were barking at a predator or alerting me to something gone terribly awry with the birds until I heard the neighbor's Pomeranian egging them on along the fence. I tend to be an early riser but woke up before even the sun. I threw on my warm purple robe and slipped my feet into a pair of tennis shoes before walking down the driveway to the coop. I opened the hens' nest area so they could get into the rest of the run when they woke up, then crept back into bed.

"The chickens are okay," I whispered to my husband, who was still fast asleep.

I kept the brooder up for a few more days, just in case they had to come back in or there was a sudden cold snap. But then it was June, and I had to admit that it seemed like my tiny eggs with legs were doing just fine in their new outdoor home. I often wondered what they thought of their new residence. It was many times larger than their brooder, and they had access to dust for bathing, sun for warming, grass and dandelions for eating, and just about anything else I thought a chicken might desire. I kept them inside the run for the first few days on the advice of strangers in online chicken forums. Apparently being "cooped up" can help teach them that this place is their home and, importantly, where they want to return to before it gets dark, so you don't have to run around your garden with a flashlight looking for a missing chicken. But even once they were allowed time out in the yard, they didn't like to go too far from their coop. Sometimes I'd pick them up and move them to another part of the lawn, trying to show them what they were missing. They were underwhelmed. An hour later, they'd be right back beside the coop again. Despite all my worry, we saw no signs of nighttime predators even though we knew there were raccoons that liked to wash their paws in our neighbors' pond at night. The dogs and chickens happily went their own ways when I put them out in the yard together.

Finally, after years of waiting, I had chickens roaming in our garden. It was what I'd dreamed of all the way back in Brooklyn. Now the only thing left was to sit back and wait for them to lay their first eggs—an Earth-tone rainbow of sky blue, olive green, and light brown.

The winter before the chicks came, I started playing flute for the first time since middle school. Picking up the instrument as an adult was more fun than I'd remembered. As a kid, every hobby came with strings attached—the ever-present question of whether I was good enough at something to do it professionally. It was the reason I hadn't taken gymnastics beyond a single tumbling class. At 5'9" by the time I was a teenager, I knew the Olympics would never be in my future. Now it was freeing to pick up skills I knew I'd never "do anything" with. I could get better at flute just for the pleasure of playing more difficult songs in the living room. My husband, the dogs, and the chickens were the only ones who'd ever hear any of it.

It was August. The chickens had been outside for a few months, and so far I hadn't had cause to worry. Though I'd kept a careful eye on the dogs and chickens when they'd been out together, I hadn't caught so much as a sideways glance between them. I usually sat outside when the animals were out together—just in case—but the weather was so nice and for once I felt like practicing scales. If you've ever played an instrument, you'll know how rare those days are when you're excited to work on technique. So I set up my music stand and flute in front of the big picture window and left the screen door open. If anything happened, I reasoned, I'd be able to see or hear something in time to stop it.

I'd been playing for less than ten minutes when my dog Mesa came into my view with something in her mouth. We had neighbor kids who were always trying to "play with" the dogs by throwing things into our yard—balls, sticks, and sometimes apples (though their dad quickly put a stop to the last one)—so when I saw what looked like a white stuffed animal in her mouth, I rolled my eyes, thinking they'd tossed her an old toy bear. I put the flute down and called the dog.

That's when I saw that whatever she was carrying didn't look stuffed at all. It flopped up and down as she walked. What I'd assumed was plush white fur were actually feathers.

It's hard to remember what I did next. A sound between a yell and a scream of terror came rushing out of me. I might have said the word "No." That's the only thought I had. No, this couldn't be happening. No, to time moving forward instead of in reverse so I could fix what had occurred. No, to my dog, who dropped what was in her mouth and didn't understand why I screamed at her to go away. No, to the moment when my brain processed that the stuffed animal was actually my white chicken, Betty, lying limp in Mesa's mouth.

The sound I made was worrying enough that my husband, who'd been working in his office upstairs, was by my side before I thought to call for him. He still gets a funny look on his face when he talks about it. "I just knew something was very, very wrong," is all he'll say about it today.

Betty's body was on the brick patio, and I picked her up, hoping she was just in shock. Her eyelids were open, but the eyes themselves were hidden behind the film of her second eyelid. It made them look murky. I don't remember what color they were when she was alive anymore, only the bluish tint they took on in that moment. She was still warm. She wasn't breathing.

When I think of a chicken that's been killed by another animal, I imagine finding worse injuries—bites and gouges. But the only injury I could find was a single streak of red next to her wing. Later that day I found a patch of feathers in the grass near the driveway and guessed that's where whatever happened took place. I felt guilty that I hadn't been outside supervising more closely. I couldn't look at my dog, who I'd raised from a puppy, much less reach out and pet her for the rest of the day. It would have been so much easier if it had been a hawk or a raccoon that took her instead of another animal that I loved. All the blame pointed back at me.

I held Betty in my hands. She was already colder. I tried to rifle through her feathers, hoping to find answers to what had happened. Had it just been a single bite? Could she have died from shock? I'd gotten Betty because her breed was supposed to lay eggs the color of the sky. In just another month or two, I'd expected her to start laying for the first time. It hurt all over again to realize I'd never get to see what she'd look like in her heftier adult body. I'd never know the exact shade of her eggs.

"I'll bury her for you. You don't have to be here for this," Lyle said, standing beside me.

There was a shady grove in our yard where tall holly trees and decades-old rhododendrons gave way to a small clearing, empty except for a broken stone fountain and a moss-covered bench. It had always felt a like a sacred place. I decided that was where she should be buried. Lyle got the shovel and started digging and digging. He had to make the hole deep enough that wild animals (and our dogs) couldn't dig Betty's body back up again. By the time he was done, the hole was more than three shovels deep. I went inside the house. I must have cried more because I remember crying a lot that afternoon.

The first pet I'd killed was a lop rabbit who I'd been carrying up the stairs when I was four. I tripped and she fell on her back and broke it. The vet had to put her down. A few years later there was the friendly yellow parakeet named Caruso, who used to sit on my shoulder and nibble my ear. I was playing with him unsupervised and accidentally killed him. When my mom and grandma discovered what I'd done, they both cried. No one wanted to look at me. After that, a mistake so scarring that I still feel guilty about it decades later, I had a better track record with animals.

Now there was Betty.

But unlike when more traditional pets had died, it felt strange to admit that I was in mourning for a chicken. I didn't know if most of my friends would understand why I was crying over a dead hen if they'd just eaten a fried chicken sandwich. Even I still ate chicken sometimes—though only the pastured kind that was raised in conditions somewhat close to my backyard coop. I'd intended for my birds to be food and to treat them as egg layers who were expected to pay "rent" in the form of eggs in exchange for food and shelter. I felt mixed up. Logically, I didn't think it was wrong to raise animals for food as long as we treated them well, but my deep sadness over losing this chicken that I'd raised from the time she was just one day old was hinting at something else.

I felt like I didn't have the right to grieve over something that was so much my fault—or at least the result of choices I'd made. If only I'd stayed outside with the dogs and the chickens, maybe I could have stopped it. If only I'd assumed that Mesa's high prey drive (she often hunted the moles in our yard and loved to chase squirrels) meant that she wasn't ever going to be a good candidate for chicken training. Lyle and I had both hoped that if we taught the dogs that the chickens were now a member of the pack, they'd decide not to chase them. I wasn't there to see what happened to Betty and her injuries were so slight. For all we know, Mesa had just tried to play a game of chase with her like she does with our other dog, Bandit, and that alone had been enough to kill the far more fragile chicken. Dogs, just like people, can cause harm without meaning to.

When I stopped crying long enough to come out of the house to check on Lyle's progress, I heard Peggy and Joan calling from their coop. Earlier I'd checked them over anxiously, worried that they too had been hurt when Betty died, before putting them away in the run where I knew they were safe. It was strange that they were so loud. Unless I was right next to the birds, I rarely heard them make a noise at all. Now their calls rang out from their coop to the front door, two hundred feet away. I took a moment to listen, as I had done so often when they were chicks. That's when the tears came again.

"It's the lost chick call," I said as I got closer to Lyle. "The sound. It's the same one they made as chicks when they were separated from the flock."

Unlike the tiny peeping they once made, this sound felt like it was being wrenched right out of their throats. It was deeper and raw, somewhere between crying and screaming. But it was the same unmistakable two-note sequence, the higher note always the louder. They called again and again. High-low, high-low, high-low. I wondered if they knew they were trying to call their flockmate back from the dead.

No one ever told me that chickens mourned, though it seems so obvious in hindsight. Most social animals mourn. Gorillas watch and groom their dead. In 2018, an orca whale named Tahlequah was seen carrying her calf Tali, who'd died shortly after birth, for seventeen days after Tali's death. Every time the calf would begin sinking to the ocean floor, Tahlequah swam underneath to keep the body close to her. Even crows have funerals for their fallen flockmates. Geese, who have monogamous relationships, grieve for mates who have died—separating from the flock to conduct vigils for their lost loves and often neglecting to eat or drink.

Many people are familiar with the fact that chicken flocks have a strict social structure commonly known as the pecking order. It determines when and where chickens get to eat, perch, or dust bathe with the flock. Chickens figuring out this order can be violent toward other flockmates until it's decided—dominant chicks start challenging and pecking others within just a few days of hatching—but few people extrapolate from these careful social relationships that chickens can have friends too. They might prefer to do their foraging or dust bathing with certain members of the flock who they've formed close relationships with. Anecdotally, it's not uncommon for grieving chickens to die of mysterious causes soon after a friend's death. They often stop laying eggs and refuse food, sitting in the corner with their feathers puffed up as if they're sick.[14] And many people have reported hearing surviving hens calling to a lost friend after a death.

The soundtrack to Betty's burial was Peggy and Joan repeating their heart-wrenching call. I carefully laid Betty's body in the bottom of the hole. It felt wrong to shovel dirt on top of her, so I scooped the first layer with my hands.

"I can finish up here," Lyle said, offering me the chance to walk away.

"I'm fine. I need to do this," I said. She was, after all, my chicken. Betty was my responsibility, even now.

I'd tried to learn so much about chicken care before getting these birds—what to feed them, how to house them, how to know if they were getting sick—and yet it was this day that showed me just how little we really knew about them. They've been living around us for generations, and yet I'd never known that chickens grieved. I'd heard this of pigs and cows (cows will bellow and mourn for hours or days when their calves are taken away from them), but few farmers have bothered to get close enough to their chickens to make this observation. Until now, I'd maintained the uneasy separation between *my* chickens that I'd raised and the other members of their species that were treated as food-production machines. I couldn't do that anymore. The day Betty died was the day I stopped eating chicken entirely. As long as I was raising these girls as pets and members of my family, I couldn't pretend other members of their species were any less deserving.

CHAPTER FOUR:
A CURE FOR CHICKENS

CHICKENS ARE FLOCK ANIMALS, AND KEEPING ONLY TWO FELT like asking for trouble. The day after Betty died, I looked for more chickens. I was about to have my first winter with pet chickens, and if anything went wrong during the cold, long nights, I wouldn't be able to get any more until spring—leaving the survivor completely alone in the coop. So, still grieving, I alternated between scrolling through potential chicken breeds and crying until I picked out four chicks to join the flock. It was a surreal day.

Though I'd chosen my initial three chickens for their egg color and prolific laying, now I threw all pretense of the birds being a practical flock out the window. Two of the chickens I wound up picking were bantam breeds, roughly half the size of a normal chicken. Another I chose entirely because the breed was known for being lovable, fluffy goofballs. The final chicken simply laid blue eggs (and I couldn't resist a blue egg-layer in the flock).

This group finally got the country music names I'd come up with so long ago. Wanda was a little black-and-white Cochin Bantam with a bustle for a tail, reminiscent of a Victorian ball gown. Emmylou, a Mille Fleur d'Uccle, was six inches tall and her brown feathers were flecked with black and white spots. Our somewhat standoffish Easter Egger, Loretta, had a sleek body and long neck and looked like she could survive in the jungle. Then there was Dolly, a fluffy cream-and-peach-colored Salmon Faverolle. Except for Loretta, who looked at me as though I was trying to poison her when I held out treats, this new flock was friendly. Once they got big enough to join Peggy and Joan in the coop, the flock and I fell into a pleasant routine. They came running to the car when I got home and trailed after me in the yard like I was the pied piper. Even when I went inside, the chickens followed as best as they could, camping out on the doorstep and occasionally pecking the door loudly enough that I thought it was UPS delivering a package. When I looked over, I saw chicken faces staring mischievously back at me.

I didn't pay much attention to the pecking order at first. The term, which has crossed over into everyday use, dates back to the 1920s and comes from a Norwegian named Thorleif Schjelderup-Ebbe, who was obsessed with a flock of chickens near his family's summer home in the country. He was only ten when he started filling out notebooks, documenting their behavior and relationships to one another.[15] Schjelderup-Ebbe quickly discovered that chickens organized themselves into a hierarchy where dominant birds enforced their status with the use of liberal pecks at underlings. He was one of the first people to pay attention to the social structure of any species, and the idea of social dominance has since spread into research on human and nonhuman animals alike.

Yet while most people think of the pecking order as a ladder with one chicken slotted into each rung all the way down, my flock seemed to be more of a pyramid.

Some things about the order were obvious: Peggy was the head hen and Joan her second in command. For a while, the rest of the younger chickens seemed equally beneath them. Then they didn't. One day I went to the coop to find Dolly's face covered in blood, half her comb hanging to the side. I quickly scooped her up and brought her into the house where I yelled for Lyle to come help. One of the other chickens must have clipped Dolly's comb near her skull. My chicken first aid kit was woefully understocked. I wrapped Dolly in a towel so she couldn't shake herself—and blood—all over me. I was glad to be wearing a black shirt. I stopped the bleeding with some styptic powder I had on hand for our dogs.

"We have to cut it," I told Lyle.

"What can I do to help?"

"One of us has to hold her still and the other has to cut that dangling piece off," I said. Now that the bleeding had slowed, the bit of comb in question had turned slightly purple.

Lyle sighed. "I guess I'll cut."

The best thing we had on hand were fingernail scissors, which I sterilized and then handed to Lyle to do "chicken surgery."

I watched his face wrinkle as he cut through the skin.

"Ugh," he said. "I think I'm going to see that in my dreams."

Dolly recovered from the injury. After a month, I'd already forgotten what she looked like with a full comb.

Guerrilla chicken surgery like this is familiar to many chicken keepers. When I go to the veterinarian with my dogs for their shots and wellness checks, I see cats, other canines, and even the occasional parrot or rabbit in the waiting room. But a chicken? Never. When I first got chickens, one of the books everyone told me I *had* to have was *The Chicken Health Handbook* by Gail Damerow, a guide to keeping chickens healthy, with symptoms of common diseases and ailments and advice on how to treat them. I've had dogs most of my life and have never encountered a book on DIY canine veterinary care. But a chicken handbook is, in fact, rather indispensable. It tells new chicken owners what symptoms might be worrying to see in their flock. (Chickens, being prey animals, often try to hide when they're sick, and it takes an experienced eye to know when something is amiss.) In most places, there's not much of a difference between "professional" veterinary care for chickens and what a well-read owner can do.

There's a simple reason for this: veterinarians don't get much practice treating chickens. On farms with good animal husbandry, a sick cow or horse or even pig might be "worth" paying the vet to do a house call. Not so for a chicken. If the birds are treated at all (culling them for dinner is much easier than wrangling a chicken for medical care), it's usually a DIY affair. Because people don't take their chickens to the vet, vets don't know how to treat chickens, which makes it hard to justify taking a chicken to a vet. . . . Now that's a real chicken-and-egg situation.

That's not to say that people have been simply ignoring their chickens' health issues. Writers of antiquity certainly had a lot to say about the care and keeping of fowl. The Roman agronomist Columella wrote about how to set up a henhouse and successfully hatch and care for chicks in *De Re Rustica*. One book by English poet and food writer Gervase Markham published in 1668 devotes large sections not only to the raising and care of chickens but also to basic veterinary care. At hatching, if a chick seems weak, Markham suggests wrapping them in wool and setting them near the fire to strengthen them. "To perfume them with a little rosemary is very wholesome also," he wrote.[16] Markham advises readers to bathe a hen in cold water to keep her from going broody (a tactic people still use today) and to cure "sore eyes" by chewing a piece of ivy and spitting into the chicken's eye (this one, unsurprisingly, seems to have fallen out of favor).

For most of history, veterinary care as practiced by laypeople was passed down orally rather than catalogued into books. The treatment and care of sick chickens usually fell to women, who were even less likely to write things down for posterity. It's little surprise that poultry medicine remained in the realm of "old wives' tales"—that's literally all there was. When veterinary schools were founded beginning in the late 1700s, most programs were dedicated to large animals like cows or horses. When anyone with medical or veterinary training considered poultry at all, their attention was focused on curing or vaccinating against diseases like chicken cholera.

By the mid-1800s, as poultry journals proliferated, people often wrote into these publications asking for remedies. While there were some commonalities in treatment (most agreed that the cure for a hen unable to pass an egg was to warm her belly and maybe give her castor oil), one poultry keeper might recommend giving a hen cayenne pepper for an ailment, while another thought homeopathic remedies were the best bet for the same thing. There were no studies to see whether the remedies worked; people simply tried something, and if their chicken got better afterward, they passed it along as gospel.

And people argued whether it was worth it to treat sick poultry at all.

An article from a 1912 issue of *Farm Poultry* states, "The value of individual specimens in egg and meat producing flocks is so small that if a man's time is worth anything at all, it is too valuable to be spent in treating sick chickens individually."[17]

This is probably why much of chicken care focused on keeping hens from getting sick in the first place. The old adage "an ounce of prevention is worth a pound of cure" appears in countless poultry articles. "Cleanliness is Essential," reads the title of a *Reliable Poultry Journal* article published in 1909.[18] "You may talk about your remedies for lice and cholera and the various diseases with which poultrymen have to contend, but there is nothing that equals cleanliness as a preventative of disease," the author writes. And it's true that chickens kept in clean and uncrowded conditions with proper lighting, ventilation, and food are less likely to become ill. But chickens, especially when free-ranging, do encounter wild animals or parasites that can make them sick. Accidents happen. Today, instead of reading poultry journals, most poultry keepers turn to Facebook groups or online forums for advice on how to treat their chickens. For every question, there might be a dozen different suggestions. Owners of sick chickens are often left treating their birds with a plan that resembles nothing so much as throwing spaghetti at the wall to see if it sticks.

The first time I brought one of my chickens to the vet (Peggy had bumblefoot, a bacterial infection on her foot pad, which can spread to other tissue and become fatal if left untreated), a man in the waiting room asked if I was holding a chicken. I'd wrapped her in a green towel and was holding her on my lap, so her wings were covered but her little gray, bearded face still stuck out. A bit later, I saw him surreptitiously take a picture, holding his phone low in the way people do when they're trying not to be so obvious about it. I couldn't blame him for wanting to capture the novelty. While many people have started considering chickens as pets, it can feel strange to spend fifty dollars or more on a vet visit for a chicken that "only cost" a dollar as a chick or—I think more importantly—can be purchased rotisserie-style for $4.99 at the local grocery store. Even at a veterinarian's office where they'll agree to treat chickens, the birds are seen as a novelty by the staff. Vet techs ooh and aah over the chicken because they've never seen one before or don't know how to handle them. Doctors complain about human patients diagnosing themselves thanks to WebMD, but chicken keepers, out of necessity, have become expert diagnosticians (or at least have tried).

All of this can make it hard to justify taking a chicken to a vet, but there's been one change in recent years that has forced chicken lovers to find one nearby: since 2017 in the United States, most antibiotics for farm animals can no longer be purchased over the counter.

⤚

Over the last decade, people have started paying more attention to the rise in antibiotic-resistant infections. According to the CDC, over 2.8 million of these occur every year in the United States alone, causing over thirty-five thousand deaths.[19] Worldwide there might be as many as 4.95 million deaths from antimicrobial-resistant bacteria a year.[20] Infection-causing bacteria have always attempted to evolve ways to survive the effects of antibiotics (within a decade of penicillin becoming available, 50 percent of staph infections were resistant to it), but until a few decades ago, drug companies continued making enough new antibiotics that it wasn't a problem.[21] There was always another antibiotic to try in the arms race against bacteria. That's no longer the case for a variety of reasons. Now if dangerous infections become immune to even our strongest, last-resort antibiotics, there might not be anything else coming to save us. People started looking at the only other option for curbing the increase in antibiotic-resistant infections: stop giving bacteria so many chances to become resistant.

Doctors overprescribing antibiotics to their human patients was one culprit, but another one that people quickly zeroed in on was the regular use of antibiotics on farms. Farmers in the 1940s discovered that subtherapeutic levels of cheap antibiotics (enough of a dose that it might potentially prevent an infection but not enough to cure one) could promote weight gain with less feed. By 1980, an estimated 40 percent of all antibiotics produced in the United States were used as feed additives.[22] This was great for business but terrible for public health. These subtherapeutic doses helped bacteria become resistant to antibiotics and pass that resistance on to their progeny or to nearby bacteria.

By the 1990s, the public started worrying about the problem of antibiotic resistance in earnest, and the meat industry began looking into their own antibiotic use as well. Purdue, the processing company, started a three-year study in 1998 to determine the effects of antibiotics on their business. (In other words, they wanted to know just how much money antibiotic use was saving them.) They discovered that the difference between a flock raised with and without antibiotics was now almost negligible thanks to breeding and changes to farming practices.[23] In 2013, the FDA instituted a voluntary plan to help the industry phase out the use of growth-promoting antibiotics and began looking into moving any farm animal antibiotic used for human health from an over-the-counter drug to something requiring a veterinarian's prescription.[24] Perdue, the fourth-largest chicken producer in the United States, stopped using growth-promoting antibiotics in feed and at their hatchery as of 2014, and other members of the poultry industry followed soon after the company's announcement. As of 2017, all medically important antibiotics that farmers might put into animal feed or drinking water became available by prescription only, and the FDA is looking into making that the case for doses given to individuals too.[25] It's questionable how well this is working to curb antibiotic use; the U.S. law still allows entire herds or flocks to be routinely dosed with antibiotics as a "preventative" under a veterinarian's oversight.[26] Stronger restrictions on farm animal antibiotic use have been put into place to greater effect in the European Union and other countries. The EU banned all routine antibiotic use in animal agriculture in 2022.

This has created a big problem for the backyard chicken community. Old posts on the popular forum *BackYard Chickens* are peppered with advice on administering antibiotics. One popular antibiotic, Tylan, was commonly used by poultry keepers to treat respiratory issues in their flocks and was phased out of farm stores between 2013 and 2017. (Of course, respiratory symptoms can have several causes, not all of which should be treated with antibiotics.) "It used to be simple to buy antibiotics for my poultry," one person wrote.[27] "I'm not sure when that all changed, but it has." While some people recommended visiting a veterinarian for a prescription, others offered suggestions for antibiotics that were still possible to get, or black-market methods like ordering medicine from eBay or using antibiotics meant for fish. For a desperate chicken lover with a sick bird, these can seem like reasonable options even though there's more chance of something going wrong (fake medicine, the wrong dosage, or an illness that never required antibiotics in the first place) than right. Anyone who raised poultry prior to 2012 was probably used to diagnosing and treating their own chickens. They would have little reason to pay hundreds of dollars in vet bills for something that they'd always done themselves. But in eliminating over-the-counter antibiotics, the FDA also nudged backyard livestock keepers to seek out a veterinarian. Between this and the rise in new chicken owners who see their "feather babies" as pets, it's no surprise that the demand for better veterinary care for fowl is on the rise.

But there still aren't many vets to go to. Statistics from the American Veterinary Medical Association show that the number of avian specialists actually went down between 2008 and 2018—from 129 to 116. The number of members of the American College of Poultry Veterinarians stayed roughly the same.[28] While veterinarians don't have to be specialists to treat chickens, it certainly helps to find someone who has experience with the birds and knows what to look for.

~

One of the flock's favorite places to linger was on the brick stoop of our front door. They'd sit there on hot days, cold days, and windy days—and almost always when they got caught in the rain—sheltered and contentedly preening. Lyle and I had learned to open the front door slowly or else risk injuring a chicken.

"Come on, chickens," I'd say while nudging the slowest ones with the door. "Off the steps." I kept a hose nearby to wash away the "leavings" that the chickens deposited.

Dolly could usually be found close to the house. Though she wasn't picked on by the rest of the flock, she didn't quite seem to have a place in it either—the kid who always went to the art room during lunch. Sometimes I'd see Peggy or Joan peck her, and Dolly would go running with a squawk to hide behind her best friend, Emmylou, who, as a bantam, was a third of Dolly's size. Dolly had always been so sensitive and so ungainly. Her breed, the Salmon Faverolle, has a large, fluffy white beard that would impress any mall Santa. She was an unusual chicken. People often refer to her breed as "barnyard comedians." I guess odd behavior really is genetic.

One day when Dolly was about a year old, we were up at the house together. She looked beautiful. She'd just molted, and her new feathers had come in so thick it seemed like my whole hand could reach into her fluff before I'd touch her skin. I sat on the stoop and picked her up to hold her in my lap. It was something I'd done a million times with the other chickens. They accepted pets for a few minutes, then jumped away. Dolly tried to do the same. She went up into the air, but instead of landing firmly on her feet, she hit the ground and rolled. Chickens may not fly very well, but their wings are always there to help them down. For whatever reason, hers weren't.

Dolly didn't fall far, no more than two feet, but when she righted herself, she held her neck at a strange angle. She squawked. I panicked. She began walking in small circles, neck twisted far enough that her beak went around and pointed nearly up at the sky again. I tried to hold her still so I could see if anything was wrong. Her neck straightened out. Then Dolly started circling backward, head nearly touching the ground. I decided to make up the cage we used when we needed to bring a chicken inside the house. Dolly rested for a day or two. She looked better.

But over the next few weeks, it seemed like she was forgetting how to get out of the coop in the morning. When I went down to check on the chickens, she would be in the nest area pacing back and forth near the door. I grabbed her and set her down. Sometimes, as if at random, her neck would twist again, or she would try to peck a treat and instead hit all around it like she couldn't see what she was doing. Dolly made a honking squawk with this tone that couldn't have been anything but frustration. It was time to take her to the vet.

The vet I take my dogs to is just a five-minute drive away, and their avian specialist would see chickens, they told me. I knew from all the poultry groups how hard it was to find a chicken vet. I brought Dolly in.

The vet, after looking Dolly over, called her a sweet girl and said it was a good sign that she was still eating and laying eggs. "It's worth giving her a shot," she said while petting Dolly. "We don't know exactly what caused this, but we can make an educated guess and treat for it. Hopefully she'll pull through." They put Dolly on the scale and were impressed by how well she cooperated.

She weighed only four pounds. The average hen of her breed weighs six and a half. There was little but skin and bone underneath all those creamy feathers.

The vet's best guess was something called "wry neck," usually caused by a nutritional deficiency. It's a symptom, not a disease. I gave Dolly supplements and antibiotics. I had to squirt gobs of liquid medicine into her beak every day for a week. Neither of us liked it. I worried about giving her too much or too little in one shot or getting it into her windpipe. She squawked and shook her head back and forth. It was like forcing a kid to take medicine. I pried her beak open over and over, hoping this was for the best.

＞—○

It feels like every pet chicken owner near Portland, Oregon, gets to know Dr. Marli Lintner of the Avian Medical Center eventually. She opened Oregon's first bird-only vet clinic in the mid-1980s and has been treating feathered pets, from parrots to chickens, ever since.

I was two years into chicken ownership when I came across her. It was a sad way to meet. She was the only one who would do a necropsy when I'd found Joan dead in the coop with no warning or signs of illness beforehand. Dr. Lintner fit it in on her lunch break. Afterward, she spent fifteen minutes talking me through what happened and how I could prevent it from happening in the rest of the flock. Joan, who had always been plump, had died from overweight. Fatty liver hemorrhagic syndrome, where fat builds up around the liver and eventually causes it to rupture, was a leading cause of death in laying hens, and I'd never even heard of it before. I'd never had a veterinarian teach me anything new about chickens or treat them with such kindness.

When Dolly's medicine didn't do anything to help her and the original vet was out of ideas, I thought of Dr. Lintner.

For months after Dolly's accident, I'd watched as her neck got better. Then it got worse again. Her tumble had happened in winter, and now it was June and Dolly couldn't get up to roost at night. She could walk up onto the doorstep but couldn't get back down without help. I started watching for her in the yard, worried that she'd get stuck while free-ranging and be unable to get down for food or water. I had to walk down to the coop just before dark every night to "tuck her in" and return first thing in the morning so she could eat and drink. I worried what would happen if my husband and I went out of town at the same time. We had a good chicken sitter but were they good enough to care for a sick chicken? I wasn't sure.

The first thing Dr. Lintner told me after looking at Dolly was that it wasn't wry neck. "It's pretty rare in a noncommercial flock," she said, though other problems with the neck can cause similar symptoms. Not that you would know this from online chicken groups, where it seems to be a favorite diagnosis. If most poultry veterinary training weren't based around the care of commercial flocks, maybe wry neck wouldn't be the go-to answer for any issue involving the neck.

Dolly, in fact, had spinal trauma, likely from the fall. "We did some manual manipulation on her neck to help the muscles relax and straighten everything out, and she was actually able to walk in a straight line afterward," Dr. Lintner said.

I'd noticed that along with everything else wrong with Dolly, her face seemed swollen. I'd mentioned it to the first vet and she'd brushed it off. But Dr. Lintner said the swelling was inflammation from the trauma. This time I got a bottle of anti-inflammatories and a brief lesson on how to give a chicken a neck massage. (Reach down through the feathers and rub the muscles while gently straightening her neck into its proper position.) Dolly seemed to love it. She got a little better, though she still often curled up on the ground like a loaf of bread, her head tucked into her chest. At least she wasn't walking in circles anymore. I wondered how much better Dolly would have been if I'd gotten the proper diagnosis in the first place and how much pain she'd probably been in for months.

Over the previous six months, Dolly had spent a lot of time inside the house. I was worried about her losing weight or that the other chickens might pick on her while she wasn't feeling well. (If anything, it seemed to be the opposite. Dolly often instigated fights with the other hens, then squawked loudly in shock when they dared peck her back in return.) We had a small crate we could set up in the TV room when a chicken was sick or broody. In between watching movies, I'd glance at Dolly, who seemed to have two modes: honk and loaf. She either sat in a fluffed-up position or honked with annoyance when she was bored. I tried to give her extra treats to help her put on weight again. She hated leafy greens but happily pecked at red berries and got bits of red stuck to her beak and face. The thing she loved most of all was plain scrambled egg. Non-chicken people might find this odd, but there's a reason chicks rely on egg yolks to make it through their first few days of life— they're nutritious for chickens too. (It's not so different from a woman eating placenta after giving birth.) I'd take one of the small eggs from the bantam chickens, crack it in a bowl, and microwave it. Once it cooled, I brought it down to Dolly and scraped it into her dish. It got to the point that when she saw me holding a bowl, she'd do a little waddle dance and start honking. Sometimes she pushed against the bars of the cage, hopeful that she'd get the egg faster.

I loved all my chickens, of course, but I got to know Dolly the best of all of them. We spent so much time together that maybe it was inevitable our relationship would change. Now when she ran away from one of the other chickens, she'd hide at my feet. One magic day, I was sitting in the driveway watching the chickens when Dolly trundled over, pushed her body against me, and went to sleep. My chickens are friendly, but none of them have ever willingly cuddled with me before or since.

I fretted over her constantly. Did she seem better or worse? Was she gaining weight? Did she seem happy? That last question was the hardest to answer. Frankly, even with all the time I spent with or thinking about chickens, I didn't really know what gave their lives joy.

I had no problem answering this for my dogs. Bandit, my Velcro-dog, would be brokenhearted if he wasn't able to follow me around the house anymore. For Mesa, who loves nothing more than sitting underneath our one-hundred-year-old deodar cedar and surveying her domain, it would be the day she couldn't enjoy hours in the sun.[29] It's not so easy with chickens.

I think one reason we, as humans, have allowed ourselves to treat chickens—the only animal exempted from the Humane Slaughter Rule—so badly is because it's more difficult to relate to a bird's life than to a mammal's.

Birds don't have facial muscles that can reveal precise emotions.[30] The presence of an unchanging beak makes it impossible to imagine a smile on their faces. Hens and roosters alike might flare their hackle feathers when they're itching for a fight and crouch or stand taller to show submissiveness or dominance. Chickens can communicate using their voices, gestures, and even the movement of their feathers, but most of this is unreadable to humans. I know the chickens like (and expect) treats and get upset when I take too long to let them out of the coop. But I often wonder if what my friends call the "chicken paradise" where my flock lives is actually just someone meeting their basic needs. Commercial farms give them so little and yet they survive it. Their "favorite activities," like perching or foraging or dust bathing, also serve utilitarian purposes.

There's only one thing I've witnessed chickens do that communicates contentment, if not outright joy. Chickens purr. It's not a common occurrence, and the sound is so quiet that unless you're sitting right next to them it would be easy to miss it. I usually hear purring on summer days when the chickens have found a particularly good dust bathing spot or a patch of sun to nap in—sometimes both together. This, more than treats or new things to peck, is the height of chicken happiness.

The last time I heard Dolly purr was that day she lay next to me in the driveway. That was in April.

She still roamed around the yard and interacted, in a limited, peck-and-run kind of way, with the rest of the flock. I saw her floppily try to take dust baths. On her worst days, I thought about putting her down. On her better days, she still behaved more or less like a chicken.

~

"One of the big differences with chickens compared to other birds is how they ambulate and how narrow a range they have of physical responses to things," Dr. Lintner told me. I was shadowing her as she treated birds at her veterinary practice. When I walked in the door, I saw a large rooster propped up in a storage tote. He had spinal trauma a while ago that, like Dolly's, was left untreated. Unlike Dolly, he couldn't use his legs or walk. The prognosis wasn't good.

On the other side of the office, a brown-and-gold-colored hen calmly walked around. She made sweet noises that had a questioning quality to them. *What is this shiny metal over here? Why are those birds making such a racket?* When she walked past a cockatoo in a cage, the parrot raised his yellow crown into a mohawk and cackled in alarm. Parrots, apparently, did not like the sight of chickens. They were both part of the class Aves but branched off after that point.

A parrot, for instance, could do all kinds of things with his beak, Dr. Lintner said. Parrots could hang upside down and fly and make a much wider range of vocalizations, including mimicry. "A chicken," she laughed, "a chicken walks. A chicken pecks. And there you have it." This didn't mean their lives were less complicated, but it did mean there were a narrower range of observable habits for them to change. "It's much more difficult in a chicken to assess pain thresholds, happiness, depression," Dr. Lintner said. A chicken not feeling well for any number of reasons might seem depressed, stop eating, and have a poopy butt. (She said these three symptoms were 90 percent of the immediately observable changes she saw in chicken patients.)

This, added to the fact that there's very little published information on treating a live chicken, made them particularly tricky to diagnose. "We know more about commercial poultry than any other animal on the planet, and yet all that knowledge is acquired at the necropsy table," Dr. Lintner said. "You have a chicken with a problem? Bring them to us, we kill them, and do a necropsy on them." Most backyard chicken owners prefer a diagnosis that leaves their pet alive to take back home after the appointment.

When Dr. Lintner got to the clinic earlier that morning, she came in carrying a Starbucks coffee and a slice of frosted lemon loaf for a midday snack. She greeted the staff and showed them photos of a calf that was just born on her farm over the weekend. Her phone had a heavy case because she had a habit of dropping it, and the protective screen was so thick it made it hard to swipe. It was the kind of small staff where everyone seemed to know each other well.

A whiteboard in the back was already full of appointments and rechecks on birds that stayed overnight. There were chickens and conures and parrots and even pigeons in the office. Occasionally, Dr. Lintner had a hawk come in from a local falconer. In the 1990s, when a pair of ostriches could be worth tens of thousands of dollars (people hoped the meat, oil, and eggs were a burgeoning market just waiting to break open), Dr. Lintner treated most of

Oregon's large, flightless birds, which are known as "ratites." There were so many of these clients that she had to hire a strong vet tech to help her hold the birds safely while treating them. A large ostrich might be over three hundred pounds and nine feet tall. "That business came and went and crashed, which was kind of nice," she said.

It was a few years after this that the chickens started coming in. There had always been some, she said, "But it didn't get Portland crazy until about fifteen years ago." That's when she started seeing chickens so often that now there was rarely a day without at least one of them on the books—usually more than one. She was one of the first to regularly use tests like bloodwork and X-rays (with and without barium to look at the gastrointestinal tract) on chickens. The latter was something she'd had to get quite good at. "They're much more prone to eat stupid things," she said. In fact, later that day I watched her necropsy a hen who'd eaten what looked like a piece of rope and died from obstructed intestines.

When chickens eat, food goes into their beak, down the esophagus, and hangs out in something called the crop. Food can stay in their crops up to twelve hours, and it's immediately apparent when a chicken has had a big meal because it protrudes in a ball on their right side. (Chicken keepers often refer to this as a "food boob.") From there, food goes into the gizzard, which is the avian answer to teeth. In the gizzard, food mixes with digestive enzymes and grit—anything from sand to pebbles—until it's ground down into something small enough to pass through the intestines and, well, out the other end. Unfortunately, if a chicken were to, say, get a hold of a diamond from your wedding ring, it would stay there forever getting a light polish. "That's why chickens and birds in general have such a problem with heavy lead and zinc poisoning," Dr. Lintner said. A flake of zinc solder will keep getting ground up and released into their bodies until it kills them.

Dr. Lintner owned chickens for many years, so she knows the quirks that are normal for hens but might worry another vet. She once had a chicken come in from another veterinarian who'd felt an egg and thought the bird was egg bound. "Well, of course there's an egg," Dr. Lintner said. "A chicken lays an egg nearly every day!" But the other vet had stuck their finger inside the bird's reproductive tract to try and move the egg and cracked it. Dr. Lintner has a radiograph showing the egg inside the chicken and the crunched spot where a finger had poked it. "It was bad."

These are the things that people miss when they don't know chickens and only have the rare hen come in for treatment.

Another difficult part about treating chickens is that most owners eat their birds' eggs. Before prescribing medicine, Dr. Lintner has to keep in mind how long of an egg withdrawal time it will have (in other words, how long before it's safe to eat the eggs again). If the hen's eggs aren't easy to tell apart from the rest of the flock's, either the chicken has to be separated or none of the eggs should be eaten. In some cases, she might suggest owners wait until fall or winter, when egg production naturally slows, before treating.

Dr. Lintner told me that it was exciting in a lot of ways to figure out how to diagnose and treat pet chickens at a time when almost no one was doing it. Money wasn't an object for the bird's owners, but, essentially, it was a lot of trial and error. "We laugh about it in vet school: 'That's why we call it veterinary *practice*,'" she said. "You get better as you do it, but you're definitely practicing." Without seeing a lot of chickens, veterinarians didn't have the cases they needed for comparison. And they were more likely to have a hard time treating problems common to backyard hens versus better-publicized commercial flock illnesses.

In July, Dolly stopped laying eggs. I couldn't help but notice that her good days weren't as good as they used to be, and the bad ones were even worse.

The worst thing about having chickens is that sometimes, no matter what you do, they die. The world's oldest chicken lived to be twenty-two years old, and I often hear about chickens living to be eight or nine, but this is uncommon.[31] Many of them get sick or are killed by predators. I know few people with chickens who didn't experience one kind of loss or another within their first years of poultry keeping. The more time you spend with the birds, the harder these losses are. They can live a long time, but they usually don't.

I wish Dolly's story had a happy ending: we found out what was wrong thanks to better chicken veterinary care and cured it. But not every problem has a solution.

Even if we'd known from the very beginning that she'd hurt her spine, there's no guarantee anything would have turned out differently. But there are a lot of other chicken owners who might have a better outcome with their birds if they could find a vet willing and able to treat their chickens.

I'd never had to decide to euthanize a pet before. I'm ashamed to say I had always assumed it was easy. Your pet is sick, unhappy, not getting better—obviously it's time. But Dolly always went back and forth between the land of the healthy and the land of the sick, and it was hard to let go of the hope of giving her more good days. It was hard to know when allowing her to continue wasn't extending her life so much as prolonging her suffering. Eventually, the day came.

In mid-August, Dolly stopped eating on her own. Her neck wrapped around itself like a corkscrew. I sat with her in the warm summer grass and hand-fed her a juicy peach. I can't say it was a good day. I tried to make it a good day for her anyway. The next morning, Lyle drove us to Dr. Lintner's office while Dolly sat on my lap wrapped in a towel. They gave her body back to me in a small white box with Dolly's name beautifully written on the lid. I buried her in the yard next to her other flockmates who had left us. I still think of her often, and not just because I loved her. She had made me wonder what gave a chicken joy and what it looked like when that joy was gone.[32] What was a good life for a chicken anyway?

CHICKENS
ON
DISPLAY

CHAPTER FIVE:
THERE'S NO BUSINESS LIKE
POULTRY SHOW BUSINESS

C HICKENS! CHICKENS! CHICKENS! WE'RE GOING TO SEE CHICKENS today," a young boy yells, skipping through the parking lot. "I can hear them," he says gleefully.

"Sounds more like quacking to me," his dad responds.

The boy hardly hears him. He runs ahead of his family, looking back every so often as though urging them to hurry up. "Chickens!" he yells again. "There's chickens in there."

It's two weeks before Thanksgiving, and it's twenty-eight degrees and sunny. The parking lot is filled with cars and trucks and tractor trailers. Noise occasionally comes from the vehicles, though their engines are all silent. Instead, birds surprise passersby with a quack or a honk or a shrill rooster's cock-a-doodle-doo. It occurs to me that the roosters crowing their hearts out can probably see the breath lingering in the air in front of their beaks.

For most Americans the second weekend in November doesn't mean much, but for chicken people it's the biggest event of the year—the Ohio National. Serious poultry breeders go to smaller local and regional shows as they perfect their birds throughout the year, but it's all just practice for the National, as people tend to call it.

Two days, 8,400 birds, and a chance to win it all as best in show.

I arrive on Friday, the load-in day before the show officially opens. The large concrete building is filled with anticipation. It's impossible to miss the gleaming wall of trophies with awards for best in breed and class and, of course, the biggest prize of them all: best in show. The rest of the building is packed with row after row of empty wire cages and only a couple signs to help people navigate throughout what's easily a few miles worth of rows. Every cage is labeled with the variety, breed, and type of bird that belongs in it along with the owner number. (No one is identified by name on their birds' cages to keep the judging fair.)

It feels like walking into a dressing room before the curtains go up. I see some black-and-white Polish chickens with their poofy hair tied up like women in a 1980s Jazzercise class. In another row, a White Silkie that undoubtedly just finished a blow-dry is nibbling water from a small red Solo cup. "It's to protect their hair," their owner says. Everyone seems to have tricks like this, their best guess at what will keep the prewashed and primped poultry looking like the best in show until judging takes place the following day.

People have camp chairs set up along the edge of the building, most of them close to their rows. I talk to a woman named Jan who just drove fourteen hours from Oklahoma to be here and is now sitting in one of the foldable chairs. She has four fluffy Black Australorps and two other birds at this year's show. She's holding a big rooster on her lap, filing his beak and trimming his nails. I ask if I can see what she's doing.

"I'm not really getting him ready, just cleaning him up after the trip," she says while brushing the rooster with what looks like a wool carder. After this, she brings him to the nearby hose and washes his feet—being careful to get between the toes. His red comb gleams. The rooster bears this all stoically, with the grace of someone used to this level of primping.

"He's so calm," I say.

"Oh, that's just because I'm holding him. He's not really tame or anything."
Jan puts him in a large wire cage, and he just stands there like this is all totally
normal. For him, it probably is. But Jan doesn't have time to spare for a lookie-
loo like me. She has five other birds that need grooming and feeding and water-
ing, and, at some point, Jan herself will need to take a break after the long drive.
She says she'll be around later if I'd like to ask her some questions, but I never
see her again—only her birds standing like Roman statues in their cages.

I leave her row and narrowly avoid running into a woman who is bringing her ducks into the room, all of them in plastic storage totes with air holes
punched into the sides, the bottoms half-filled with water. While chickens are
in the majority at the Ohio National, there are poultry of all kinds—geese as
large as German Shepherds; prehistoric-looking guinea fowl; turkeys taking
turns showing off and cooing to each other; small, delicate quail; and more.

"You letting it walk or trying to catch it?" one man in a Carhartt jacket
says to another who is wearing a hat and walking calmly after a Sebastopol
goose with frilled feathers that make it look like the bird is wearing a tutu.

"Oh, just letting it walk," he says as they promenade together around the
turkey cages. Eventually he decides the goose has gotten enough exercise. He
whisks the bird into his arms with a smile and proceeds to join a group of
people in conversation.

It smells like fresh straw. At some point, the room goes from empty to full—
sound ricochets throughout the building. It's so loud that even though I hold my
tape recorder as close to people as I can while I talk to them, later it's still hard to
make out the human conversation over the cacophony that surrounds us.

I overhear a woman at the info station, one of the volunteers who helps
organize and run the Ohio National year after year, say that she's been here
every day for the last five weekends and is looking forward to doing nothing
next week when it's all over. Putting on the National, which has run nearly
every year since 1957, is serious business.

⤙⤚

I was there, cold despite my layers, because poultry shows were the catalyst for
chicken culture as we know it today. People who keep chickens generally fall

into three categories. They might keep chickens as food animals or have the birds as beloved pets. Both of these practices are familiar to the general public. But the third category, keeping chickens as show animals, is something outsiders don't know much about. Most people, whether 4-H kids or backyard hobbyists, find out about show poultry because local shows are the only way to get certain breeds of chickens that hatcheries don't carry. While the Ohio National usually gets local (and sometimes national) media coverage, smaller shows are often held in barns or warehouses and are only advertised by word of mouth.

I grew up in the kind of dog-loving family that would tune into the Westminster or Crufts dog shows when they were put on television. My mom and I would ooh and aah over the dogs and declare this one to be our favorite, or actually this one, no, this one! The Whippets on screen were like the Whippets I grew up with, but somehow different. Show dogs had an air of professionalism about them, like if you met one at a party you'd immediately wonder if they were famous for something. The dogs had all been raised for the moments in the ring where, freshly bathed and groomed and fussed over, they'd walk in a few circles and stand politely while a judge gave them the once-over. Dog shows are a big deal. They're shown on national television and Americans spend $330 million a year, including travel costs, to compete in them.[33] But dog shows only got to where they are today by basing themselves on something that was even more popular when it first started—the poultry show. The first dog show came thirty years after poultry shows were already established and wildly popular events. If it weren't for chickens, who knows if the Westminster Kennel Club Dog Show would even exist today?

People often act like the growing infatuation over chickens as pets is a brand-new phenomenon. They scoff at the two-thousand-dollar chicken coop from Williams-Sonoma or the wealthy Silicon Valley types buying a chicken for $350, thinking it's some new form of excess.[34] But compared to one moment in the past, today's chicken lovers are almost restrained in their spending.

⟿

Starting in the 1840s, something between obsession and mania took hold in England and then spread to other countries, including America. Chicken shows, like many agricultural shows or fairs, were nothing new, but in 1842, a stir began in the United Kingdom after Queen Victoria received seven chickens—five hens and two cocks. These birds were taller than any chicken England had ever seen and had long yellow legs and feathers that hugged tightly to their bodies, giving them a predator's air. Though they were called Cochin Chinas after the part of Vietnam where they'd reportedly been collected (Cochin China was a colonialist term for Southern Vietnam), the birds were closer to what we know today as Malays.

The queen was so delighted by these unusual and large fowl that she immediately had a new aviary constructed for them. The final building had to have been one of the grandest chicken coops ever constructed. The semi-Gothic building had fenced runs for the chickens with gravel paths bordered by grass. Inside, the birds' accommodations were spacious and warm. Nests were formed from twigs of heather, hawthorn, and lichen and were made "to resemble the dark, bramble-covered recess of their original jungles," wrote self-described "amateur poultry keeper" J. J. Nolan.[35] It doesn't seem as though the expense of this fowl house was much of a concern for the young queen, who was, at the time, only in her early twenties.

Newspapers covered the chickens and the design of the new poultry house. As the Cochin Chinas—of various shapes and sizes—began to hatch chicks, Victoria gifted their offspring to other royal families.[36] Thanks to all the press around the queen's trendsetting new chickens, London held its first poultry show in 1845. Though it was a small affair held at the zoo, the public couldn't get enough of it. Everyone had to have Asiatic fowl. Clipper ships from the newly opened Port of Shanghai began carrying exotic chickens along with other cargo. In 1846, the queen received some large, fluffy chickens with feathery legs and tails that looked like bustles. They arrived from Shanghai, and the public lumped them in with the original Cochin Chinas, though today these downy chickens alone are called Cochins.[37] (The fact that something akin to a Malay actually started the poultry craze was forgotten largely due to the naming confusion.) Queen Victoria sent a delegation of her new Cochins to Dublin, where they were exhibited at the show of the Royal Dublin Agricultural Society.[38] This show was when "Hen Fever" or "Cochin Mania" became truly virulent.

"Immediately the Cochin *furore* commenced," wrote famed publisher

Samuel Orchard Beeton in *Beeton's Book of Poultry and Domestic Animals.*[39] "As soon as it was discovered, despite the most strenuous efforts to keep the secret, that a certain dealer was possessed of a pair of these birds, straightaway the avenues to that dealer's shop were blocked by broughams, chariots, and hack-cabs until the sly poulterer had been tempted by a sufficiently high sum to part with his treasures," Beeton elaborated. "Bank notes were exchanged for Cochin chicks, and Cochin eggs were in as great demand as though they had been laid by the fabled golden goose."

The madness over these fowl was telegraphed across the pond and quickly took hold in the United States too.

Within a few years, many influential men in America had become obsessed with exotic poultry. They paid for chickens to be sent from breeders in the United Kingdom or even shipped all the way from Asia. Yet as "the fancy," as it was sometimes known, became more popular and unusual fowl proliferated in chicken coops throughout New England, it became impossible to tell whether one man's chickens were better than another's. Other than taking a person at their word, there wasn't much to go against. So in October 1849, Dr. John C. Bennett wrote a letter to the editor of influential farm journal *The Boston Cultivator*, declaring his intention to organize a poultry show. He hoped to show off "perfect samples of the full-blooded domestic fowls," which, Bennett wrote, "comprise some of the handsomest and best fowls in the world."[40] He initially proposed Quincy Market as a venue, but *The Cultivator's* editor, believing this show would be more popular than Bennett imagined, suggested using the larger Public Gardens and even charging an admission fee to the many visitors who were sure to want to come.

A month after this letter, 1,423 fowl were sent to be put on display at this show from 219 exhibitors—most of them from close to Boston but some from other nearby states. Over ten thousand members of the public paid the four-pence admission price to see them.[41] Until then, chickens had simply been "straggling and starving" in Boston backyards, "unknown, unhonored, and unsung," as poultry fancier George P. Burnham wrote in his book *The History of the Hen Fever.*[42] Newspapers covered this first-of-its-kind show, remarking both on the ornate fowl and the prominent men who came to show their chickens, including the famed orator, lawyer, and politician Daniel Webster. (He brought seven geese and two Java barnyard fowl to the show.)[43]

"Unheard-of prices were asked, and readily paid, for all sorts of fowls," Burnham wrote, recalling this first poultry show. "As high as thirteen dollars was paid by one man (who soon afterwards became an inmate of a lunatic asylum) for a single pair of domestic fowls."

That's the equivalent of roughly $480 today.

Word of these rare chickens (and the prices paid for them) convinced many people that they should get into the poultry business themselves. Some chickens were priced and sold for as high as fifty dollars a pair (or over $1800 today). In 1854, the famous showman P. T. Barnum even held national poultry shows in New York City, the first in February and another in October. But by the time the second show rolled around, the bubble—or the Hen Fever—had finally broken.

Poultry that sold for tens of dollars a pair a few months before could hardly find a buyer at half price. Men who'd ordered chickens from abroad at great expense found that the hens were no longer even worth the price of a trip by the time their ships docked in America. Those, like George Burnham, who got into the fancy early likely did okay, while others were ruined. *

Fancy breeds of poultry continued to be valued by hobbyists but at much more reasonable prices. Chicken shows, when they popped up throughout the country, rarely got the same numbers and media attention as they had in the 1800s. People forgot that chickens had once been a cultural phenomenon; they were just birds again.

But not for everyone.

～

---

* As Burnham put it in his book, "Kings and queens and nobility, senators and governors, mayors and councilmen, ministers, doctors and lawyers, merchants and tradesmen, the aristocrat and the humble, farmers and mechanics, gentlemen and commoners, old men and young men, women and children, rich and poor, white, black and grey—everybody was more or less seriously affected by this curious epidemic."

"A lot of people ask what I like to do in my free time, and I tell them, 'I show chickens.' People are really surprised by it," says Chad Satterfield. But maybe it was meant to be. He's spent most of his life around chickens. "When I was nine years old, I started working at commercial chicken houses," he says. There were some within walking distance of where he grew up in South Carolina. Then he purchased some Cornish Bantams, a small but stocky bird with a short beak and round eyes, to keep in the backyard. "I had chickens all the way up through when I was fifteen or sixteen. But then I started driving, got out of the chicken business, and went into horses and different things." His family usually had a few laying hens around, but it wasn't the same. When a work friend mentioned that he kept show chickens, Satterfield jumped at the chance to get back in the poultry game. "I started doing it with my son. He was eleven or twelve then when he got his first, and I just got me some, and we started working together, and to this day he has his and I have mine," Satterfield recalls in a pleasant Carolinas lilt. "We spend a lot of time fooling around with our birds."

Today Satterfield is in his late forties. For the last thirteen years, he's worked six or seven days a week in manufacturing before coming home to tend to his show chickens. "I can do all the chores within forty-five minutes, but then when you go out there, you like to comb through stuff." Often he winds up spending closer to four hours with the birds, he says, though he doesn't ignore things like his daughter's softball lessons or working in the home garden just to hang around the fowl.

Satterfield is the kind of man who might be called imposing if friendliness didn't ooze out of him. When I meet him at the National, he tells me to look for someone in a bright blue shirt. It's impossible to miss him. The blue brings out his deep tan. He seems taller than his six feet.

People like to say that dogs look like their owners (or the other way around), but in chickens, it's always a bit of a surprise to find out what breed someone gravitates toward. For Satterfield, it's the Quail d'Anver. Seven years ago, he bought them for his son, who "didn't like them and didn't want them." Satterfield wound up adding the birds to his flock instead. The birds had so much character and the females were sweet as can be, he says. He'd already taken a shine to them when he started bringing the birds to shows—and winning.

The d'Anver is what's known as a "true bantam," a small chicken breed that doesn't have a full-size variation. They have small delicate faces except for their large black eyes and fluffy beards that puff out like someone tucked an oversize scarf into a winter jacket. Their legs seem short because of the birds' habit of holding their wings at a downward angle, swept back like coattails. They are impossibly cute and seem especially small next to Satterfield, who could fit one in each hand and have room to spare.

The National had placed them in a row that was nearly all d'Anvers, one cage after another of tiny, bearded hens and squeaky roosters staring up at me. There was some order in the chicken chaos. Birds of the same breed were put together so the judges could make easy comparisons. Fowl were largely organized around the room according to the class divisions within *The American Standard of Perfection*, a book published in 1874 to define the ideal for each breed. Finding Satterfield's birds was a bit like playing a trivia game: I had to know both his birds' breed and that they were Rose Comb Clean Legged Bantams. (While the full-size chicken classes refer to the breed's geographical origins—American, Asiatic, Continental, English, or Mediterranean, as well as a grab-bag All Other Standard Breeds—the bantam classes tend to describe the birds' looks, like their comb shape and whether their legs are feathered.)

He scoops a squawking hen out of her cage and cradles her in his hands as we talk. Satterfield scratches her beard absentmindedly. The hen closes her eyes. No matter how much the chickens don't want to come out of their cage, they seem to relax as soon as Satterfield holds them. You may not be able to guess what kind of chicken someone would show based on looks, but you can tell a lot about a person based on how they treat their birds—and how the birds respond in kind.

The Ohio National takes place at a time of year when most chickens start molting, losing their feathers so new, stronger ones can grow in. A lot of breeders pin their hopes on a chicken with best in show potential only to have him lose all his feathers a week before the show and have to stay at home. But even the most beautiful chickens need a little bit of work before they're show quality. Satterfield's birds all got baths before the ten-hour drive to the National. It's a complicated affair involving buckets of soapy and clean water, glycerin (to make feathers shine), and maybe bluing for white birds whose feathers have yellowed from the sun, over and over for all twenty chickens

Satterfield brought with him. The chickens look pretty good from where I'm standing, but he isn't done yet.

Satterfield grabs a plastic toolbox he stashed underneath the wire cages, pulls out a stool, and gets to work. There are wipes and clippers and tweezers and a "special potion" he feeds to the chickens upon arrival to give them a little pep.

First, he wipes their feet and combs with a mixture of alcohol, witch hazel, and what he describes only as "something I found at Dollar General." While some products overlap between chicken breeders, everyone has their own special cocktail of treatments they think work best on their birds. They're not secrets exactly, but few people broadcast their tricks of the trade. He also sprays some sheen spray on a cloth and rubs it over the birds' feathers. When he's done, the impact isn't dissimilar to giving a clean pair of leather boots a good polish and shine. Back in their cages, the birds seem to stand up taller. Whether it's from the strange feeling of their express spa treatment or the way they look is hard to say.

When I ask Satterfield what it is that makes him put all this time and effort into breeding, raising, and showing his birds, he tells me he loves the birds and then pauses to look down at the d'Anver, whose beak needs a small trim. But it's more than that; he could love the birds just as easily by staying home. "I've met a lot of friends doing this that I don't get to see unless I come here. Yeah, we can talk on Facebook, but you know," he trails off. Without the excuse of the National to make the ten-hour drive, it's unlikely they'd ever see each other.

This is the case for most people I talk to at the National. There are meetings scheduled left and right for various breed groups and annual dinners marked on people's calendars. I'm at the National during the Trump presidency, and people in opposite political parties are more likely to immediately block someone on social media than try to have a conversation, and yet I can't help but notice how many different groups of people chickens manage to bring together. I see MAGA hats but also Obama/Biden stickers. During the second day of the show, I'm walking through the parking lot when I see two forty-something women spot each other.

"Tiffany!" one yells like a middle schooler on the first day after summer break.

They run toward each other.

"How are you?" the first one asks.

"I'm married!" Tiffany says, shining a large ring in the air. The two laugh and hug and stand in the cold catching up.

All day, people sit by their birds in the pop-up camping chairs that line the outer edges of the show floor and talk. It's hard to maintain friendships as an adult, but everyone can get together at the chicken show.

I ask Satterfield what he talks about at these get-togethers that he can't say over text.

"We're talking about life," Satterfield says. "We're talking about chickens."

~

"The chicken business is an interesting thing. There's millionaires in here. There's poor people. There's doctors, judges. You don't know who the hell they are," says Clell Agler. "And nobody cares." He's been involved with poultry shows for most of his life, the National in particular, but doesn't think anyone here could say what he does for a living outside of chickens. Agler has been heavily involved in putting the show together since 1964, and the show's growth is more than a little thanks to his efforts. By 1973, less than four years after he took over running things, the National was the biggest show in the country.

"I don't like to brag because it's not healthy, I don't think. But we're really the only show people talk about," says Agler. The Ohio National has technically been around since 1957, though, as Agler tells it, for the first few years "we were a little six-hundred-bird, piece-of-garbage show nobody came to." He's proud of what it's become.

Showing chickens is a lot of work for little monetary reward. Even before the hours spent getting each bird cleaned up and ready for show, there's the travel and the expense of housing so many birds and a lot of chores too. Unlike the dog business, where people can sell a puppy for thousands of dollars, or large livestock, which can go for tens of thousands, even the highest-quality show chicken from the best breeders won't sell for more than a couple hundred. Today, as far as animal shows are concerned, chickens are the great equalizer. You can get a good quality show chicken for eighty dollars (or even for free if you find the right mentor) and build your own coop for only a little bit more money. Entry fees for most shows hover around thirty dollars. It's why people from all backgrounds gravitate to chickens—the main requirement for the hobby is a love of poultry.

Throughout the time I sit talking to Agler about the beginnings of the National and how it's changed over the years, we're interrupted constantly. Judges in white lab coats walk up to him, asking which breeds and classes still need judging. A few people ask for a recommendation for who to buy a chicken from. One woman tells him that a chicken from the junior show has gone missing, a Black Cochin Bantam. (This, Agler says, happens every show. "Most of them get out or . . . something. Okay, sometimes you get a thief." That's all he wants to say on the subject.) Throughout the show, I've seen Agler talking with one breeder or another—deep in conversation and laughter. Now he's holding court at the info booth, and his expertise, apparently, is in high demand.

The most important thing he tries to get across to me is how much chicken shows have changed since he was a boy. "Back in the day, it was an old man's game," Agler recalls. They'd let younger people like him into the shows but were never welcoming. The older showmen would ignore newcomers outright or make fun of them. "They'd only pay attention to kids after they'd been there for two or three years and took their abuse," Agler says. As for women? Forget about it.

While backyard poultry was the province of women, show poultry (and its high-value birds) has always been a man's game. The names of famous or wealthy men show up constantly in stories or ledgers showing the prices people paid for poultry during Hen Fever. Other than Queen Victoria herself, I never saw another woman mentioned. This trend, it seems, continued for over a century after poultry shows began. Things only started changing in the 1980s when youth shows were created and families started coming to poultry shows together—making it the kind of place where women might feel welcome for the first time.

Today there are still more men than women involved in show poultry, but it's far from male dominated anymore. When the judging ends and championships are announced on the last day, more than a few women win champion or reserve champion for their bird's class. One of these is Jan Brett, whose Polish Bantam chickens frequently win best in breed or class. She is a Grandmaster and Master Breeder in the American Poultry Association and American Bantam Association shows respectively—both titles that take a lot of wins within the same breed to obtain. I can tell she's been a fixture at the show for many years because she gets one of the loudest rounds of applause when her best in class win is announced at the awards ceremony.

~

When I first see Brett at the National, she's wearing a black sweater and a black knit hat with a white poof on top. She's holding one of her Polish Bantam chickens, black with a white crest of feathers. I realize, with a jolt, that she's dressed to match her chickens. Even her bag has a black-and-white Polish painted on the side. This attention to detail is less surprising from her than from the other breeders (though I've noticed that chicken-themed clothing and accessorizing is customary, particularly for women). The first time I was looking through lists of winning breeders, I stopped when I came to Brett's name because hers is one that's been familiar to me since I can remember. Brett is a bestselling author of children's books, which she writes and illustrates herself. I have three of her books, carefully tucked away on my shelf, that I've been carrying around since toddlerhood. I was thrilled to find out she was a chicken lady too.

It was a children's book that first brought Brett back to chickens. She'd written three books that had chickens in them and figured she should probably get some if she was going to keep drawing them. She'd had them as a little girl and knew that with handling, the birds could go from flighty to friendly in no time. (One of her childhood chickens got so friendly it sometimes sat on her handlebars and joined her on a bike ride.) Twenty years ago she got some chicks from the feed store and hasn't been without a flock since.

What started as a desire to get a small flock of chickens soon turned into an obsession when she stumbled onto the world of show poultry. Today the birds travel all over the country with her from her home in Norwell, Massachusetts, both to shows and to their summer home in the Berkshires—her husband is a Boston Symphony Orchestra bassist who plays at Tanglewood during the summer. The chickens have gorgeous and spacious accommodations at each home. Take out the shavings and nest boxes and these buildings could be popular rentals on Airbnb.

To move between their properties, Brett and her husband used to load over fifty chickens and ten ducks into the backs of a Jaguar and a Toyota Prius to make the drive, but now she has a dedicated trailer for the chickens. (The two used to get a lot of looks when they stopped for gas.)

Brett describes herself as a competitive person, and it shows in her successful chicken breeding. But there are some things she does that are different from the average breeder. To get chickens that better conform to the Standard of Perfection—a platonic ideal for every breed of chicken, taken from the book of the same name—breeders have to breed and hatch out many generations of chickens. Not all of those hatched will make the grade. Having too many roosters in with the hens can be hard on the girls, whose feathers get rubbed away from overmating, and not all of the birds—of any gender—will be show quality. This means that all poultry breeders have to cull some of their flock. For many, this means killing the extra birds. Brett doesn't go that route.

When she hatches out her new chickens for the year, one hundred chicks the year we talk, she uses a broody hen to do it rather than an incubator. She's never had luck with the machines, which seemed to always be breaking or turning off during a power outage, so she keeps a breed that often goes broody just to be mothers to her flock. "I'll be the only person who shows poultry and doesn't use an incubator or brooder—it's much harder to do," she says. "The hens are always stealing each other's chicks!"

Brett then raises these one hundred chicks throughout their adolescence until they're about six months old, spoiling them the whole time, so she can see whether they're show quality. At the end of that time, if any of them have flaws, like a white tip on their wings, she simply takes them to shows, where she sells them as pet quality. At the end of the National, all Brett's cages in the sale area are empty.

"I find it very fulfilling," Brett says of her chickens. She works eight hours a day on her books but spends an hour with the birds in the morning and another hour at night. Some of that time is spent on chores like cleaning the pens or vaccinating chicks—a multi-hour process that she does by hand—but it also entails giving the birds treats and just spending time together. "I love the bird mind. They're really quite smart about some things but also very transparent," she explains with a smile. "Sometimes I see a chicken and think, 'That chicken is tiptoeing. It's trying to sneak by me,'" Brett says, then sings a few bars of the *Pink Panther* theme. She tells me that they sometimes crouch down as though they think she can't see them if they stay very still. Brett can't help but laugh at them. "They're all my little friends," she says.

～～

Other than conversing with people, I spend most of my time at the National simply wandering from cage to cage looking at all the birds. (If you think you can't spend two or three days looking at chickens without getting bored, you've never met a chicken person.) The only thing better than looking at the chickens is watching people's reactions to them. I walk past a tabletop show for Seramas, the smallest chicken breed in the world. They range in height from six to ten inches tall and stand with their tails high and chests puffed out like soldiers at attention. While most other birds are judged in their cages, Seramas have a special type of show where they're put onto a table and judged not just for looks but also on how well they strut. Chicken people often call this "vigor." There are two judges at the table, a man and a woman, and whenever the Serama does something showy—walking around, standing upright—the woman says, "Good boy!" I've never seen a crowd of people get so excited to watch a chicken flap his wings. When one rooster crows, the group huddled around the table bursts into applause.

I, too, can't help but be impressed by the birds.

At one point, I'm admiring the White Faverolles—I'd only ever known the breed to come in salmon color—when a couple, dressed as though they'd just stepped off their motorcycles, walks up next to me.[44]

"Do you have one?" the woman asks.

I don't, but I briefly mention Dolly, my "pet quality" Salmon Faverolle.

"They're so sweet," the man says. His front teeth are chipped, which gives him a bit of a lisp.

"Too sweet for their own good sometimes," I say, and we laugh.

The couple tell me about their own chickens. They started with twenty-five and now have over two hundred birds in total—Faverolles and Cochins in just about every color. "We have a Cochin rooster that comes up to here," the woman says, pointing at her knee. "But he's a big baby."

There's such a spark in their eyes when they talk about their own flock. As they speak, they lean in closer to each other. Now, side by side, they hold hands. They coo over the chickens like some people coo over babies. Their love for each other seems somehow tied up in their love for chickens, for their home, and for the flock they'd be returning to when the show was over.

~~o~~

Though the show is technically Saturday and Sunday (with Friday setup), when I arrive early on Sunday morning, it already feels like things are wrapping up. Best in class birds were transferred to champion row the night before. Despite the pomp of the glittering trophy display, the awards ceremony feels oddly perfunctory. Except for best in show, most people already seem to know what they're going to get. Going into this weekend, I'd thought the awards show would be the culmination of the event—isn't showing poultry about winning? But it hardly seems to matter.

I find Andrew Miles, a twenty-year-old from Pennsylvania who brought his Silkies to the show. He started raising chickens in 4-H, then moved into youth poultry shows, and now competes as an adult. I ask him how he feels he did this year, only getting slightly distracted by the Muppet-meets-cottonball look of his Silkies in nearby cages. He tells me that while the Bearded Silkies didn't do as well, he won best in breed for his Non-Bearded White Silkies. Still, he says he's happy because he achieved the goals he set for his breeding program this year.

"I'm so surprised that people don't seem more disappointed not to win best in class or show," I tell him. "What's that all about?"

"Even though it's called the Standard of Perfection, we all interpret 'perfection' differently," he says. "That's what makes the hobby fun; you never know what's going to happen. My bird that won out of five thousand last year won't win at the next show."

It's not about big prizes so much as consistency. Miles and everyone else I speak with say that they're happy when this year's birds are better than the year before. It's all so wholesome that sometimes I can hardly stand it. Of course, people gossip and say so-and-so's birds deserved to win and the occasional bird gets stolen, but the chicken world doesn't have a seedy underbelly like the horse or dog world does. Everyone is just so nice and welcoming and more concerned with improving their personal best than winning. They're in love with their birds, who almost always cost more to raise than they bring in. Differences in politics and socioeconomic status are largely ignored in favor of what everyone has in common—chickens. It feels like a utopia.

When the award ceremony ends at 10:04 a.m., entire rows of birds have already been emptied. The floor is covered in wet blotches where people have dumped out their birds' water cups. As I walk, I step on discarded show tags that have fluttered to the floor. I head up to the mezzanine and watch the room clear out from above. It gets quieter as people push trolleys full of poultry to their cars. One woman manages to put a turkey under each arm and walks out the door. The birds came; they were judged; they went home.

There must be a German word for what I'm feeling. There's sadness mixed in my chest with a fullness from being around all these birds and the people who love them. It feels like it was over too quickly.

I think back to one of my end-of-day calls with Lyle to tell him about all the wonderful chickens I'd seen. On industrial farms, chickens are bred to be little more than animal machines and they're treated as copies of one another. At poultry shows, chickens are celebrated as individuals. My praise for them was effusive. Lyle laughed, happy that I was doing a reporting trip that brought me such joy. "Of course you love it," he said. "This is exactly your kind of place."

Sitting on the mezzanine, I think about how Jan Brett mentioned she once "made the mistake" of using the National as one of the stops on her book tour. It didn't go badly, but she said, adamantly, that she would never do it again. "I like to be a chicken person when I'm there and not anything other than that," she told me. "I want to attend as a chicken person." Even though all of my chickens are back home and I have no idea how many ways my birds probably deviate from their breed standards, I've felt swept up in being a chicken person too.

In normal life, I often wonder if I'm talking too much about my chickens. There's a popular social media meme that shows a photo of a barely full swear jar on one side, and on the other is a jar bursting with coins, titled, "Telling people about chickens when I wasn't asked." I think about it often. I rarely bring my chickens up in conversation, but once someone else does, all bets are off. (I imagine people are either happy or miserable sitting next to me at a party.) That's not a worry here.

I think of that couple staring lovingly at the Faverolles and how many other people have become smitten with the strange and beautiful creatures that are chickens—both now and throughout history.

A show quality chicken may not cost as much as it did in the 1850s, but Hen Fever never really went away.

CHAPTER SIX:

4-H IS FOR THE BIRDS

I T'S THE FIRST WEEKEND IN APRIL, AND SEATTLE IS A BALMY SIXTY-two degrees. People tending their spring gardens quickly lose their jackets and work bare-armed in T-shirts. It's the kind of weather that invites everyone to go outside and do something. But at two in the afternoon, a small group of six kids and three adults are all inside talking about chickens.

"If a hen has red earlobes, what color eggs is it most likely to lay?" asks Barb, a woman with glasses and dark brown hair.

One of the girls tentatively gives the correct answer: "Brown?"

"What mineral is most important for good shell formation?" Barb quizzes again.

This time everyone shouts out the answer: "Calcium!"

In a few months, these kids, members of a 4-H group called Cooped Up in Seattle, will be showing their poultry at the fair. There they'll be judged on how well they handle their birds and answer questions like these. Barb is one of the parent leaders of the group and has been involved for nine

years. Cooped Up, which started in 2010, also does other projects like sewing, cooking, and gardening. Those projects can simply be dropped off for
judging at the fair; that's not the case with animal projects. Their knowledge
counts just as much or even more than the bird's quality.

"This one will be easy for you to answer," Barb says. "Do you need a
rooster for a hen to lay an egg?"

One young girl, a newer member who has been holding her chicken,
Blanche, on her lap during a large portion of the meeting, shouts, "No!"

Gina, who has an undercut in her short hair that makes her far more styl-
ish than I ever remember being at twelve, mentions that one of her neighbors
once asked if her chicken was pregnant. The group laughs knowingly. "She
was talking about our Jersey Giant, who is really big and fat," Gina says.

The 4-H'ers go around and talk about their chickens next. This is not the
usual conversation people have about their pets. Instead of names and how
old the hens are or the quirky things they do, the kids talk about what class
the birds fit in and how they stand up to the Standard of Perfection. Some of
them are prepared with the answers. Others need to study more.

After almost a year of monthly meetings, it's only two months until the
poultry show. Usually they'd be doing this meeting in person, schlepping
their chickens across Seattle to practice handling them, but in the midst of the
pandemic, everything has taken place over Zoom. It means that in addition
to the frames of on-screen people in bedrooms, living rooms, and backyards,
there's often one or more chickens making an appearance. Their beaks face
the screen, making it feel like they're attentive club members. Of course, with
eyes that don't face forward, they're looking everywhere but at the computers
in front of them. Sometimes the hens stand still, but often they tolerate only
so much petting before flying off in a whirl of feathers. Despite not getting to
meet anyone in person, I'm deeply familiar with dining rooms, living rooms,
backyards, and even the occasional unmade bed in the background.

Like everything everywhere in this unprecedented year, things in 4-H
clubs are the same but different. In past years, 4-H'ers would all get together
to wash their chickens a few days before the show. That's not happening at
all this year, Barb says, though it wouldn't hurt to make sure their chickens
are clean. (Even if just for their own sake while handling the birds.) Next, she

brings up the dress code for showing poultry—a white button-down shirt with black slacks and black close-toed shoes. Even for a chicken show on Zoom, she cautions, the kids shouldn't wear flip-flops.

"My aunt is a 4-H club leader, and she says showmanship is pretending the judge has one hundred dollars and is going to buy the bird presented best in the group," Katie says. "You want to sell them your bird and be a knowledgeable person." Katie is Barb's daughter. She has long brown hair, glasses, and a matter-of-fact attitude when it comes to talking about chickens. She and her mom joined Cooped Up when Katie was in first grade. She's seventeen now and a junior in high school. She's often an encyclopedia of chicken knowledge and is quick to look up anything she doesn't know.

"Depending on the judge, they might ask you to show specific things, like show the tail or wing or ask *you* to evaluate your bird," Katie warns. She grabs a stuffed chicken toy and uses it to demonstrate how you'd turn it to show every part from head to toe. There's one move where she flips the bird upside down, resting its back against her chest, to show off the bird's keel bone—or where it would be if the stuffed animal had bones at all. There's a proper way to hold a show chicken and it's not anything that people with chickens in their backyards come to without being taught: two fingers slip between the legs to palm the chicken like a football while another hand rests on the chicken's back to keep them from flapping away. It takes practice to get it right.

Even today, when it's become normal to have a chicken coop in a suburban yard, there's something incongruous about watching Gen Z learn how to show a chicken. They might have TikTok, but their conversations about raising chickens, the Standard of Perfection, and chicken biology aren't all that different than they were over one hundred years ago when 4-H first started. But it's hard to imagine that the people who started 4-H as a series of agricultural youth programs and contests in the early 1900s could have ever imagined their program spreading to kids in cities throughout the country. Today there are roughly six million kids in 4-H programs in the United States. They can learn about everything from robotics to sewing to raising cattle to sell at auction. It's a big shift from something that started with groups with names like the "Tomato Club" or "Corn Growing Club."

When 4-H started, most farmers produced the food that they ate and kept a little bit to sell. Rather than using machinery to plant and harvest crops, they relied on their families for help. Only the wealthiest farmers could afford to try new "progressive" methods of farming that were being developed at land grant universities. A divide was forming. Progressives judged farmers doing things the old-fashioned, unproductive way. Poorer farmers, wrote Gabriel Rosenberg in his book, *The 4-H Harvest*, reasonably felt condescended to and scorned any advice that came their way as "book farming."[45] Those who wanted to see farming come into the twentieth century figured that teaching new methods to children might be the best way to change what farming looked like in America. In 1900, one of the first programs like this "offered as much [corn seed] as could be sent for one cent of postage to any boy under eighteen," Rosenberg wrote. The program promised cash prizes and farm equipment to those who had the best results.[46] To win, the boys simply had to attend a farmers' institute where their corn could be judged by a college professor. It had been hard for education programs to coax even a few farmers into attendance, but hundreds of boys—and their parents—showed up. Just four years later, enrollment grew to eight thousand boys a year.[47] "While those same families . . . might reject the USDA's book farming, club work enticed them by appealing to their pride and pocketbooks," Rosenberg wrote.[48]

The first official 4-H club was created by an Iowa superintendent named Jessie Field Shambaugh. She had run clubs at a rural school, but when she became the superintendent of Page County's 130 country schools in 1906, she established boys' corn clubs and girls' "home" clubs (which taught skills like baking, sewing, and cleaning) at each of them.[49] To promote the program, Shambaugh designed a badge that looked like a three-leaf clover with one "H" on each leaf. (The three H's stand for "head, hands, and heart." In 1910 she added another "H" to stand for "home.")

These clubs continued in a somewhat piecemeal fashion until the passage of the Smith-Lever Act in 1914, which funded state extension programs that in turn supported local 4-H programs.[50] Other youth programs like the Girl and Boy Scouts or YMCA had existed since the 1800s, but 4-H was the only program made for people in rural areas.[51] The Smith-Lever Act formalized agricultural clubs under Shambaugh's emblem and name: 4-H.

4-H programs continued offering gendered home economics or agricultural projects, Rosenberg wrote, but the most popular projects appealed to both sexes. Even then, poultry was a top pick.[52]

From 1945 to 1948, my own grandma was a 4-H'er doing poultry projects in North Dakota. I stumbled across a document in one of her scrapbooks titled "Chickens: my poultry project" that she wrote when she was sixteen. She described starting her flock by ordering Leghorn cockerels from a Minnesota hatchery that only charged her for shipping. "People only want pullets and people otherwise drown the cockerels," she wrote. She got three hundred chicks for only $7.76. When she sold them as "friers" a few months later, she made over $156 in profit and reinvested it further into chicken businesses in eggs and meat. The following year, my grandma wrote that she'd ordered 500 Leghorn and 400 Austra-White cockerels as well as 250 Austra-White pullets. She made over six hundred dollars, which she used to pay for clothes, books, and "other high school expenses." When I asked my grandma about all of this, she had no memory of her years as a poultry mogul. In fairness, she had just turned eighty-nine; 4-H was a long time ago. But tucked next to the poultry-keeping records in the scrapbook were blue ribbons her project had won at the county fair and an old cap with a 4-H clover printed on the front of it.

Today, 4-H isn't a rural program anymore. Even back in 1965, fewer than half of all 4-H'ers lived on farms, and those statistics haven't changed much since.[53] Roughly a quarter of all members live in smaller cities or suburbs.[54]

The Seattle kids in the Cooped-Up 4-H group do not have hundreds of chickens. Most of them didn't track how much it cost to raise their birds (or if they'd saved any money versus buying eggs directly from a grocery store). But the fact that they could answer questions about chicken biology and how the fowl were raised make them agricultural experts compared to the majority of other urban children.

One 2013 study that interviewed kids at a summer camp in Long Beach, California, found that young people generally have very little knowledge about farming or animals raised for food.[55] One girl, describing how she'd seen cows with brown spots and ones with black spots, explained that if she had a farm, "I would pick the one that got brown spots because the one that has black spots just gives out regular white milk, but the one with brown spots gives out chocolate milk." (Of course, many adults in developed nations aren't much better off when it comes to talking about where food comes from.)

"I know more now about the work you have to put in, not just with chickens but other animals too," says Kathleen, Cooped Up's club president. Every 4-H club has a formal structure with democratically elected presidents, treasurers, secretaries, and so on (in addition to adult volunteer leaders), and Kathleen became president in fall 2020 at the beginning of her senior year of high school. Kathleen has blonde, wavy hair and dark eyebrows. She's eighteen when I first meet her but has been in 4-H since 2013.

She remembers going up to other 4-H kids every summer at the fair to strike up conversations about their animals. In addition to the chickens, there are usually rabbits, freshly blow-dried cows, goats, lambs, and horses. Even at a working farm, visitors would rarely find so many different animals in one place. "Everyone is around your age at the fairs," Kathleen says. "It's easy to go up to them and say, 'Tell me about your cow.'"

Kathleen joined 4-H for the same reason many kids do: she had an interest and wanted to meet other kids who liked the same things. Her family got chickens when she was six years old, so she doesn't remember much about the decision-making process that led to adding chicks to the family. What she does remember is that from the very beginning, the chickens felt like hers. "We had two cats as well, but my parents got them before I was born. They were never really *my* cats," Kathleen says. "We have pictures on the Christmas card from that year where I'm holding all the eggs they'd laid and have a giant smile on my face." Chickens are really accessible animals for kids, Kathleen says, and there's been more to learn as she's gotten older and can now talk about anatomy and breeds and veterinary care in addition to just collecting eggs. Schools often do "hatching projects," where students learn about how a chicken develops inside of an egg as the eggs incubate—and eventually hatch into fuzzy chicks—right in front of them. (Unfortunately, many of these projects end badly if teachers don't think about how to care for the chicks once they've hatched, or what to do with any roosters that come from the project.) But when Kathleen was little, no one she knew had chickens.

4-H was a place where she could meet kids her age who also took part in what was still a niche urban hobby.

For the first few years, Kathleen says, she was shy. "I just wanted to hide behind my mom for the first little bit," she laughs. From what she tells me about her early time in 4-H, it's impressive she stuck with it. She was too scared to talk to anyone, and when she showed her chicken, Chippy, for the first time, the hen flew right off the table. "It's a disqualification," Kathleen says. "I was a little scared to show my chicken for a couple years after that."

This year, at the virtual fair, she'll be showing Chippy again. The size of her flock has gone up and down over the years, but now, with Kathleen about to leave for college, they're down to one hen: Chippy. The orange-and-black hen is nine years old, ancient in chicken years. Chippy's face, which is only lightly feathered, seems small for the rest of her body. Today she's much more comfortable being picked up and petted than she was that first year in 4-H. Even as Kathleen has been busy with high school and other commitments, she's continued making time for Chippy. "She has this one spot on the side of the house that she goes to take a dirt bath in," she says with a smile. Kathleen refills it with dirt every so often so Chippy has enough to throw around her feathers. Chippy also gets VIP access to a rosebush with tasty petals to peck off and snack on. All of Kathleen's friends know Chippy. When she had a Zoom presentation in calculus class this past year, Chippy got a special introduction.

It may seem like keeping chickens as pets is a new, particularly twenty-first-century phenomenon, but it's been happening in some form for as long as farms have had children on them. It would have been hard for a child to argue in favor of saving a beloved cow or pig from slaughter—they cost a lot of money to raise and could provide a lot of income (or meals) after their deaths—but chickens were unobtrusive. A pint-sized bantam could almost fend for itself where food was concerned.

It's hard to know when the first child saw a particular chicken in their parents' flock and decided to make them a pet, but there are stories of it happening all over. As Katherine Grier writes in *Pets in America,* chickens were common urban livestock in the early 1900s, and many families kept a couple bantams as pets.[56] I've found many old newspaper articles with stories about boys bringing their pet chickens to school. One twelve-year-old girl wrote a long letter to her local paper about her pet hen. The bantam only laid two eggs a year, liked to ride in cars, once was almost carried away by a bald eagle, and died at the age of "eight years and five months," at which point she was buried in the flower bed.[57] The girl felt the editor should know about her pet.

The Southern writer Flannery O'Connor may have been known for having pet peacocks that roamed her yard, but chickens were her gateway drug into poultry. At the age of five, she became obsessed with chickens, particularly any fowl with strange features like mismatched eyes or crooked combs. She even made clothes for her chickens, dressing Colonel Eggbert, a gray bantam, in a "white piqué coat with a lace collar and two buttons at the back," as she wrote in an essay.[58] On farms, where dogs were often for guarding livestock or hunting, and a cat's worth was tied to how many rats and mice he caught in the barn, chickens were the ones who became pets.

﹏

When I ask her, Sophia has to use her fingers to count how many chickens she has. "I think we have ten," she laughs. "And three ducks." She's thirteen and has had chickens for eight years, but this was her first year in 4-H. Over the past year she's learned about chickens like never before. "I like to research things when I get really into a topic," she says. She started going on chicken forums as well as using "more official sources" like the Standard of Perfection to learn about chicken health issues, how to improve their coops, and more. Being home during the pandemic was part of it too; suddenly, the chickens became the most interesting thing around. She spends at least half an hour a day with her chickens in the backyard. Some of the time is spent just hanging out, while another portion is reserved for work. Learning how to handle chickens leading up to the fair wasn't something she could do in a day.

It took her a long time—and a lot of watching 4-H kids showing their chickens on YouTube—for her to feel like she'd gotten the hang of it. "Getting my chicken to be still and be quiet was hard," she says, even though she practiced with her smallest chicken. Most younger kids use bantams for show chickens since they're easier for small hands to wrap around, though there's no requirement that older 4-H'ers have to show large fowl. "I just held her for a long time to get her used to it," Sophia says.

Whether someone is doing agility with their dog, truffle hunting with a pig, or showmanship with a chicken, having an activity to do *with* an animal—especially one that requires their cooperation—is very different from simply having them around. A 2014 study about dogs and their owners found that people who regularly do activities with their dog believe they have a closer relationship with them than those who don't.[59] With pets, as with humans, it's not the quantity of time that matters in a relationship, it's the quality.

As a kid, I did 4-H with my pet sheep. I'm sure I would have liked the sheep anyway, but having to train them to wear a halter and stand still with their legs stacked neatly underneath them made our relationship something more than child and pet; we became a team. It made me see them as more than wooly creatures who munched grass all day and liked head scratches. To this day, whenever I see a picture of sheep, I'm overwhelmed by a combination of love and nostalgia. I have no doubt that I would love to have sheep again someday.

~

At a normal summertime fair, there are livestock barns with rows of everything from poultry to cows to rabbits to horses. The vast majority of the animals are shown by teens and children even if those kids have a family farm. Some stalls have the name of the farm's business and a logo hanging above it, while many others have posters for the 4-H group (or another club, like Future Farmers of America) printed on it. These barns, whether at county or state fairs, are the closest most Americans get to the animals we raise for food.

And some of the animals do, in fact, become food when the fair is over. So-called "market projects" involve raising animals like cattle or pigs to market weight and auctioning the animals off at the end of the fair. The idea is to teach potential future farmers to weigh income against expenses and to lavish care on their animals before letting them go. It's not uncommon to see tears from kids saying goodbye on auction day. Though my grandma did a market project decades ago, it seems to be less common in poultry these days—at least at the East and West Coast fairs I've been to.

Like many 4-H groups in the first years of the pandemic, Cooped Up canceled their in-person poultry show. (Many state and local fairs did open back up in 2021 in the United States, but some individual clubs chose to continue the virtual model.) Instead of 4-H kids from clubs all across the county or state competing against each other, it was just the Cooped-Up group showing their birds on Zoom. But showing poultry in 4-H is often more of an exercise in doing better than you could at the beginning of the year than a competition against other kids.

Even over Zoom, the show is unbelievably sweet. Many of the moms show up in their own Zoom screens wearing the club's 4-H shirts. Kathleen wears a white long-sleeve shirt. Katie, unsurprisingly, is dressed exactly as she would for an in-person show: white button-down shirt and her hair pulled back in braids. I can't see her shoes, but I would wager she's wearing regulation close-toed black ones. Gina is there but in a purple long-sleeve shirt because the white button-down in her closet doesn't fit anymore. A few other kids are there with their chickens at the ready, but the biggest surprise is Sophia. When she logs in, everyone quickly sees that her family has set up a black backdrop behind her. She's almost in full view in her show uniform. There's a table in front of her that she's set her chicken onto. Somehow Sophia has taken a virtual 4-H show and made it look professional.

Cooped Up used club money to hire a judge for their show, a woman named Kimberly Burt, who shows up wearing a blue collared shirt, her blonde hair pulled into a bun on top of her head. She's immediately friendly, saying that she raised chickens from the time she was three years old. "I'm going to hang out with you today and we'll have a little fun," she tells the 4-H'ers. "Please don't ever feel wrong about saying, 'I don't know.' It's okay to do that with me or any other judge." She smiles. There's a big difference between the atmosphere of this 4-H event and the white-coated, silent judges of the Ohio National.

First Kimberly asks everyone to grab their chickens and hold out the wing. Gina has some trouble getting her Buff Leghorn hen, Brandie, to cooperate. She and Kathleen are the only ones not showing bantams, and Gina's bird is so much fluffier than Chippy, she's already starting at a disadvantage.

"Okay, now show me the tail," Kimberly says.

It looks like a little dance. The girls all have a hand on each side of their hen, and the fluffy butts face the camera as the birds' tails are tilted back and forth. Some of the chickens can't help but grumble.

When Kimberly asks to see the keels of the birds, each 4-H'er picks their chicken up and rests the hen's back onto their shoulder so they can part the feathers around the bone running along the bottom of the bird.

Some of the birds stand on the table without moving while the 4-H'ers answer questions. This is a routine the hens have been through before. Gina keeps a hand on Brandie's wing at all times, holding her in place. Sophia's bird is largely well behaved but occasionally tries to run off the table. Sometimes, while another 4-H'er is answering a question, I see Sophia calmly reach out for her runaway chicken and settle her again. Everyone pets their birds with long strokes over the hens' backs.

The questions Kimberly asks them range from simple ones about certain chicken breeds to ones that even stump me. She asks Gina if she knows what "hen feathering" is. She doesn't. Kathleen doesn't either. Finally, Katie gives the right answer: it's when males have hen-like characteristics like rounded feathers versus pointed.

Next she asks Sophia a genetics question about whether a self-blue or regular blue chicken would "breed true" to the color in future generations. It's a good thing that Kimberly never seems disappointed when someone doesn't know the answer to a question.

It's after this question that Kimberly goes back to easier ones like asking each girl with a bantam to name all the large fowl classes and vice versa. Other than Katie, no one is prepared for this question.

"This is an area I would recommend focusing on in your studies," Kimberly says kindly. "When I first started, I didn't even pay attention to large fowl classes because I didn't care. But if you have a large bird on the table, I will ask you about bantam classes to trip you up a little." In the early years of 4-H participation, it's usually enough to know about your own bird. But judges will expect kids who have been in poultry 4-H for a long time to know about everything to do with poultry, from how to manage diseases like mites or egg abnormalities (both questions Kimberly asks) to the classes in the Standard of Perfection and what would count as a defect or disqualification in different chicken breeds.

It's over in roughly twenty minutes, and Kimberly tells everyone that they did a great job. "Can we say, Miss Sophia, for a novice, holy cow! If I didn't have to follow 4-H rules, you should be on the intermediate table. Your birds did fantastic and are well handled."

Sophia beams. Her chicken squawks.

Everyone gets a blue ribbon. (It is a small group after all.)

The poultry show is the thing 4-H'ers are ostensibly working toward throughout the year, but it's all the parts that come before it that really matter. The time spent with other people who love the thing you love. The time spent doing something with your chickens besides giving them snacks and watching them do chicken things in the yard.

Chickens have infiltrated the 4-H'ers' lives. Throughout the year I often see people come to meetings wearing shirts with chickens on them. When I interview the 4-H'ers, I ask each one whether they have a lot of chicken things in their homes and bedrooms. At first, Gina tells me there aren't any, then looks closer. "I have chicken stickers some places. I have a chicken cup for my pencils." She pauses, mentally cataloguing the items in the room that have sprung up over the years so thoroughly she's forgotten they were even there. "That was a lie. I have a moderate amount of chicken things. Not too many though," she says, without elaborating on what too many would mean. Everyone's home is like this. There's just something about chickens.

A few weeks after the poultry show, I ask Gina why she likes her chickens so much. She pauses. "This will sound really stupid, but they're like my therapists," she says. She loved the chickens from the moment she met them, but during the pandemic, stuck at home all the time, they'd become an even more important presence in her life. "I didn't do it as much before Covid because I had less time, but I go out there and talk to them. Sometimes I sing to them," she admits. "They don't judge me or say mean things back." But they are good listeners. She talks to the chickens; the chickens burble back in their comforting language. "I just let all my emotions out even though I know they don't care," she says. "It puts a smile on my face every day."

CHAPTER SEVEN:
CHEEP THERAPY

I've seen chickens on TikTok but not in person," the student says as she wanders over to the table. Her eyes are wide, as though she can't quite believe the rumors are true: there really is a therapy chicken sitting in front of her. Melissa* has long brown hair and eyeliner drawn in a perfect cat eye. A black mask covers the lower half of her face. She reaches for the ball of fluff on the table and gives the chicken a couple light strokes at first, then starts gently raking her fingers into the bird's feathers. Tilly, short for Atilla the Hen, sinks down into her woven cloth basket. The chicken is a sooty white with flecks of gray and black. She looks more like a hat than a hen.

"What kind of chicken is this?" Melissa asks.

"It's called a Silkie," answers Tanya Bailey, the woman standing next to me. Bailey has a crown of curly blonde hair on her head and wears pink pants and a floral-patterned shirt. She tells Melissa that if you look at a feather

---

* Not her real name.

under a microscope, it looks like Velcro—covered in tiny hooks, called barbicels, that allow the feather to zipper together. "That's what makes birds look so sleek. Silkies don't have that gene. That's why they just look like big poofs," she laughs. With no barbicels, Silkies can't fly at all.

Some version of the breed has been around so long that its exact origins have been lost to history, though in the thirteenth century Marco Polo wrote of chickens with hair like cats. Unscrupulous sellers have, on occasion, tried to pass Silkies off as a cross between a chicken and a rabbit—a genetic impossibility that nonetheless is a pretty accurate description. Handling Tilly feels like touching a furry cloud.

Melissa pets Tilly for another minute before Bailey asks her how school is. Melissa just shrugs.

"Are you a first-year?" Bailey asks her.

"Yeah."

"How's it going?" Bailey asks with light concern in her voice.

"It's pretty good," Melissa says, looking down as though she's talking to Tilly. "I've had to learn to manage my time wisely, actually. There's assignments for each class posted online every day. It's hard to keep track of them all," she says with an attempt at a laugh. "The other night all I did was homework and that was for, like, eight hours."

Tilly nestles herself lower into the basket as Melissa pets her. I can't see the lower half of the young woman's face but get the feeling that this is something she's been wanting to admit to someone for a while.

Bailey commiserates, saying that she was someone who needed a large chunk of free time to get anything done when she was in school. "It was hard for me," she says.

Melissa nods. When another student walks up to Tilly, Melissa thanks Bailey and says goodbye. This is exactly the kind of exchange that Pet Away Worry and Stress, or PAWS, was meant to create at the University of Minnesota, Twin Cities. It's not meant to be therapy, Bailey says of the program, though she is a licensed therapist. Her chickens, as well as the dogs, cats, rabbits, and even a miniature horse that sometimes visit the program, are just a way to make it easier to connect. "They're a bridge for human-to-human interaction," Bailey says. Students can feel overwhelmed by the thought of going to the campus mental health clinic or feel like their problems aren't bad enough to talk to anyone about. But it's easy to pet a chicken.

Bailey remembers one student who came every week throughout her entire four years at the university and cried during every session. "When we have students who are struggling, I'm able to pull them aside and say, 'Here are some additional resources we have,'" Bailey says. "It helps get them in through the back door."

And it's clear that the chickens are a big draw. During the three days that I observe the program, multiple students mention that they'd heard PAWS has chickens and had to see it for themselves. Everyone's reaction is different. Memorably, one young man just laughs while he puts his fingers in Tilly's feathers. Another observes the hen closely from all angles as though he's trying to make a 3D scan with his eyes. Some girls ask a lot of questions but don't do much petting. One petite student visits two days in a row but hangs silently in the background like she's hoping for a moment to be with the chicken one-on-one.

Bailey usually rotates her four therapy chickens on a weekly schedule— each coming to a week's sessions then taking three weeks off—but she brings a different hen every day for my benefit. Unfortunately, I don't get to meet Henley, who prefers walking on the table to sitting in her basket and will come up to cuddle any student who puts their arms out as if they're asking for a hug. (She's feeling broody the week of my visit.) But after Tilly, I meet Hennifer, who is brown with copper highlights, and then Layla, who has a combination of gold and gray feathers referred to as "blue merle." They all have slightly different personalities. (Hennifer is the most talkative of the hens and grumbles pleasantly as though having a conversation when people talk to her.)

Unlike the dogs, who happily endure being petted by as many as eight students at a time, rolling onto their sides for better access to belly rubs, there's only so much real estate on a Silkie. Students linger in the background while someone strokes a hen, and Bailey often has to urge kids to "get in there." In most cases, each group of students within earshot gets the same spiel.

As soon as Bailey establishes that this is, in fact, a chicken, she instructs students on the right way to pet one of the hens. "She loves her back. Not a huge fan of the top of her head. The more you pet her, the more she'll do what she's doing." After a few pets, the Silkie's back is nearly flat with the top of the basket. "She's relaxed because you're giving her a massage. Thank you for giving my chicken a massage," she laughs.

Bailey repeats the same quips many times. They're new to the hundreds of different students who come through to give the hens a quick pet, and Bailey manages to act like she's never told them before. "They're called Silkies but should be called fluffies. Just look at them!" Or that to become therapy chickens, "They all have to sit through an exam, just like you do." In fairness, there's only so many topics of small talk when you're petting a chicken, and Bailey has been using chickens as therapy animals for decades.

In 1999, Bailey started a therapeutic farm nonprofit outside the Twin Cities where she'd planned to have horses and sheep and dogs and cats. After talking to fellow social workers about kids' reactions to different animals and thinking about it more, Bailey realized they should probably have chickens too. Dogs could be scary for some kids. Horses were big. "The chicken is an animal that, if you think about it, they're part of everybody's culture," Bailey says. "They don't really have a lot of negative connotations."

Because chickens always came in a flock, the birds brought up some surprising conversations. "It gave me a unique way to talk about human relationships," Bailey says. "I had two hens that both sat on eggs and raised thirteen chicks together—you have a same-sex marriage there. I had a rooster killed defending the flock—you have a widowed hen and the trauma of losing a father," she recalls. "You name it and I have had it happen in my flock and had conversations with people about how the flock healed and managed it." Animals are often referred to as a social lubricant because they provide a safe space for strangers to talk to each other ("Can I pet your dog?"), but they're also a proxy for topics like loss that can be hard to talk about.

Bailey soon realized that for some people, chickens weren't just a curiosity—they were the main event. One group of autistic boys was scheduled to come out to the farm twice a week for equine therapy, and on the second week they stopped, transfixed, in front of the chicken coop. At first, Bailey tried to rush them along to the animals they were supposed to be interacting with, but the boys insisted on seeing the chickens. "I knew then, horses were off the table." She smiles. "For the next twelve weeks we focused on chickens." The boys trained the birds, learned about them, and even brought the chickens to school for a final show-and-tell in front of their peers. From that point forward, Bailey decided she would always work with therapy chickens. "The people I worked with weren't just one type of person," she says. So why wouldn't she have a diverse group of animals too?

❦

I've had many different pets in my life—rabbits, sheep, fish, small parrots, dogs, cats, and even a peacock—but there's something special about chickens. Some of it comes from the fact that (though I rarely admit it) they don't really need me. Of course, they rely on me for food and shelter and are better off thanks to a few necessary trips to the vet, but chickens aren't dogs. I've never gotten the sense that they miss me when I go out of town. They don't get sad if I don't play with them. As long as someone is giving them treats and cleaning the coop, I could be any two-legged creature in the world. I can't even excuse it by saying they don't know who I am. Chickens can distinguish between familiar and unfamiliar faces of their own and other species.[60] They hardly blink when my dogs are nearby, but when we had a strange dog come to visit, they fluttered in alarm when the Golden Retriever politely sniffed the coop.

That doesn't mean they aren't curious about me. When we're out in the yard, they walk up to me and peck my jeans or shoes. I assume they're either checking to see if my clothing is food or hoping I'll dispense treats at the push of a beak. It's freeing. While I love the deep connection I have with my dogs, sometimes it's nice to spend time with an animal that can take you or leave you. I only spend time with the chickens when I want to. And I find that I want to be around them often.

There's nothing more Zen than watching chickens in the garden. It's a bit like sitting on the beach as the waves come in—nothing is happening and yet there's so much going on. Whatever the girls are doing, they're utterly focused on it. People often say animals live in the moment, but my dogs wistfully lay on the floor while looking at the door, hoping I'll get the hint and let them out. When I had sheep, they liked to come bounding down the hill at the sight of me and nudge my shoulder until I scratched their foreheads. Even the peacock had plans—displaying his feathers whenever my mother was nearby, hoping for romance. The chickens just are.

Watching them, my brain is lulled into the kind of state that I imagine other people find from meditation. The girls talk to each other with chirps and grumbles, rumbling sounds that give my ears a pleasant tickle to listen to. Sometimes they stop to preen, grabbing oil from the pimple-like gland at the base of their tails and spreading it carefully over each feather until they gleam. The girls peck and scratch in the grass and leaves, grabbing up worms or other morsels too small for me to see them. I've lost count of the number of times Emmylou's large, feathered feet have kicked dirt onto me. On wet days, which come often in the Pacific Northwest, the smell of damp earth follows the chickens around like a perfume trail in a hallway. They rustle the fall leaves. Sometimes they stop what they're doing because they've found a patch of sun they like and fall slowly onto their sides, fanning out a wing. I sit in the sun next to them and watch as their eyes close, then open, then close again as another chicken decides to join them.

On occasion I've seen the entire flock sunning themselves next to each other, and I suppose I should include myself in the group too. It's hard to watch the chickens for long without wanting to join in whatever they're doing. When they peck in the grass, I get out my garden tools to weed and they run to join me. Sometimes they're so enthusiastic that they get underfoot, rushing to examine whatever holes I've opened in the dirt. I don't mind. Hours pass this way. Time spent with the flock seems to move differently than it does in the rest of my life.

Since I was a teenager, I've struggled against depression and anxiety. I have to manage my mental health in the same way that, now that I'm getting older, I have to stretch every day or risk discovering aches and pains popping up like Whac-A-Mole throughout my body. I take medication and drink herbal tea and exercise and take breaks from work to deal with frequent burnout. But it still seems like either things are going well or my brain is telling me that nothing will ever be good again. Spending time with the chickens, which, yes, means going outside into the fresh air and sunlight too, puts me in a rare middle ground. Everything gets quiet. When I'm with the chickens, I can just be, too.

I don't talk to the chickens other than to coo at them for a cute thing they've done or call them to come to me for treats, but it would be hard to find a therapist as immediately effective. Over the past few years, I've found myself using the phrase "it is what it is" a lot, and I think it started creeping into my vocabulary in the months after I got the chickens. Some things aren't changeable and it's easier to accept that and move forward than get stuck in a losing battle.

During the first year of the pandemic, chicken watching became my main hobby. (Not that there were many other options.) When the news got to be too overwhelming, watching the chickens was how I reset. Obviously, I'm not the first one to discover the therapeutic power of chickens. Once I talked to a veteran who told me that the army wanted to give him a service dog for his PTSD, but he didn't have time for a pet that needed so much from him. So he got service chickens instead.[61] I've heard from people who said their chickens helped them get through cancer treatment or the loss of a loved one. For other people, sitting with the ladies is the only way they can relax after a stressful day at work. Some people pour themselves a glass of wine; others stare at chickens.

The appeal of animals doesn't have an age limit, but it's impressive to see how much chicken therapy spans generations. There are kids barely in grade school who have become deeply attached to their birds, who are pets and confidantes. Now programs are popping up around the world as people realize that chicken therapy can play a special role in helping the elderly too.

ᴒ

Jos Forester-Melville used to visit care homes in England to do arts projects with elderly residents. She'd been working at a nonprofit called Equal Arts for nearly a decade when one resident in 2012 changed everything. "There was an older man who would get very agitated and frustrated at certain times of the day," she recalls. "He shook the doors and windows and tried to get out." The man's name was Billy and he had dementia, but his behavior was still confusing to the staff and unsettling to the other residents. Even more mysteriously, he repeated the same female names over and over: Tilly, Esther, Rosie, Sweetpea, and Cookie. Forester-Melville and the staff eventually discovered that Billy wasn't asking for friends or lost loves, he was calling for his chickens. Specifically, the flock he'd kept when he was a much younger man. "He was rattling the door because he wanted to feed the hens and collect the eggs," Forester-Melville says.

So she brought six hens from home. They were each a different kind to help residents tell them apart. Forester-Melville ferried them to the care home in a large cardboard box with holes cut in the side for ventilation and let Billy open it. "The moment he opened it, he smiled and was animated and lively," she recalls. "It was like he'd found his purpose." And Billy wasn't the only one. Everyone seemed drawn to the chickens.

Though many care homes she visited had gardens, Forester-Melville noticed that most residents didn't use them. There were clipped grass lawns and manicured shrubs, maybe some spring bulbs, but it rarely enticed anyone to go outside or even spend much time looking out the window. As soon as the hens moved into their garden coop and started free-ranging in the grass, everything changed. Suddenly, residents—Billy and others—were asking to go outside. The chicken coop was placed in front of a large window so people could enjoy them even in bad weather. Chickens became a popular theme in arts activities at the home. People drew them or even wrote songs about the hens.

Forester-Melville says that care home staff often found it difficult to get older men engaged. "Historically, women are more sociable and find it easier to chat with each other. Men withdraw into themselves and don't go out." They were also less likely to enjoy typical activities like crafts, music, or dance. But many male residents had kept chickens at some point in their past. It was part of their history.[62]

Other care homes heard about the program and wanted to try out having a chicken coop of their own. Forester-Melville soon had eight care homes taking part in their program, now called Henpower. Residents could sign up to be Henpower volunteers (they began calling themselves "hensioners" as a play on the word "pensioner") and go out into the community to talk about chickens. Loneliness can be a major problem for elderly people, but these hensioners often brought their knowledge—and even a few chickens—to local schools or festivals. It was more than just petting or watching chickens, it was a bridge to their old lives. Forester-Melville told me that many care homes reported that the use of antipsychotic medication went down, and staff stuck around longer too. Today, over forty homes in the U.K. and Australia have Henpower programs for their residents.

Henpower isn't the only one doing this kind of work. In the United

States, there are nursing homes, schools for kids with various disabilities, and even prison programs that include spending time with and caring for chickens as part of their therapeutic programming. More often, individuals and their therapy chickens are getting registered as volunteer teams. Not that there are many places that will register a chicken. Some have done it in the past and then stopped. Qualifications can vary considerably. Intermountain Therapy Animals, based in Utah, has only qualified a few chickens in part because the organization requires that experts in the species be on hand to make sure the animals like the work too.

⇀

Just like not every dog is cut out for this kind of work, it takes a special hen to be a therapy animal. Tanya Bailey's hens are registered with Intermountain and have to get reregistered every two years. But the work starts long before exam day. As soon as she gets her hens as chicks, Bailey starts handling them and picking them up regularly to see if they enjoy it or get flustered. (She has a fifth hen at home who indicated early on that she would not love to be brought into a bright room to be petted and handled, thank you very much. She is not a therapy animal.)

"Could I make a chicken do things I wanted it to do? Probably," Bailey says. "But my philosophy is that the animals that do this work have a choice. It's my job to read the behaviors and cues that they give me."

A lot of the training involves getting the hens comfortable staying inside their baskets. Bailey gives them positive reinforcement in the form of shredded cheese. "They like little worms too, but I can't stand to touch them," Bailey says with a shudder. Unfortunately, her hens have started associating cheddar orange colors with food, which means giving curious pecks at students who come wearing orange nail polish. Bailey sighs. "I might have to think of something different."

The hens don't have to learn commands like "sit" or "come" like a dog would, but their test is extensive. Intermountain sent me the qualification score sheet they use for handler-and-chicken teams. Handlers are scored on such things as whether they are paying attention to their chicken's mood, but the chickens have to be far more than competent to pass. They are supposed to be "calm and polite," stay inside their basket at all times, not react too strongly to "exuberant or clumsy petting," and not just be neat and clean but also be "irresistibly attractive—a people magnet!" (I'm not sure if I would pass.)

During different sections of the test, the hens have to remain calm in their baskets during an encounter with a dog-and-human therapy team, while people are yelling angrily nearby, while multiple people pet the chicken at once, and while a large pan or other object is dropped loudly on the floor. "I always startle," Bailey says. The hens, luckily, are professionals.

Bailey would go so far as to consider her hens coworkers and says it's her job to know when they need a day off. "Frankly, I'm asking this chicken to do something that they didn't sign up for," she says with real passion in her voice. "Shame on me if I didn't interpret them correctly." When that happens, it doesn't just put the hen in danger and break her trust, it makes it less fun for the humans who have come too.

"They give us clear signals if they're not happy," I hear Bailey tell a student who asked how she knows her chickens wanted to become therapy animals. "They have their bad days just like we do. That's why they're such good role models for us." They never put too many items on their to-do lists or worry they aren't living up to the flock's expectations. A chicken is always happy to say no.

CHAPTER EIGHT:
HOW TO TRAIN YOUR CHICKEN

UST HOW SMART IS THE AVERAGE CHICKEN? CROWS CAN RECOGNIZE and remember faces of those who have wronged them, mourn, and solve complex tasks. Parrots can talk—Alex the gray parrot, who might have been a linguistic genius for his species, learned and could use over one hundred words and might have accomplished even more had he not died young. The male bowerbird is an artist. They create bowers, complicated structures made of sticks, rocks, and colorful found objects, in order to attract a female, who chooses her mate based entirely on how much she likes his aesthetic sensibility. I've seen many similar couplings at art school.

Chickens can't mimic human speech. They don't make art (unless you count rearranging their humans' carefully tended gardens). If a chicken's smarts come up in conversation, people are likely to recall the phrase "running around like a chicken with its head cut off," which is a direct reference to one of the most famous chickens of the mid-1900s, Mike the headless chicken. This poor bird lived for eighteen months after a farmer's ill-fated attempt to eat him for dinner—cutting off the bird's head but somehow keeping part of the brain stem intact. His owner toured Mike around the U.S. as a sideshow attraction. The rooster was fed with a dropper that put food and water directly into his esophagus. The bird's hometown of Fruita, Colorado, has held an annual festival in the rooster's honor every year since 1999. This might be good PR for the city of Fruita, which has a Mike statue downtown, but it wasn't great for the reputation of the chicken.

A reasonable person might extrapolate from the story that if Mike could do chicken things like scratch in the dirt and stay alive for almost two years without a head, there must not be a whole lot happening in a chicken's noggin. But the chicken has been unfairly maligned. They may not be able to speak human language, but they make about thirty distinct sounds and calls and may even have special chickenese names for their owners.[63] The average hen might not be able to solve a puzzle the way a crow can, but she can discriminate between different colors and shapes. She can be trained.

Many owners of backyard flocks have already trained their chickens in small accidental ways. When I come outside and the ladies hear the door shut, they start making their most annoying sounds, usually a squeaky screech or a honk that sounds like someone forgot to oil a goose. They know doors equal people, which equal treats. If it's seven in the morning and the chickens are shrieking, I will go down and give them treats to shut them up. I wince every time. I know I'm teaching them that they'll be fed delicious snacks if they're loud, but we do have neighbors.

I whistle for the girls so they can find me when we're on opposite ends of the half-acre yard. They call; I respond. Marco! Polo! If it's time for them to go back in the coop, I walk carefully down the driveway as they speed-waddle by my feet, their feathered pantaloons bouncing. Then they run inside the open door to their enclosed run because they know treats are coming. I toss them a handful of mealworms, count my chickens to make sure everyone is inside, and close the door behind them. The ladies have learned that they will get treats if they follow me, whether I'm taking photos of them or closing them in their coop. This is a form of training. But they're capable of so much more.

➶

The workshop seems ordinary. There are rows of tables and chairs, a large screen for PowerPoint presentations, and an area for coffee and snacks. If it weren't for the dusty smell when you walk in the door and the sounds coming from downstairs, this could be a 101 workshop in any conference room in the U.S. The spell is broken quickly when I hear a *Ba-Kawk* from downstairs. Someone has laid an egg.

This is Chicken Camp, a multiday class that is ostensibly all about clicker training chickens. Most people in the workshop work with animals: some are professionals, while others just want to learn how to train their puppy when they get back home. One woman does wildlife rehabilitation; another is a primate researcher; a few of them work with feral cats.

But for the next few days (or longer for those who stay for both the beginning and advanced chicken training classes), we will learn how to clicker train chickens to do all kinds of things a chicken doesn't normally do. Some will teeter across balance beams. Others will walk confidently around a parking cone. They will complete obstacle courses and matching games. These hungry chickens will do amazing things in exchange for food. But for now, they know very little. Nothing has ever been expected of them besides laying the occasional egg.

Today that's all about to change.

～

Terry Ryan, who started her career in the late 1960s as a dog trainer, has been teaching chicken training classes since 1993. She's since taught chicken camps all over the world. You supply the chickens and she'll teach a class! The people who orchestrated the workshop are from a group called Kitsap Animal Rescue and Education in the state of Washington. They love animals and treat the chickens well, but there's a joking-not-joking quality to the workshop. The training supplies are all put into buckets from KFC. The Colonel's black-and-white face stares at the chickens every time they're put on the table to work. Behave or else.

These days, there are plenty of people who have never seen a chicken up close, much less attempted to hold and train one. A dog trainer from South Korea who has worked with Ryan before (but never with chickens) says that she's worried about the hens "biting" her. Some birds can have sharp beaks, but most of the time a hard peck is more surprising than painful.

"People don't know chickens," Ryan says at the beginning of class, standing in front of the projector while wearing a smock with colorful chickens printed all over it. "People are possibly afraid of chickens." She says all of this by way of explaining why so many people—this class included—have paid her to teach them how to train an animal they probably have no intention of working with.

There's a common quip in the dog training world: "The only thing two trainers can agree on is that the third trainer is wrong." But few people have strong opinions about the best way to train a chicken.

So rather than trying to challenge a lifetime of core beliefs about how to train *their* animals, chicken training starts everyone back at ground zero—focusing on the mechanics of clicker training and how animals learn. When a Special Forces K-9 team, big men with big Belgian Malinois, called Ryan to ask her to teach a class, she said, "If you really want to learn, you should start with chickens." She shows the class a photo of the men, who are all wearing camouflage. Their faces are blurred out for national security reasons (or maybe out of worry that the Special Forces might seem a little less special if people saw photos of their nation's defenders holding chickens).

The average hen will tolerate you in exchange for treats and is generally pretty good-natured, but her patience is thin. She does not crave your approval the way a dog does. "Dogs are special creatures," Ryan says. "They will learn no matter what silly things the human is doing to them." Most of our dogs learn in spite of our well-intentioned training because they so desperately want to do the thing we're asking them to do. Chickens require more finesse.

~⊷

When we go downstairs to meet the chickens we're about to work with, the people are divided into pairs. I'm not participating in the class but eagerly watch from the sidelines with the enthusiasm of someone who can judge what's working and not working for everyone else without ever having to do it myself in front of other people. Each pair will take turns being either the trainer or the "coach," who does anything from giving constructive criticism to being an extra pair of hands to reset the chicken and clear spare food off the table.

Ryan spends thirty minutes showing us how to hold a chicken, keeping one hand firmly on the top of the hen's wings so she can't flap you in the face, something the chicken internet has taken to calling a "chitchslap."

Then, in one final note, Ryan says, "It's likely that at some point, a chicken will fly off the table. If that happens, yell 'chicken down' and remain calm." She or Jade Fountain, an animal trainer from Australia who is assisting the class, will get the chicken. I imagine that twenty adults stampeding to catch one wayward chicken in an enclosed space would not end well for anyone. Though it would be fun to watch.

Upon first meeting the chickens, the class is immediately so entranced by them that Ryan has to use her whistle to get everyone's attention. The birds flutter their wings, and feather fragments fly into the air. It's dusty and though the animal rescue hosting the class has done an excellent job of keeping the chickens' cages clean, poop happens. The chickens are noisy and impatient. Two of the hens have laid an egg since they arrived last night.

For the first task, each pair finds their hen, opens her cage door a crack, and tries to let the chicken peck from the food bowl exactly three times before whisking the dish out and closing the cage. The trainers repeat this for a few minutes, trying to get it right.

The chickens do not want to play along with this game. In other words, they cheat. Oh, how they cheat! Each hen does it with a personal flair. I see one hen pecking in such a way that she barely raises her head out of the dish, pecking three, four, five times before her human manages to get the cup away from her. ("That's a tricky chicken," Ryan says as she walks by.) Another hen lowers her head in powerful downward strokes, causing food to spill all around her.

The food bowls all have a clicker attached to the handle. The clicker makes a quick metallic sound. Multiplied by a room full of people using them at once, it's a bit like listening to popcorn in the microwave. Clickers are what is known in the training community as a "bridge." They're increasingly popular in dog training. Rather than stopping to tell a dog, "Who is such a good boy? Yes, you are! Yes, you are!" every time he does the correct behavior, you simply click and then give a treat. Eventually the dog will associate the sound of the clicker with the reward that's to come (like Pavlov's dog, who learned to salivate at the sound of a bell), making the treat less necessary. It's no different when someone is training a chicken.

The clicker is also useful because it's fast and can "mark" the correct behavior more precisely than most people can with their voices. This is especially important when training trickier animals like chickens or cats or hawks, all of whom are disinclined to ponder over what the trainer meant to teach them if the mark isn't perfectly timed.

A simple task like "walk across this piece of wood" actually has to be taught in a series of small steps. This is known as "shaping" and is an idea that was developed by psychologist and accidental animal trainer B. F. Skinner. First, the chicken has to learn that she's supposed to step toward the wood. *Click, treat.* Then step onto the board. *Click, treat.* Then do all that and continue taking a few steps forward. *Click, treat. Click, treat. Click, treat.* If you want to train a chicken, you have to be fast and you have to be precise, but you also have to think of the best way to break a "big" trick down into smaller steps. As it turns out, it's hard to train someone when you can't use language to explain it—whether they're a hen or a human.

~

Lest anyone think that a chicken's bird brain is why they need so much coaxing to do a simple activity like walk across a board, we try something at Chicken Camp known as the shaping game. The game is straightforward: try to train a human to complete a simple activity using only the sound of a clicker. No words. No explanations. All the trainee knows is that they're supposed to be completing a task and that *click* equals good. Our human trainee, unfortunately, doesn't do nearly so well as the chickens.

Fountain sets up a table in the middle of the room with several different objects on top of it. She's already decided on a behavior she wants to see from her student and clicks every time the student, Ms. X, as I'll call her, gets close to her goal.

Ms. X is ready to learn. Her eyes are wide, face flushed. She picks up differently colored sticks and moves them around the table. *Click.* Ms. X looks up at Fountain, excited, hopeful. She tries to retrace her steps. No click. Ms. X moves the items randomly again.

The class crowds around the table. I feel for Ms. X. Her face reddens. She looks lost as she grabs one stick and moves it on top of another, tries to put them into piles, even separates them by color. She gets the satisfaction of a *click* but then can't figure out what she was doing right. Her eyebrows furrow. Each guess gets more frantic than the last as she starts feeling like, no matter what she tries, the click isn't going to come.

We watch her fail. Ms. X can't figure out that "all" she has to do is put two sticks on top of a card in the corner of the table. It's such a simple action but ludicrously complicated without the use of language or pantomime. Just when Ms. X seems like she's about to shut down entirely, I look down at the floor. (If she was a chicken, she would have pooped and flown away a long time ago.) I can't watch. It feels too private a moment for us to crowd around it.

"That was a hard one," Fountain says abruptly. She stops the exercise and explains how the challenge was supposed to go. I notice that Ms. X, who had been a frequent volunteer earlier in the session, doesn't raise her hand quite so often after the shaping game is over.

The game is a rare exercise that compares animals and humans while putting them on almost equal footing. People regularly test animals to see if they can do things that we're pretty sure we can do better. We try to see whether parrots can be taught English and proudly declare that they're smarter than a toddler but not, of course, the average adult human. I'm not sure whether these tests teach us much. Their main goal seems to be to rank animals in a hierarchy in which humans remain on top. Animals know exactly as much as they need to survive. This often involves the use of skills that we don't have or value (like a chicken's ability to see ultraviolet light). Yet we act like animals are lesser because they don't appreciate music or art or know advanced physics when plenty of humans don't either.

I start to feel like everyone could benefit from going to a chicken training camp. There are a lot of important lessons in training an animal. Because the key to success is understanding what an animal's body language means, it teaches empathy. You also have to know yourself well enough to notice when you're in a bad mood or frustrated and take a break; you can't teach anyone if you're not able to connect with them. Just think of how much better off we'd be if the next time we found ourselves in the midst of a miscommunication, we stopped to wonder how we could make our desire clearer to the other person or thought about what we might have accidentally indicated that led them astray?

❦

Terry Ryan never intended to be in the chicken training business, though she certainly has developed a fondness for the fluffy creatures over the decades. In the 1990s, her dog training classes had gotten so popular that it had created a problem—how could she teach without making people lug their dogs halfway across the country (or the world)?

"What about chickens?" suggested a trainer who just so happened to have a brooder full of peeping chicks in her house at that very moment.

Ryan thought that it seemed like a fine choice, and the birds worked well in her workshops. She used ex-battery hens from an egg farmer first. They were smart birds, she says, though she had to have them peck padded targets because hard surfaces were painful for their previously cauterized beaks. Eventually, Ryan got a flock of her own. In the beginning, participants often did a unit working with dogs and then a practical section focused on the mechanics of clicker training where the chickens were center stage. As her classes got more popular, she realized that she needed someone else to take over the chicken workshops.

"Contact Marian Breland and see if she'll do it for you," another trainer suggested.

"Who?" asked Ryan, not recognizing the name.

The friend burst out laughing. "Haven't you heard of B. F. Skinner?"

Of course, Ryan had.

"Well, then surely you've heard of Marian and Keller Breland."

Ryan is the type of person who cites even the smallest phrase in casual conversation. When she references a study in class, she can remember not just the authors' names but their university affiliations as well. Feeling chastened, Ryan went to her bookshelf and discovered that there were lots of references to the Brelands. "All this stuff was highlighted and underlined," she says. "I'd just forgotten along the way."

❦

People have been training animals as long as we've had working relationships with them: "Hey, dog, please let go of that mammoth so I can get a bite," or "Hawk, come back to my arm when you're done hunting rabbits and don't go flying off into the wild," or "Hi horse, I'm going to sit on you and would like you to figure out that when I push my heels into your sides or pull the reins attached to your mouth that you should speed up or slow down." Yet our approach to training has changed quite a bit over the years. Thankfully.

A few hundred years ago, people believed that the sound of a dog whimpering was no different from a cog creaking in a machine. Scientists regularly conducted cruel experiments on animals with no anesthetic because they believed that, lacking a soul, animals couldn't feel pain or joy. We required obedience of our animals, but relationships between ourselves and working "beasts" were rare.

That all began to shift a little bit thanks to a man named B. F. Skinner, a psychologist known today as the father of "operant conditioning," which showed that behavior could be shaped by reward or punishment. He put rats into a Skinner Box, an enclosed space with stimulus like lights and a loudspeaker, a food and water dispenser, an electrified floor that could be turned on and off, and levers or buttons that the rat inside was taught to press. Skinner used "negative reinforcement" by playing loud music until a rat pressed a lever, at which point the music stopped. Skinner also might use "positive reinforcement," giving the rat a tasty treat when he did the desired behavior. It all sounds simple today but was groundbreaking at the time.* Though we talk a lot about positive reinforcement today when we're training pets, managing employees, or raising baby humans, the idea that you catch more flies with honey than with vinegar was little more than an aphorism until Skinner proved that it had scientific merit.

During World War II, Skinner joined scientists throughout the world in putting their expertise to work aiding the war effort. This great mind decided that the best way he could help was by training pigeons to guide bombs. Seriously. Skinner wrote in his memoir, *The Shaping of a Behaviorist*, that he was looking out the train window, thinking of the Nazis' recent

---

* Despite this, Skinner was also one of many scientists at the time who firmly believed that animals had neither emotions nor even feelings.

invasion of Norway and Denmark and how everyone should fight back against the Germans, when he saw "a flock of birds lifting and wheeling in formation as they flew alongside the train."[64] Once home, Skinner purchased some pigeons and got to work.

Bombs of the era were an "aim and drop" model so imprecise that wind could easily shift them as they fell to the earth.[65] To have any hope of hitting a given target, the military had to drop a lot of bombs, which meant collateral damage (not to mention the expense) was high. Skinner believed that a bomb could be guided toward its target, and who better to guide it than one or more pigeons placed inside the bomb as it fell.

The birds were food-motivated, could be found in every city in the United States, had keen eyesight, and (presumably) weren't scared of heights. He began to work on the project in the early 1940s at the University of Minnesota, where he was teaching. Skinner harnessed the pigeons in a jacket so they were immobilized except for their head and neck, which had to be left free to peck and eat. "The bird could ascend by lifting its head, descend by lowering it, and travel from side to side by moving appropriately," Skinner described nearly twenty years later, once the project was finally declassified.[66]

The original contraption was mounted on wheels so the pigeon could move himself in space toward a bullseye, filled with food, mounted on a wall across the room. That image is worth sitting with for a moment—a pigeon in a harness bobbing his head in all directions as he travelled from one side of the room to the other. "The pigeon learned to reach any target within reach of the hoist," Skinner said. The idea was that the bullseye in the real world would be the bomb target, and the harnessed pigeon—inside a bomb—would peck his way to a strike.

The university didn't think much of Skinner's "crackpot idea" and, in an age where mechanics and chemistry and math were helping to win the war, the military wasn't too sure about putting pigeons in charge of its bombs. But as Japan launched kamikaze attacks on Allied forces, Skinner continued to believe that fighting back without risking the lives of soldiers was a worthwhile proposition.[67]

He found support from the General Mills company, which provided Skinner with not only grant funding but also space for a pigeon laboratory on the top floor of an old grain mill. Skinner closed his lab and enlisted two of his graduate students to drop out and help him in this important mission. Those researchers were Keller and Marian Breland. (The pair met at university and had married a year later.[68]) There was a lot of downtime during Project Pigeon while the team waited "for Washington to make up its collective mind," as Skinner recalled.[69] The bored behaviorists decided to see what else their trained pigeons could do. They taught one to play a baseball tune on the piano called "Over the Fence Is Out, Boys." This probably gave them their next idea—teaching a pigeon to hit a ball. Both tasks were accomplished within just a few minutes.

Pigeons never did guide bombs in the war, but the project (and the pigeons' extracurricular tricks) set a lightbulb off in the Brelands' minds. As soon as the war was over, they promised each other, they'd find a way to turn shaping into a business.[70]

Their first attempt was to advertise a new humane way of dog training, but nobody was interested. At that time, trainers working with a dog didn't "teach" dogs anything so much as they regularly pinched a dog's ear or hit the dog until the animal did the desired behavior.[71] Neither owners nor trainers were interested in learning a new way to do things. They'd been pinching dogs' ears and teaching them to sit for hundreds of years. People felt that, clearly, they were great at training dogs already, thank you very much. Marian said that they kept the dogs but quickly abandoned the idea of a training school.[72]

~

The Brelands trained just about every animal someone could get at the local pet store but still didn't have a way to turn training into money until they remembered their old friends at General Mills. The war was over and Larro Feed, a division of the company, was in the farm animal feed business. In 1947, Keller went to them and pitched a chicken show with trained hens that could be used at fairs and conventions to bring in a crowd. Larro Feed loved it.

The Brelands got to work constructing a hen-sized stage with a feeder that would dispense grain to the chicken like an audience throwing roses at a diva's feet after her performance. They also made or found props that the chickens could interact with. For one trick they taught a hen to use her beak to play a five-note tune on a toy piano. The pianos quickly showed signs of use with beak scratches and tiny gouges from being pecked over and over again.

In another show, the hen had specially made shoes and a costume and would "tap dance" on command. This being the 1940s and long before the days of the buy-anything-anonymously internet, I have to imagine that Marian made the chicken clothing and shoes herself, at least initially. There was also an even more interactive show where the audience could call out a number between one and eight and the hen would roll out that many wooden eggs from a nest box.

According to the contract with General Mills, the Brelands would "furnish units of trained chickens" and a couple trained hogs to Larro Feed employees who would then take the animals on the road after a crash course in animal training.[73] These coaching sessions with General Mills employees were the first-ever chicken training workshops. After only one or two days of training, the handlers ran performances throughout the United States. The Brelands did the initial training of the chickens and then shipped The Talent throughout the U.S. "The birds played thousands of performances without a single failure, except for an occasional sluggish performance due to ill health or overfeeding," the Brelands later wrote.[74] They added, "The acts proved to be unprecedented crowd-stoppers . . . showing to as many as 5,000 people in a day."

The public couldn't get enough of the trained chickens, and neither could General Mills. The Brelands' newly formed business, Animal Behavior Enterprises (ABE), quickly became profitable. They received $150 a month for each "act" and brainstormed new ones constantly.[75] They taught baby chicks to run up a ramp to a platform where the little fluffs could reach a feed hopper. To get a bite, the next one in line had to push the chick in front of her out of the way, sliding the fed chick onto the stage floor. The Brelands trained sixty to one hundred chicks for each show and could run it indefinitely with ten chicks on stage at any given time. "When the group becomes sleepy they are replaced by a fresh batch," the Brelands wrote.[76] The finished product was an "endless chain of baby chicks running up the ramp and sliding off."

~

Within a few years, the Brelands outgrew their facility in Minnesota and moved to a 260-acre property that had previously been a dairy farm in Hot

Springs, Arkansas. They christened the place the IQ Zoo and opened it to the public in 1955.

Opening during the peak of car culture and the Great American Road Trip, the IQ Zoo was a hit. It was regularly covered by local media and even got a spread in *Life* and *Time* magazines. Guests who stopped in were first ushered into a dimly lit room with a row of boxes all along the walls. A voice would describe the Brelands' training methods and invite viewers to take a look at the first window. It illuminated just enough to see the "colorfully lit technicolor setting" of what looked like a small stage behind glass, as an article about the IQ Zoo exhibits described.[77] From there, each window would illuminate and go dark on timers as real animals performed in their boxes in sequence: a mallard duck playing "Happy Birthday" on a piano, a candle flickering in the background; a rabbit planting a kiss on his girlfriend; a raccoon playing basketball; and so on.

When the automated show ended, guests were ushered into the next room for another live performance, a more traditional stage show that had a human emcee and a cast of trained animals: a chicken, duck, raccoon, and rabbit. Unlike the previous show, which ran entirely without human interference, this one relied on audience participation. In one popular act, the audience asked a raccoon a simple mathematical question, which the furry bandit would answer by dunking a basketball the correct number of times. The emcee urged the audience to defeat the animals—a fun but ultimately impossible proposition since the games were all rigged. Nobody seemed to mind, and guests of the IQ Zoo left feeling mystified but delighted. After the two shows, the audiences were urged to exit through the gift shop, where guests could send postcards with photos of their favorite animal acts to friends and family throughout the world.

One of the most popular acts was the "Bird Brain," a chicken in a modified Skinner Box with nothing to do besides play humans in tic-tac-toe, winning every time. In the mid-1970s, ABE sent hundreds of these units to arcades and mom-and-pop roadside amusement parks. There was apparently even a Bird Brain in Tokyo. When the chicken at the Mott Street arcade in New York's Chinatown died in 1993, it had become such a beloved part of the city that the *New York Times* ran an obituary for the bird, who the owners called Willy.

But the heyday of the trained chicken was waning. Some people thought it was cruel. Others didn't see the point. The trained chicken, the arcade owners said, wasn't a moneymaker compared to their electronic games. "People came here because of the chicken, which is mentioned in tourist guides, but they did not play it so much," the Mott Street owner told the *New York Times* obituary writer.[78] Even less popular was the dancing chicken located in the back of the arcade, its song hidden amidst the loud hum and dings of the more modern games. Put in a couple quarters and she would kick her legs on a rotating stage, bob her head, and maybe give her tail a little shake from side to side. These birds responded so quickly to their commands that a passerby might almost forget that it was a living creature at all.

The Bird Brain was invented not by the Brelands but by an animal trainer named Bob Bailey, who had been hired by the Brelands in 1965 to work at ABE, just a few months before Keller Breland died of a heart attack at age fifty. Bob and Marian continued working together and finally married a decade later. Bailey tried a version of tic-tac-toe where the chicken sometimes lost, but, as he said in an interview, "it didn't improve our income at all."[79] Maybe the impulse to play against a chicken and lose is the same thing that keeps us going to magic shows long after we're old enough to know that it's all illusion and sleight of hand. There's magic in pulling off an invisible trick, a pleasure we humans get in being conned artfully, even if it's just out of a few spare quarters.

Eventually, as Y2K crept closer and people walking by did so with places to be—cell phones against their faces or headphones trailing toward the Walkman in their bags—the extraordinary chickens of Mott Street didn't seem worth the time or the quarters. What was once amazing had become little more than a curiosity. Before the new millennium, the last Bird Brain on Mott Street died and was replaced by an electronic game that didn't have to be fed or trained. This time the chicken didn't get an obituary; she simply disappeared.

Marian's and Keller's (and, later, Bob Bailey's) work tap-danced into the public consciousness in a time when animal attractions were on the rise. Disneyland opened to the public in 1955. The first Six Flags, which was then called Six Flags Over Texas, opened in 1961. Years before documentaries like *Blackfish* tarnished the idea of orcas or other large sea mammals kept in pools for public amusement, the first SeaWorld awed the public with its trained animal acts in 1964. Its training director was a former employee of ABE.[80] Many of these parks' animal acts were trained either directly by the Brelands or by handlers who used methods the pioneering behaviorists had perfected for use in animal entertainment. Every time you see an animal in a television show—whether a parakeet, dog, or tiger—remember the Brelands (and the chickens that started it all). Without them we might still be in a dark time of animal training, pinching ears until Fido finally rolls over on cue.

⤙

After just a few days at Chicken Camp, I find myself watching the birds with a strange feeling in my chest—pride. They've come so far in such a short amount of time. The trainers are faster too. If someone spills food on the table, the coach sweeps it up without a second glance. When the chicken has to be "reset" by placing her back at the start of an activity, people grab the bird confidently (always making sure to cover those big wings).

People were slightly more dressed up on the first day of camp but have gone full animal-person by day two. Some of the women have shirts with dogs on them ("My Patronus is a Border Collie") or show off swag from chicken camps they've been to in the past ("Give a cluck," one shirt says). I see one woman with a T-shirt that says, "Keep calm and treat on," and watch her do both things admirably throughout the remainder of the day. By the time I count four people wearing chicken shirts, we've gotten through the easy stuff. The chickens have already learned how to peck at a target—a red poker chip dropped on the table. Now the chickens are being taught to *only* peck at the red target after adding in blue and green and yellow targets and shuffling them around every time like a game of Three-Card Monte.

If the hens had done it all easily, it would have been less impressive. I probably would have walked away feeling like all chickens naturally love pecking at red poker chips! But sometimes the trainer would set the hen on the table and before the hen made a move, she would stop and stare and think. Humans rarely get the opportunity to watch animals think—really think. It was like watching a student sent up to the chalkboard to solve a particularly difficult math problem. The little red hen had learned enough to know that there was an answer that got her treats and many that didn't. Now she wanted to be right.

When the beginning class ends, a few students go home and others (who had been to Chicken Camp before) join. Though the beginning class made a lot of improvement, the smaller size and higher skill of this new group means that the chickens are being taught more interesting skills. Everyone is so fast with their clickers that the sound ping-pongs around the room. The exercise where the hen pecked at the red poker chip now becomes "match to sample." The trainer shows their chicken a flash card with either a blue triangle or a green square and the hen has to peck the corresponding shape on the table.

Soon everyone is building chicken obstacle courses and training their birds to walk through them, one trick at a time. In one, a chicken walks through a tunnel then over a bridge. Another group trains their chicken to walk around a traffic cone, a seemingly simple task that takes the better part of two days. A few people's chickens learn to weave in an S-shape between poles. Some teams add things to their course, like having their hen "roll" dice by pecking at it or "go fish" by plucking a small plastic goldfish out of a cup. The hens all add their personal flair to this last trick. While some calmly pick up and drop the fish, others hold it in their beaks and rattle it back and forth like they're trying to kill their prey.

There are smiles all around the room. I'm sure people are proud of themselves, but they seem proud of their chickens too. Each chicken is officially identified by a number on her cage, but some people prefer to give their hens nicknames instead. I notice "Jaws," who was given the name after she gave her trainer a hard peck at the beginning of the class, being cooed to affectionately as she goes back into her cage. "You're a good chicken," her trainer says. "Such a smart girl."

Grace Peck, a student and dog trainer who had taken the class the year before, pulls out her phone when we're sitting next to each other on the last day. She has her own flock of "agility chickens" in Portland, and I've asked her to show me the tricks she's been teaching her own girls. They fly up onto the tops of their coops and jump to her arm after a quick word of encouragement. She's even set up obstacle courses for them in her own backyard. A chicken may never learn how to speak English or appreciate works of art. But to some extent, what they can learn is only limited by the trainer's imagination and how much time you want to spend with a treat cup and clicker in your hand.

In 2013, undergraduate students at an Australian university were given the option of taking a chicken training workshop as part of their practical requirement. Students were given a questionnaire to fill out at the beginning and end of the class. It asked whether they thought chickens were intelligent or slow learners, if students felt like they were good animal trainers, and whether students believed chickens had "individual personalities." Roughly half the class had kept chickens at some point and a quarter had never had contact with a chicken in their life—other than, presumably, at the grocery store. In the beginning, only 49 percent believed chickens were "intelligent animals" and roughly 7 percent thought it would be easy to teach chickens how to do tricks. Yet by the end of the eight-week class, the number of students who thought chickens were smart increased by 27 percent, and more than 60 percent now believed it was easy to teach chickens. A study of the class, published in the journal *Animals,* hinted that "greater knowledge of the cognitive abilities of an animal may lead to more positive attitudes to that animal."[81]

I was never surprised that chickens were smart. I'd spent enough time with my own birds to know that they had a great amount of specialized intelligence. What Chicken Camp impressed upon me was just how much they could do that wasn't related to the business of being a chicken.

Within a few days of getting my first chicks, I knew that one belonged in the chicken version of a gifted class. Peggy, even when she was just a little gray ball of fluff, was clearly a very smart chicken. She was the first to learn that she could roost on top of the heat plate the chicks relied on to stay warm. She was the first to fly to my shoulder as an awkward tween chicken. As an adult, she became the flock's head hen and often warned the rest of the chickens when a hawk was nearby.

Of course, none of these skills were tricks: they were just part of being a chicken. The obstacle courses are fun to watch, and people are often surprised to hear that a "dumb chicken" can be trained. But maybe it's not the training that changes people's minds about these birds; maybe spending time with them is all it takes to make people realize how great they are all by themselves.

CHICKENS

IN

THE WILD

CHAPTER NINE:
WINTER EGGS

T's April and Peggy has gone broody again. I go to collect eggs from the nest box and find it full of gray down. When I open the door, Peggy is fluffed up like a pufferfish. She screams at me and the noise makes me feel like I'm in Jurassic Park. Some chickens are more likely to go broody than others, and since she started laying eggs at six months old, Peggy spends the spring and summer in an almost constant state of chick fever.

The nest box is full of gray feathers because she's plucked them out of her own chest to make a "brood patch" that allows better heat transfer from her 105-degree body to the eggs. She hoards eggs from the other chickens and sits on those too. She screams at anyone—human or chicken—who comes too close to *her* nest. She also stops laying eggs since, according to her hormones, she's busy hatching out the clutch she already has.

Though there are multiple nest boxes, it's a well-known phenomenon that hens often use the same one. I often find Peggy ruffled and clucking while another chicken has squeezed in beside her to try and lay an egg. Last year I walked in on Peggy sitting on top of Emmylou, my tiny Mille Fleur d'Uccle Bantam. Emmylou seemed rather perturbed by the whole thing, while Peggy acted so proud you could have been fooled into thinking she'd hatched Emmylou out herself.

If we had a rooster around, Peggy would sit on a clutch of eggs for twenty-one days, hatch her chicks, and soon be showing her brood what it means to be a chicken. As it is, Peggy would sit forever waiting for eggs to hatch that never will. For people in the egg business, a broody laying hen is a problem because she stops laying eggs. But it's a problem for me too. Because while Peggy is broody she'll only get off the nest a couple times a day to eat and drink a little.* She will lose weight fast. Being a mother is hard work even when you're not gestating offspring. Peggy won't even leave the nest to cool off with a dust bath during a heatwave, which can be dangerous for her already dehydrated body.

Soon, I know, I'll be sending Peggy to jail.

These days, you can buy an incubator for as little as thirty dollars. But a broody hen was once an important part of farm life; she was the only way that people could get more chicks for free. Today most urban chicken keepers need to practice family planning with their flocks, either because of limits on the number of chickens they can keep in their yards or because roosters aren't allowed. Thus, there are thousands of posts on backyard poultry forums asking for advice on "breaking" a broody hen.

Some of these methods are strange and of dubious value. People have recommended sticking your hen in a tub of cool water or putting a frozen water bottle underneath her, theorizing that it will cool down her hormonal instinct to mother some chicks. (It calls to mind the phrase, "mad as a wet hen.") Others suggest closing off access to the nest area in the hope that if the hen thinks her eggs have stopped incubating, maybe she'll snap out of it, though this affects the rest of the flock as well. I use a different tactic. When I see Peggy has gone broody, I give it a few weeks and then haul a small wire dog crate from the garage into the house.

---

* Broody hens also cut down on the number of times they go to the bathroom, resulting in the evacuation of a substance known to chicken keepers as a "broody poop." I'll leave this one up to your imagination.

I put food and water in the cage and newspaper on the bottom and bring Peggy inside. She promptly makes herself big on the hard bottom and growls as she closes her eyes. Imagine an angry ball of lint. She'll waffle through phases of nesting, clucking with disappointment while pacing back and forth in the cage, and standing on and spilling her food and water all over the floor. For the first few days, she fluffs herself as large as she can and fans out her tail when I walk past. By day three, she's usually back to her normal self, but I always keep her in jail an extra day just to be sure. I know she's done being broody if I let her out of the crate and she doesn't beeline right for the nest box.

We both hate this routine. I do try to bring her treats like strawberry tops, dandelion greens, or mealworms to smooth things over and keep her occupied, but I always feel bad to leave her in such barren conditions. Short of giving her chicks to hatch, there isn't much of a choice. The first time she went broody, I left her to her own devices for six weeks before she seemed so thin and sad that I knew it couldn't go on any longer.

The chickens all behave strangely when they're about to nest. My tiny Emmylou has never gone completely broody but goes through phases where she dances with the idea of motherhood. She likes to hide clutches of eggs around the yard from time to time, tucking them under bushes, unused wheelbarrows, or the camouflage of fallen leaves. Chickens are exceptionally good at hiding nests, and I only find them when I see Emmylou coming out from her hiding spot.

She never tries to hatch these hidden clutches, but I catch her camping out on eggs in the nest boxes from time to time. If I try to take the eggs from under her, she stays still, fluffed up as big as she can get. She's roughly the size of my hand but can fit as many as an impressive ten eggs underneath her small body. If another hen walks into the coop she puffs and screeches enough that the hen thinks better of it and usually turns right back around.

I've never needed jail for Emmylou. As soon as I take the eggs away, she goes right back to normal. But it's usually around this time that I catch her picking fights with some of the other hens. Maybe they've committed a grave offense, but from my outside perspective it seems like Emmylou just didn't like the way they looked at her. Chickens aren't mammals and they don't menstruate, so I can't call it PMS, but I'm certainly not the first chicken owner to notice something that looks suspiciously like a hormonal mood swing in certain hens.*

Most of my other hens have had the gene for mothering bred right out of them. Humans have gotten so good at artificial incubation that, for us, the most efficient way to keep *Gallus gallus domesticus* going is to keep them from wanting to reproduce at all. It's strange. Some breeds of poultry are so large and strangely proportioned that they physically can't mate naturally anymore. Commercial flocks of Broad-Breasted White turkeys—commonly served at Thanksgiving—actually require artificial insemination. The Cornish Cross, the quintessential grocery store chicken, grows so fast that the birds are usually slaughtered at just seven to nine weeks of age. As the "broilers" (chickens raised for meat) get older and bigger, they're likely to keel over from heart attacks or stop being able to walk because they've grown too quickly for their bones to support them. "Broiler breeders," the parents of these birds, are put on severe diets as soon as a week after hatching so they can live long enough to mate. Though some European countries have outlawed the practice, in the United States and abroad many of these breeding birds are fed only every other day to keep them slim.[82]

Peggy's broodiness harkens back to how her ancestors would have hatched eggs but is not quite the same. The red junglefowl, the precursor to the modern chicken, only lays ten to fifteen eggs per year in the springtime.[83] When Peggy was three, past her prime egg-laying days already, she laid well over 160.

Every time she goes broody, I feel bad that I can't let her hatch out some eggs. I worry about the inevitable roosters we can't keep, and, on our suburban lot, I'm already inching toward the maximum number of chickens that's reasonable for me to care for. Buying chicks is predictable; nature is not. But I often wonder what Peggy's missing out on by not being allowed to follow the instinct for mothering that she's somehow managed to retain despite years of human breeding. Hens are well known for their ability to be caring mothers. One of my favorite photos of chickens that makes the rounds on the internet from time to time is one of a drenched hen standing in the rain. She spreads her wings wide like an umbrella to shelter her chicks, who are hiding beneath

---

* Pre-Broody Syndrome?

her to stay dry. The chicks are so hidden in her down that all you can see of them are their little stick legs.

People who decided chickens were cowardly have never seen a mother hen raise herself up to protect her chicks. They can easily make themselves look twice as big and three times more threatening than in everyday life. Chickens have different alarm calls for ground predators versus ones in the sky, and studies have shown that a hen without chicks won't sound an alarm for a small hawk, but one with chicks will.[84] They're aware of danger not just to themselves but to their brood as well.

It's impossible to know what hens are missing out on by not having chicks, but it seems clear that chicks are at a disadvantage when they aren't hatched by a hen. Playing Mozart for a baby in utero may not ensure that a child gets into college, but the sound of a mother hen's voice talking to an incubating chick *does* affect a chicken's brain development. Studies have found that exposing an incubating egg to the sounds of a mother hen kick-starts their brains.[85] Their hippocampus, which plays a major role in learning and memory, develops faster and with greater synaptic density. These chicks can also solve mazes faster than chicks hatched without sound. The impacts don't stop there. After hatching, chicks raised by hens are kinder to each other. Disagreements between chickens are less likely to devolve into an all-out brawl of feather-pulling and pecks hard enough to draw blood if they've been raised by a real mother.[86] Even after they've outgrown the care of their mothers, brooded chickens will get closer to new objects than those raised artificially.[87] They're also more social. Studies in mammals show that being raised in an enriched environment creates "more complex, flexible brains," as animal welfare professor Christine Nicol notes in her book *The Behavioural Biology of Chickens*.[88] There's no reason why this shouldn't be the case in chickens too. My flock likes to sing the egg song loudly after laying, and I've heard from other chicken keepers that if a flock starts with chickens who tend not to sing, new girls in the flock won't sing either. Bad and good habits both spread through flocks because chickens are social learners.[89] In other words, chickens have culture. There are things mother hens pass on to their chicks, who would pass it onto theirs, and so on, but we incubate them artificially, so every generation is, in effect, starting from scratch. It makes me wonder how we would see the species and how they might change as well if we let them behave more naturally beginning with their development inside of an egg.

～～

While we haven't completely bred out natural instincts like mothering or the ability to mate, we have found ways to change a chicken's environment to moderate natural behaviors. We're used to having eggs year-round, but even our domesticated chickens stop laying when the days get shorter. (Until I started storing our summer and fall egg surplus in a refrigerator, we had to buy eggs from the grocery store in winter when the girls stopped laying.) Most people don't even know eggs are meant to be a seasonal product.

Old recipe books are full of instructions on how to preserve eggs to keep them through the wintertime. This often meant storing shelled eggs in pickling lime or covering them with salt. Fresh eggs in the winter were a rare delicacy that could cost four or five times as much as during the plentiful summer.[90] Around the holidays, newspapers printed recipes for eggless cakes for the frugal housewife.

In the 1930s, laying hens moved out of farmyard coops into large battery farm sheds where they never went outside. We have a seemingly unlimited supply of eggs because the egg industry retires and slaughters hens when they pass prime laying age of one and a half to two years old. Hens are also given supplemental lighting throughout the winter to trick their bodies into thinking it's spring year-round. By the 1960s, mentions of "winter eggs" disappeared from newspapers. Most people forgot that there ever was such a thing as an egg season. Even now, many backyard chicken keepers put lights in their coops to keep their girls laying year-round. I think they deserve the vacation. An ISA Brown hen, a common egg-laying breed, typically lays an egg that's 3 percent of her body weight.[91] For a 170-pound woman, that would be like giving birth to a five-pound baby multiple times a week. It's a lot of work, it's not natural for them to do it so often, and there's a reason why so many hens die from reproductive issues.

In many ways, we know so much about chickens. They're the most numerous farm animal on the planet and were the first farm animal to have their genome sequenced. There are countless studies on chicken management and the best way to get them to become "productive" but fairly few that look at them as a bird.[92] We know everything about the chicken as it relates to human uses, but we don't really know chickens at all. Who are the birds without people caring for them or even a coop to roost in?

It was time to go off in search of wild chickens.

CHAPTER TEN:
CHICKS GONE WILD

IN SOME WAYS, CHICKENS ARE HARD TO MISS IN FITZGERALD, GEORGIA. There's a restaurant called Chicken Coop and five-foot metal rooster statues and murals of chickens on a few old buildings downtown. When I visit in the summer of 2021, they're also in the last stages of constructing a sixty-two-foot topiary chicken. The local government hopes it will get people to take a thirty-minute detour from the highway to come visit the small southern town. It'll have the dubious distinction of being the largest chicken topiary in the world if completed as planned. But it takes a little more work to find the wild chickens.

There was a time in the town's history when it was impossible to go anywhere without encountering a live chicken. They took up residence in the parks downtown, scratching out spots to dust bathe under the bushes and occasionally getting ornery when someone came out of a bakery and didn't want to share their crumbs. Everyone who's lived here seems to have a story about traffic jams caused by hens and their chicks—locally referred to as "biddies"—crossing the street. Sometimes the chickens bypassed the roads altogether and simply soared to the other side. Drivers slammed on their brakes as chickens flew past their windshields. The occasional chicken hit-and-run was inevitable. In Fitzgerald, a bird sanctuary, the chickens are protected and have the right of way. At times, it felt to people like their hometown was being overrun by birds. Some people, lucky or unlucky depending on how they felt about the fowl, might have as many as thirty chickens scratching the days away in their front yards. Both tempers and the fowl population have calmed down somewhat since the last big fight over the future of the chickens in the early 2000s. These days, the best way to find Fitzgerald's wild chickens is to follow the sound of crowing.

~

"They were going to be game birds," says Fitzgerald's resident chicken advocate, Jan Gelders, about the birds' strange origin story. Following World War II, hunters and conservationists sounded the alarm that native animals were disappearing from the forests thanks to habitat loss and deadlier rifles.[93] Gardiner Bump, chief of game conservation in New York convinced the U.S. Fish and Wildlife Service that the solution to this problem was to import exciting and exotic game species from abroad. He sent dozens of species back home to the United States, but none of them took to their new surroundings, as Andrew Lawler chronicles in *Why Did the Chicken Cross the World?*

That's when Bump went looking for red junglefowl. These birds, the ancestor of the domesticated chicken, were known to British hunters living in India as challenging game. They're small enough to fly high into trees to roost, and the hens have drab brown feathers that allow them to blend into the warm wooded areas they like to call home. It can't have hurt that the roosters seemed designed to become striking trophies with their colorful black, gold, and orange feathers and dark gray legs. Between 1960 and 1961, Bump sent back 115 wild red junglefowl that he'd had trapped in Northern India.[94] State game managers in four southern states divvied up the birds and eventually raised ten thousand U.S.–hatched junglefowl that they prepared to release throughout the South in 1963, Lawler writes.[95] Two thousand of those birds were sent into the pine forests at Bowens Mill fish hatchery, roughly ten miles north of Fitzgerald.[96]

"They turned them loose, but they couldn't find them," Gelders scoffs. The vast majority of the junglefowl released into the wild were never seen again. "That just sounds rural Georgia to me, and it sounds like a bunch of idiots were running that project," she says in a pleasant southern drawl, throwing her hands in the air with exasperation.

We're sitting in her kitchen on a hot summer night, a ceiling fan spinning above our heads. Gelders's dark hair is cut in a chic bob with a streak of gray near her temple. Everywhere I look in the small room, there are chickens. I see chickens on towels, wire baskets shaped like chickens that have been filled with potatoes, chicken magnets, salt and pepper shakers roosting on top of the stove, framed photos Gelders has taken of the wild chickens in her yard, and even a clock with a rooster on it that used to crow on the hour until she took the battery out to keep it quiet. Some of these are items Gelders bought for herself over the years. Many more are things people gifted her. "Some things were ugly," she laughs. "I put them kind of off to the side."

Gelders's family has been in Fitzgerald since it was first settled by veterans of the Civil War—both Confederate and Union soldiers. (Even today the streets are named after generals from both sides.) She moved away in the mid-1960s when she was sixteen, went to college, and had a career designing bags and matching tennis racket cases for Lilly Pulitzer. "I came back in 1984, and a couple blocks away from here, I saw chickens in the road," she recalls. "I didn't think much about it. Just what everybody thinks: that they got out of a coop." She mentioned it to her father, who had once been the editor of the local newspaper (and his father before him). She'd come back to Fitzgerald to take care of him after he was diagnosed with terminal cancer. He told her that what she'd seen were probably some of the wild chickens. Wild chickens? Gelders had never heard of such a thing. She started researching it and even called someone in Hawaii after she learned they had wild chickens of their own. Key West had a population too. In fact, it seemed like "wild" chickens were all over.

But none of them were quite like the birds in Fitzgerald.

Everyone else's birds were simply feral. By definition this means domesticated chickens that either escaped or were released. "It's not the same thing. These came from India!" Gelders says, pounding on the table for emphasis. I can tell she's been arguing this point with people for decades.

But at the same time that Gelders was learning what made this chicken population so special, people in town were starting to complain to the city government about the birds. Members of the local garden club were particularly vocal enemies of the chickens. The birds scratched up the pine straw locals used for mulch and made it impossible to keep pansies in the ground.

"These chickens were real political," Gelders says. She and her late husband printed out pamphlets about the chickens, paid for ads in the paper, and got local and national news coverage of the birds. "The only protection the chickens had was the attention they were getting," Gelders says. So she and a group of about twenty people showed up to every city council meeting that had chickens on the agenda, armed with pro-chicken signs. "You can't imagine coming up against chicken haters, going to city council and telling those men there, 'They look like chickens, but chickens don't fly, you know.'" Gelders rolls her eyes as if remembering the sheer stupidity she had to put up with.

Throughout our conversation, I hear roosters crowing in Gelders's yard. The crows are subtly different from what I'm used to hearing. While domestic roosters have the standard *cock-a-doodle-doo!*, red junglefowl sound like someone is strangling them right as they sing the last syllable. Usually the Fitzgerald chickens are shy, but they clearly know this is a safe space. Gelders notes in an offhand way, "They get real loud at roosting time," before we walk outside to watch them. This is an understatement. There's an explosion of sound as soon as she opens the door. Roosters run around and tussle on the ground. Others line up on the fence and fly into the tree one by one.

Mosquitoes are out in full force, and her large orange cat, aptly named Mr. Fluff, noses his way onto my lap but I'm too mesmerized by what I'm seeing to pay either much mind. The chickens fly high into the tree one after another until at least twenty hens and roosters are hunkered down two stories above our heads. I can hear them clucking amongst themselves. Even in the trees, there's a lot of annoyed grumbling and jostling for the best position on the branches.

Gelders has spent a lot of time observing them over the decades and is only too happy to tell me about the things that make them seem different from domestic chickens—the most obvious being their ability to flutter straight up into a tree. "These chickens have developed all kinds of survival techniques," Gelders says. "I mean, they're going on sixty years and no one's really helped them." Instead of walking across dangerous roads, they started flying across them. They nest in empty yards and stay far away from the ones with dogs (or chicken haters) in residence. More than once, she's had a hen lay eggs on the roof of her house, out of reach of predators. But the most striking example of what makes them different from domestic fowl, Gelders says, is the way they communicate with each other. She calls it the chicken telegraph system. Groups of birds live in small habitats throughout town, and whenever there's trouble—a loose dog, a hawk, or even someone walking underneath a tree where they're roosting—the alarm call goes up from the nearest rooster. What happens next is like when the beacons of Gondor were lit in *The Lord of the Rings*: one rooster after another picks up the call and passes it through town. "When danger stops, a rooster makes a special final sound and they all go silent like that," Gelders says, snapping her fingers. To some people in town, this is just a lot of noise; to Gelders, it's a sign of their intelligence.

"I didn't consider them chickens," Gelders says as we look into the trees. "That's what makes them so special."

When we domesticated wolves to turn them into the dogs that live in our homes (and sometimes sleep in our beds), we altered almost everything about them. We reduced their long, tapered snouts into the smushed faces of breeds like pugs and bulldogs. Some dogs are taller than the average man when they stand on their hind legs; others can fit into a handbag. Dog breeds developed the ability to raise their inner eyebrows, while wolves cannot.[97] Their behavior changed too. They've evolved to see humans as teammates if not family. Studies have shown that when asked to solve a problem, dogs make eye contact with their humans as if to ask for help.[98]

Obviously, chickens were domesticated for very different reasons than dogs. Fowl have been bred to have aesthetically appealing feather patterns, gain weight quickly, lay a lot of eggs, or lay eggs with various colors. The average domestic chicken looks very different from their wild cousins living in Asia. Red junglefowl typically have dark gray legs (not yellow), and the color white is minimal in wild junglefowl. They're small and light, which makes it easy for them to fly to safe roosting spots. The process of domestication itself, which requires animals to lose their fear of humans, is where the change from junglefowl to chicken began. A group of researchers at Linköping University in Sweden bred red junglefowl for tameness and after only three generations found that the birds "grew larger, laid larger eggs, and generated larger off-spring."[99] After a few more generations, the tamed junglefowl became less scared of new things and their gene expression began to change in notable ways from previous generations. The simple act of taming animals, not even breeding them for specific traits, changes their very genetics.

But on a fundamental level, domesticated and wild chickens are two sides of the same coin.[100] Most domesticated chickens are just as smart and capable as chickens in the wild. Even their language is still similar—a wild rooster's *cock-a-doodle-doo*, compared to a domestic chicken's, sounds like the same word spoken with an accent. "People often assume that domestic animals are so badly maladapted that they're only going to go feral one time in a million," biologist Eben Gering tells me. "But that doesn't really seem to be the case."

We're sitting on the patio of a coffee shop in Florida, where he currently teaches at Nova Southeastern University. He's wearing a button-down shirt with a fish print on it and his practical shoes have colorful striped socks peeking out of them. Gering started studying feral chickens on Kauai with another evolutionary biologist, Dominic Wright, in 2013. Chickens have likely been on the Hawaiian Islands as long as people have. When Polynesians took their outrigger canoes to the open seas, traveling thousands of miles to places like Hawaii and Easter Island, they brought the fowl on board. Today, even though Hawaiian chickens are part of island culture (showing up in ancient myths as well as on souvenir T-shirts), they've also proliferated in the last few decades to become a local annoyance.* When I was there a few years ago, I saw multiple restaurants with hand-painted signs asking people not to feed the chickens. I also went to a few restaurants where people had clearly ignored the signs and fowl swarmed the place, going so far as to jump up on tables to beg for food like a flock of colorful seagulls. People started noticing a chicken boom in the years after Hurricanes Iwa and Iniki in 1982 and 1992. A popular theory is that the storms destroyed coops, sending domesticated chickens

---

* Many tourist shops on Kauai sell T-shirts with the slogan "World's most annoying alarm clock" printed next to a picture of a crowing rooster.

into the jungle to mingle, perhaps with populations dating back to the early Polynesians. Everyone agreed the chickens were all over the island, but no one knew what they *were*. Figuring out the answer was more important than just assuaging casual curiosity. Hawaii state law protected wild chickens but considered loose domestic chickens pests that should be eradicated.[101]

To figure out the mysteries of Kauai chicken DNA, the biologists first had to catch the birds. "They can be pretty difficult to trap sometimes, and they learn," Gering says of the experience. First, he and Wright tried catching the birds with a net gun. The net gun looks like a flashlight, but instead of a bulb in the front, there's a carefully packed net ready to fly out and ensnare prey with the help of a little push from compressed CO_2 cartridges. Online videos of people using net guns to ensnare their (willing) friends make it look like a lot of fun to use, but alas, it wasn't much good against feral chickens. "We never caught a single bird with that thing," Gering sighs.

Then it was the whimsically named "whoosh trap," which uses a system of poles and bungee cords to throw a net over birds in a manner that reminds me of trying to make the bed in a hurry. It required a large area to work—hard to come by in Hawaii's tropical forests—and every time they sprung the net it spooked the chickens, Gering recalls. They finally had some luck thanks to two relatively low-tech methods: using a gull net, which closes over birds who investigate the feed tray like a soccer goal closing over their heads, and simply building a pen then pulling the door shut behind the chickens when they wandered in.

The birds are (rightfully) suspicious of new things in their environment. Gering says they had to leave the gull nets in place for a few days and cover the edges with leaves or grass before the chickens would step into them. "Otherwise, they'll walk to it and lean over it with their heads but won't step into it," he says. "It's really cute."

From there the work was relatively easy. They removed the birds from the trap and wrapped them in a towel "like a little burrito," Gering says. They'd take a blood sample, feather sample, and some other measurements, then let the birds go. Each bird took about five minutes to process. Not that it was a pleasant job. At times, they couldn't wear bug spray or sunscreen or they'd risk getting the chemicals on the birds and potentially contaminating data. They did a lot of their work in the early morning, but this is a tropical island near the equator—the sun is harsh and the bugs are everywhere. "Then there are the worms," Gering says with a tinge of lingering horror in his voice. "Almost every single bird has worms in their eyes. It's really disturbing." The life of a field biologist is fascinating but rarely glamorous.

When they got the DNA results back, the conclusions were surprising. Gering and Wright found that the birds weren't junglefowl or domestic: they were both. They were something new.

"In general, if you ask biologists or laypeople which genes will win, they'd say the wild genes because domestic chickens will stare at the sky and drown when it rains," Gering laughs.* But Kauai's birds had selective sweeps—beneficial genetic mutations that become common among a population—from domestic breeds that are associated with increased growth and reproduction.[102] Interestingly, the roosters also tended to have much larger combs and wattles than those seen in wild chicken species. The hens just couldn't resist a man with a fleshy red face. These are all traits that human breeding helped select into existence. While it's possible that traits for higher reproduction and growth might have developed naturally given enough time and genetic mutation, human care and selection sure made it easier. In the feral population, chickens had junglefowl genes that were linked to brooding chicks, a trait that has mostly been bred out of domestics. Farmers don't like it when their chickens go broody, but, in the wild, the only way to keep the population going is to have good mother hens. There's also evidence that Kauai's chickens lay eggs seasonally like junglefowl.

The birds can't undo domestication even when they live in the wild, but what they've become is more impressive than the label "feral" might lead us to believe. These aren't just chickens who are surviving: Kauai's wild chickens are thriving. They've taken the best of human selection and combined it with the traits that are important to their survival in the wild almost like avian cyborgs.

"I've never had anybody overestimate what those feral animals can achieve," Gering says. People talk about feral animals like it's a fixed state, he tells me. But

---

* For the record, this is a myth that comes from turkeys. Both turkeys and chickens can drown if enough rain turns into flooding, but neither species is likely to do so while staring at the sky.

he prefers to think about feralization as a verb, a process. A domestic animal is released into the wild. He survives long enough to make himself at home. He goes feral. But as feral mothers have offspring and meet with differently adapted members of the species and new environments, the animals keep changing.

I can't help but wonder whether if we left them alone long enough, maybe these chickens could surpass their "feral" label to become a subspecies—similar enough to interbreed with domestic and wild chickens but perfectly and specially adapted to their island environment.

One thing that's not in question is whether chickens are capable of surviving in the right wild climate. But that doesn't mean they aren't better off with a helping hand. In Fitzgerald, that person is Jan Gelders. In Ybor City, it's a man named Dylan Breese.

Ybor City is a historic neighborhood that was founded in the 1880s when Cuban cigar manufacturers Vincente Martinez-Ybor and Ignacio Haya were looking for cheap land close to Cuba where they could build a cigar factory town. They found it in an undeveloped area next to Tampa, Florida. The high wages and good working conditions brought waves of Cuban, Jewish, Spanish, Italian, Chinese, and German immigrants to work in Ybor's cigar factory and the many others that sprung up in the growing city. The new arrivals brought their animals with them—horses, of course, and also chickens, which were used for food and cockfighting. At the time, this kind of mixing between ethnic groups was unusual, but in Ybor it was an overall success. By 1890, the area had grown from little more than a swamp with palmetto trees into a city of six thousand. At its peak, Ybor City had over two hundred cigar factories producing over half a billion cigars a year.

That all changed when mechanization made cigars easier (and cheaper) to roll at the same time that the Great Depression cut down on the number of people who could afford such a luxury. Ybor's population began to decline, leaving behind empty brick buildings that had once housed cigar factories or social clubs, boarded-up wooden houses, and—at least according to some people—the chickens that immigrants had brought with them to Ybor all those decades before.

"Aside from the factory buildings and the brick roads, the chickens are the only lasting piece of that history dating back 140 years," Breese says. It's a summer weekend in Ybor City, and Breese and I have arranged to meet at Centennial Park just before dusk. It's not just for my benefit. Every day around "bedtime" he walks through the park to make sure the chickens are all okay. A few of the days when I'm there, I don't even make plans to meet up with Breese but run into him at the park anyway. He's an easy man to find. "I get my steps in," he laughs. It's a nice park, bordered by arching live oak trees, but the only people who regularly use it seem to be a group of homeless men and, of course, the chickens.

Today, Ybor's population of feral chickens fluctuates between two hundred and four hundred, according to Breese. The park easily houses fifty to one hundred of them. Depending on where you look in the rest of Ybor, you might not see chickens at all. The birds are surprisingly territorial. Breese tells me that even within the park, the chickens have divided it into quadrants. "They have their zone, and they stay in their zone and reproduce in their zone," he says. A few roosters wander into the middle of the square during the day, but at night each bird returns to the same spot on the same tree. There are other chicken cliques who live in the bushes outside of certain parking lots—only coming out in the morning to eat discarded pizza crusts and snacks left behind by nighttime revelers—or in shrubby bushes near the train tracks that run through the middle of town.

Breese tells me about a "cute couple" he knows, a hen and a rooster from different trees who nonetheless spend their entire day together. "Toward bedtime they'd do this game like, am I going to stay with you tonight or are you going to stay with me tonight?" he laughs. "Without fail they wound up going their separate ways, but it looked like they were trying to talk the other one into coming to their tree."

Jan Gelders is trying to protect the Fitzgerald chickens to save a species, but Breese sees each of the chickens as individuals—with all the individual dramas that go along with it. If I'm curious about any of the Centennial Park chickens, all I have to do is point and Breese can tell me their name along with their backstory. They look beautiful as they jump up to roost in the trees, green oak leaves dotted with flecks of red and gold and white feathers. Breese tells me that he often sees tourists looking up, open-mouthed, at the birds roosting—and pooping—directly above them. I shut mine firmly as soon as he says it.

Breese is in his early forties, though he doesn't look it. Every time I see him, he's wearing a backwards baseball cap and surprisingly well-kept sneakers. Nothing about him screams "this man has devoted his life to chickens," and yet here he is.

"Hey! Why are you crossing the road?" someone shouts from a car as a rooster stands in the middle of the street.

Breese rolls his eyes. "If I had a dollar every time I heard somebody say that."

He'd lived in Ybor for a few years before he really noticed the chickens. "My whole thing with the chickens started just across the street," he says, pointing to a group of businesses near the park. A hen had just hatched some chicks, and the small family lived in the bushes outside of an art gallery. This was in 2016, just after he'd been laid off. Breese started visiting (and feeding) those fourteen birds every day just to get out of the house.

"The owner caught me," Breese says. "I thought I'd be in trouble, but he gave me the keys instead." Breese started working at the gallery, which has a large window facing the park. Every day he saw the way people interacted with the park chickens. Some people were kind, but not everyone. Kids chased them. Once, Breese saw a father take off his shoe and give it to his son so the kid could throw it at a rooster. "I decided they needed some people to be on their side," Breese tells me. After work, he started taking hour-long walks to check on the birds. "I was already there and it happened organically," Breese says. "It became part of the routine." It wasn't long before he started social media accounts for the newly formed Ybor Chickens Society to get more people interested in advocating for the birds.

"To a certain extent, I think it worked because now people yell at *me* if I'm trying to help a hurt chicken," Breese says, smiling. People know the chickens are protected. But sometimes birds are clearly sick, suffering from foot or eye infections or bloodied from a particularly bad fight. Without Breese, they would likely die, either from their injuries or by being picked at by the rest of the chickens in the area. Chickens aren't particularly tolerant of weakness.

I ask Breese if his childhood self would be surprised to see him become so passionate about these birds. "I started this when I was thirty-six, and I think my thirty-five-year-old self would be surprised," he says with a laugh. Breese thinks about the question a bit more and gets quiet. "Without getting too personal, I didn't have a great childhood, so small, vulnerable things. . . ." He trails off. "It took a while for it to come out, I guess." But the fact that he became a champion for Ybor's chickens is more happenstance than fate. "If Ybor had monkeys or mini goats or anything that was small and vulnerable out on the street, it would have been that. It just happened to be chickens."

When I visit, his backyard has been converted into a chicken micro-sanctuary for birds who can't hack it on the streets of Ybor for one reason or another. Soon he will be expanding into even more nearby space. The core group of the Ybor Chickens Society consists of Nayeli Robledo, a friend who was with Breese the day he discovered the hen and her chicks outside the art gallery, and Anahy Gutierrez, Breese's girlfriend. I meet both of the women at a Friday night "Sweep-n-Sleep," where volunteers show up, clean up after the birds, and watch the chickens fly up to their roosts. It's not the kind of nightlife most people expect to find in Ybor.

Breese might be the face of the Ybor Chickens Society, but Gutierrez is just as committed to helping the birds. She's spent most of her life in Ybor. As a child she remembers hearing chicks that had gotten stuck in the storm drain and telling her mother that she wished someone would help them. Gutierrez is a teacher and met Breese when he came (with some chickens) to speak to the kids in her class. When things got serious enough to tell her mom about her relationship, Gutierrez led with the fact that not only was someone finally helping those chicks, that person was her new boyfriend. She used to say she wanted to live on a farm someday; a yard full of chickens isn't so far off.

These days, the chickens are a central figure in their lives. Even Breese's small car has been turned into a mobile chicken rescue unit. When we walk over to it, I immediately note that the passenger seat seems to have a mixture of sunflower and millet seeds on the floor.

Breese sighs. "Every car I get, I tell myself this isn't going to be a chicken car and before long. . . ." He throws his hands up. The evidence speaks for itself. The trunk is so stuffed with rescue gear that I'm surprised he has room to get groceries. Breese pulls out an expandable net he uses to get chicks that have fallen into the city's many cavernous storm drains. There's a crowbar for lifting manhole covers. Two other large nets are for nabbing chickens on the street. We look at his trunk and he shakes his head as though seeing the car through an outsider's eyes for the first time in a while. "My poor car," he sighs again. "My poor series of cars."

After Ybor was revitalized into a thriving nightlife spot during the 1990s, rents started going up. Some of the original wooden casitas are still downtown, but they're often right next to new luxury condo buildings. Not everyone likes the pastoral vibe of loose chickens in the streets. But like so many places with feral chickens, Tampa is a bird sanctuary where wild fowl of all kinds are untouchable, though domestic fowl raised in captivity for human consumption are not. While some Ybor residents have pushed back on the chickens' protections, Breese has always argued that the feral chickens—at least some of them—are descendants of the original fowl that people brought with them to Ybor. As such, they deserve to be protected. But that's not the only explanation for where the chickens came from.

One possibility is that the chickens are the descendants of forty backyard game birds who went free when a large storm destroyed local resident Cephas Gilbert's coop in the 1990s.[103] The chickens went forth and multiplied.

Another origin story traces the birds back to a man, Tommy Stephens, who did more than anyone—until Breese—to popularize Ybor's chickens. Decades ago, Stephens started feeding the fowl that frequented his backyard, including a handsome cock he came to name James E. Rooster. When the rooster was killed by a dog, Stephens decided on a whim to hold a New Orleans–style funeral on Seventh Avenue. The event was so much fun, it happened on and off for two decades. No one minded the parade, but his neighbors complained about the fowl in Stephens's backyard. If they were proven to be his pets, the city could fine him. To get out of a jam, Stephens called around until he found a friend, the grandson of Vincente Martinez-Ybor, and asked him to corroborate the story that the chickens had been there since Ybor's earliest days.[104]

There's no doubt that drop-offs of domesticated chickens have added to the Ybor chicken gene pool over the decades, but that doesn't mean Stephens's fib wasn't accidentally the truth. With condos going up, old residents being priced out, and cigar shops that seem to remain just for the sake of tourists, the chickens feel like a link to Ybor's past. It doesn't really matter if the chickens are descendants from Ybor's founding days; the story allowed Stephens to argue at a contentious city council meeting that the birds deserved to stay. Ybor is a historic district, but it's the chickens, more than anything else, that help the neighborhood feel like a place frozen in time.

Breese tells me about an encounter he had a year before. A woman walked up to him and asked if he was "the chicken man." He flinched before answering because that conversation can easily go in two directions. The woman told him that she grew up in Puerto Rico and all her family still lived there. Her grandmother was getting old and had dementia; when the woman wanted to FaceTime her abuela, she came to the park so the old woman could hear the chickens and think her granddaughter was still at home in Puerto Rico. She thanked him for making sure the chickens had a home in Ybor. Breese has seen other people bring their families to the park and tell the kids that this is what it's like where Mom and Dad came from.

One evening while I'm in Ybor, I'm watching the chickens jump into the trees at night when I see a Russian man on a video call with someone. The man walks around, pointing his phone at the chickens. I can hear his friend laughing. Despite all the bars and live music on Seventh Avenue a few blocks away, that isn't the part of Ybor the man wants to show off. The chickens are what make it special.

⚬⟋⟍

In some ways, Ybor's feral fowl might be a victim of their own success. And I'm not talking about the noise complaints or the people who think there's too much chicken poop on the ground. Ybor is dotted with signs that say "NO" in large lettering and then in a smaller font underneath, "Pet abandonment is a crime." They're decorated with small rooster silhouettes.

Breese is glad that there are chickens on the sign but wishes the city would have been more specific about the type of pets being abandoned. "People don't consider chickens pets," he says. Dogs and cats aren't the ones being regularly abandoned in Ybor, so why not come out and say it? "Chicken abandonment is a crime." During just the few days I'm in Ybor, Breese gets three separate calls about chickens—hens and roosters—who have been dumped on the streets. Even with the relatively small population of feral birds in Ybor compared to Hawaii or even Key West, Breese is spread thin. "There's so little of me and so many birds."

People hear about Ybor's chickens, see the birds living their best lives in the park, and think it's the perfect place to get rid of old hens or roosters they can't or don't want to keep. Breese has found roosters dumped with crow collars, a Velcro necklace that makes it hard for the birds to crow at full volume, still wrapped around their throats. It's a strangling waiting to happen. A hurricane passes through town the day before I arrive, and just before it hit, someone dumped an old rooster in the park whose wings were clipped, so he had no hope of safely roosting in the tree. Without Breese coming to scoop the confused rooster up, it would likely have been a death sentence. A few days later, two gold Orpington roosters were also dumped in the street.

Abandonment is a constant issue that can quickly inflate the population of feral birds in an area. Some people either don't know or don't care enough to try to rehome chickens and take the easy route of dropping the birds off instead. But others are simply caught in the catch-22 of living in a place where feral chickens or hens in the backyard is legal but having a pet rooster is not. Unfortunately, most people don't think about what happens to all the unwanted roosters until they have one of their own to rehome.

CHAPTER ELEVEN:
WHAT TO DO WITH ALL THE ROOS?

TARTING IN LATE SPRING, CHICKEN GROUPS THROUGHOUT THE world are filled with photos of young chickens and a frantic question: "Can you please tell me whether this is a hen or a roo?" It's not uncommon for a poster to ask this about chicks who are hardly older than a week or two. Often the answer to the question is a simple "It's too early to tell." Though people can't be completely sure of a chicken's sex until they start laying eggs or growing telltale hackle and saddle feathers—feathers on the neck and at the base of the tail that grow distinctively long and thin on roosters—there are a few signs, like a rapidly reddening comb and larger size, that make people wonder.

Even if your bird is sexed with a 100 percent guarantee, it only means that you'll get your money back if your pullet is actually a cockerel. If you can't keep him, you're the one who has to find a place for him to go. Back when most people's chickens were dual-purpose breeds that could be used for eggs or meat, roosters weren't "unwanted" so much as "the first ones to wind up the star of Sunday dinner." For people whose chickens are less livestock and more "pets that make breakfast," the thought of slaughtering one in the backyard is horrifying. And for chicken keepers in suburban or urban areas, it's not exactly neighborly behavior either. Thinking of chickens as pets has created a new problem—the question of what to do with unwanted roosters if you're unwilling to sell them for food.

Backyard poultry might be taking off around the world, but most cities that welcome a reasonable number of hens in an urban backyard will not allow a rooster. In places where people *can* keep roosters, there's the problem of too many boys in a small space. Though half of all chickens are male, common flock-keeping wisdom dictates that a happy flock shouldn't have more than one rooster for every four hens (though many people think closer to one rooster for every ten hens is a happier number). This is because, other than protecting his flock, a rooster's main "job" is to breed with hens vigorously and often. Chicken sex is over quickly. But when it happens too regularly, it can result in overbred hens whose back feathers have been grabbed so often they have bald patches. It's such a common problem that there's a healthy market for "hen aprons," a piece of cloth worn as a protective layer to allow an overbred hen's feathers the chance to grow back without risking further injury in the meantime.

While part of wanting to know the sex of the birds is simple curiosity, the impatience for this knowledge seems new. It should be easy for posters to just wait and see, except for one fact: no one wants to get attached to a chick who might have to find a new home. It's why even small farmers treat meat chickens differently from their laying hens. They're happy to dote upon The Girls (who usually stick around for a few years before they're "retired") but rarely spend time getting to know meat birds, knowing that they'll be going to slaughter at just a few months old.

—

For the first two years of my chicken-keeping journey, I'd scoffed at people who asked about the sex of birds who were clearly roosters. I'd scroll through the spring flush of photos showing fleshy red wattles and the kind of colorful feathers that would never wind up on a hen. People only want a second opinion when the news is bad. I knew that if sexing was only 90 percent accurate, then mathematically speaking, for every ten chicks I added to the flock, at least one of them would be an oopsie-rooster. But that's the funny thing about statistics; for every lucky person who never gets a sexing error, there are bound to be those who encounter multiples. Until now, I'd been one of the lucky ones.[105]

It was spring, and with the arrival of my five new chicks, I had ordered a total of twelve sexed pullets since starting my flock. I named the newest group of girls after fictional female detectives: Olivia of Law & Order: SVU, Scully from The X-Files, Phryne from Miss Fisher's Murder Mysteries, Harriet (the Spy), and perhaps my favorite name of the group, Miss Marple of the Agatha Christie novels. Per usual, each was a different breed: two bantams and three full-size. I'd fretted over who the best Miss Marple would be and decided to bestow it on my Partridge Cochin chick. I'd wanted a full-size Cochin ever since I learned they were partially responsible for starting the chicken obsession known as Hen Fever.

Miss Marple was a giant chick with a chocolate-brown head, gray downy breast, and fuzzy socks that ran down her two outer toes (all "booted" chicken breeds have these as chicks). I soon noticed that while the other chicks peeped their lost chick call and struggled to get back to the brooder whenever I took them out to handle them, Miss Marple was content to snuggle into my palms. When the chicks got old enough to hop out of the brooder, Miss Marple flew right to my leg and nestled there for a nap. I loved them all, of course, but I loved Miss Marple especially.

In every new batch of chicks, one has always made me worry she might be a he, whether because of her size or personality or larger and redder comb. People who get the same breed of chicken have an easier time with this since they can compare development between chicks who will look essentially the same when grown. I'd never even gotten two hens of the same breed. So when the now month-old birds entered their awkward teens and Miss Marple's comb seemed to be growing in a little faster than everyone else's, I tried not to worry. When she became nearly twice as big as even my other full-size breeds, I chalked it up to Cochins being particularly large. But at nearly six weeks old, Miss Marple's upright posture combined with the bright red (though still small) comb and wattle led me to post in a chicken group. Hen or roo? Most people said she was a hen. I was relieved.

Then the iridescent blue and mahogany feathers started coming in.

Unless a chick is "sex-linked," bred so the males and females are different colors from the moment they hatch, male and female chicks don't start to differ until their adult feathers come in. In many breeds, hens and roosters have the same general feather coloring. This is not the case with Partridge Cochins. The hens have a pattern known as "double lacing," where each feather is covered in a series of arches in alternating colors—mahogany, black, mahogany, black—getting smaller to the bottom of the feather. For whatever reason, the first coat of feathers to replace the chick down is always double laced on both sexes; on males the delicate patterns are later replaced by adult feathers in a mix of mahogany, orange, black, and iridescent blue.

I tried to deny the truth one more time, posting an updated photo of Miss Marple in a chicken forum. The answers were again unanimous. But this time everyone said Miss Marple was, in fact, Mr. Marple.

He hadn't started crowing yet, but it was only a matter of time. Mr. Marple was just eight weeks old when I started looking for his new home. I wanted to start as soon as possible, knowing all too well how hard it can be to find someone to take in an oopsie-roo.

≁

The first time I call Mary Britton Clouse, co-founder of Chicken Run Rescue in Minnesota, I hear a rooster before she even says hello. More than one, actually. They appear to be having a crowing competition. I hear her talking to the chickens in the same kind of baby talk I can't help but use around animals. Then she gives me a hurried greeting in her usual warm voice. Britton Clouse adds, "Rather than having the boys serenade you over the phone, I'll head back to the office. I'm just leaving the boys' room right now." This room has tile floors and a large glass door leading out to a brick patio. In another home, it might be the perfect place for a home office. But, as I learn when I visit in person a few months later, the room smells faintly of cleaning products and nearly every available bit of wall space is filled with dog kennels stacked carefully on top of each other. Each one has a clean towel to line it and a small name tag with a photo of the chicken who makes that kennel his roost at night.

Chicken Run Rescue (CRR) started in 2001, a few years before the backyard chicken boom began. Britton Clouse found out about a cockfighting bust that left six roosters without anywhere to go. "Neither of us had ever held a chicken before," she says of herself and her husband, Bert Clouse, who runs the rescue with her. Both have long gray hair these days and have been together so long that Britton Clouse often forgets she has to introduce him. It's so obvious that wherever she is, he simply must be also.

They liked birds fine and Britton Clouse had a pet parakeet as a kid, but it wasn't like the heavens opened up upon their first interaction with a chicken. "We chose to help chickens because no one else was helping them," she says. That and because animal control started calling the couple every time they picked up a stray chicken. "As far as finding the chickens charming or amazing or intelligent—that all came later," she says.

They started with those six roosters their first year. It's gone up a lot since then.

CRR has taken in over 1,100 chickens over the years, finding homes or fosters for some, while keeping others in their long-term care. Every year they might get requests to take in anywhere from 150 to 500 chickens. Britton Clouse started keeping a document in 2009 that lists every surrender inquiry they've ever gotten. Since then, her small rescue has been contacted about rehoming 3,400 animals, mostly chickens (though there was the occasional duck or guinea fowl). It's far more than the rescue could ever handle. They currently house roughly sixty birds. The stories from people who want to surrender birds are sad ones—if not for the chickens than for the humans giving them up. Britton Clouse has categories with the reason for each surrender request: domestic abuse, moving, stray chickens, school hatching projects, seizures from neglect cases, don't want anymore, and of course, "oops, it's a rooster."

Sometimes the requests come from families looking to rehome spoiled pet chickens whose owners have gotten too sick to care for them or died. There's an email from someone who found out the male chicks at a pop-up petting zoo would be drowned when the fair was over. Could Britton Clouse find a place for them? Another person knows someone who was planning to let their chickens loose to "fend for themselves" in Minnesota even though it meant a certain death when winter came, if not sooner. Most people mention that they want to find a good home for their chickens because they can't bear the thought of giving them to someone who would eat their pets for dinner.

Though most of the requests are from people in Minnesota, people contact CRR from all over the country. One woman in California emailed because while she tried local animal shelters, she "couldn't find an option that won't end their lives." In the United States, most shelters only take typical domestic pets. I talked to multiple shelters that do take chickens, and in every case people told me that hens—even ones too old to lay regularly—get adopted quickly. Roosters tend to linger.

With rooster bans in most cities, male chickens are the new Pit Bull: laws make it hard for many people who want them as pets to have them. (And people who have chickens as part of a small farm only need a few roosters unless they're raised for meat.) Often the only reason roosters leave shelters is because they're taken in by a place like CRR, a rescue that will commit to caring for these birds until the end of their lives.

I send a lot of emails back and forth with Britton Clouse; she's so busy it's the easiest way to contact her. When she writes back, she often adds a story about one of the chickens in her care along with a photo. It reminds me of a proud parent eager to show off their kids, and it's hard not to smile when I open her emails. There's a beautiful bronze-and-gray hen looking almost stoned as she stares into a so-called "happy light" during the darkest days of winter. In another, two roosters are happily taking a dust bath together in the "dirt yurt" Britton Clouse sets up for the purpose—a small pop-up kennel filled with topsoil and leaves. Britton Clouse always refers to each of the chickens by name and has stories about each one. It's why she started the surrender database in the first place. She wants to know each animal as an individual. "I used the database to record absolutely every detail about their past life and future I could gather because it matters to them and us," she says in one of her emails.

It's not a stretch to say that chickens have changed Mary's and Bert's lives. The couple moved themselves and the rescue to a new location in the country a few years ago. The entire bottom floor of the house is dedicated to chickens. Mary and Bert transformed the gardens into a seamless blend of plants, trees, and fencing to keep the chickens corralled into separate groups during the warmer time of the year. Britton Clouse wears a uniform of thick jeans and work boots so she can care for the chickens but puts the kind of dresses over them that hint at the fact that she's an artist too.

I ask her to walk me through a typical day and feel tired on her behalf just listening to her describe it. She gets up at five a.m. and her day is filled with making sure the chickens are cared for and the house is clean. "Usually, the day doesn't wind down until eight or eight thirty," she says. "Then I'll drag my sorry ass up the stairs and figure out what we're going to eat for dinner and fall asleep at the table and go to bed." Britton Clouse laughs, though I have a feeling it isn't a joke.

"It's a hell of a lot of work," she says. "But everyone's pretty happy here."

Britton Clouse wasn't always a chicken person. "Dogs were my first love ever since I was a child, but chickens are dogs with feathers," she says. One of her roosters regularly follows Britton Clouse from room to room while she does her rounds with the other birds. "I call them rooster puppies," she laughs.

While she's glad if having backyard chickens gives people the chance to get to know these birds, she thinks the whole system of urban flocks is based on a fantasy. "It's this idealized rural nostalgia," she says. Cities allow hens and not roosters, ignoring the fact that it leaves half of the birds unwanted and with no place to go. Hens get too old to lay. Some people put their houses up for sale with a backyard coop and include the flock of chickens in the deal, like they're an appliance or patio furniture. "When people contact us to take in a rooster they inadvertently wound up with, the story is always the same: 'Our city says we can't have them, but we love them and they're really sweet!'" she mimics, rolling her eyes. "If you love them, then you need to fight for them! Because we're full and can't take them anymore and the problem is endless." One of the walls downstairs has a string with over twenty of the chicken name tags and photos clipped to it. When I ask her about it, she starts getting choked up. None of the chickens in the photos are still alive and the tags represent only a few years' worth of rescued birds she's eventually said goodbye to. The rest of the tags are saved in boxes in the house until she can create the proper memorial for them.

"Roosters are totally screwed," she says. "The only way it's going to change for them is if our entire relationship with animals changes." Some people think loosening up restrictions on roosters would help the problem, but for Britton Clouse, who has been vegan for decades, the only answer is ending animal agriculture altogether. "Exploitation of the female is the basis of animal agriculture," she explains. "It isn't just the roosters. The same thing happens with dairy goats or with cows, where male calves are sold as veal. There's so much more to it than what to do with the roosters." Really the only reason we're talking about this at all is that an animal used for agriculture is increasingly becoming a beloved pet. And you don't kill a pet you can't keep; you rehome him. Or at least you try.

~

The Massachusetts Society for the Prevention of Cruelty to Animals (MSPCA) at Nevins Farm has been around for over a hundred years. When it started, it was a "rest home" for horses who had spent their lives working, says MSPCA's director of adoption centers and programs, Michael Keiley. Today, Nevins Farm, just one of three shelters in the MSPCA system, has the usual dogs and cats waiting for adopters but also rabbits, pigs, horses, and poultry of all kinds. The numbers fluctuate, but, when I talk to Keiley, there are seventy animals waiting for adoption, fourteen of them—a full 20 percent—are roosters.

"There's no question that backyard chicken ownership has increased the number of chickens we get," Keiley says. Nevins Farm used to be focused on horses and livestock animals, but the number of surrender requests for chickens kept creeping up. "In the last ten years we went through construction to increase capacity for birds on our property because we just kept getting more." Every summer they're flooded with requests from people who got spring chicks and now have roosters they're not allowed to keep. (In 2021, they had to stop taking owner-surrendered roosters because there were simply too many and now only accept roosters that come from law enforcement or animal control.)

"People who were more traditional pet owners are keeping and treating chickens more like pets than an animal to have for use," Keiley says. There are some good things with that—it's becoming more normal to bring your chicken to the vet—but also some challenges. Chickens often wind up in shelters that aren't focused on farm animals and don't know what to do with them. Frankly, Keiley says, nobody is prepared. It doesn't help that town ordinances are all over the map when it comes to chicken ownership regulations. "I feel sad when there's a person who can care for a rooster but has to surrender it because of an ordinance." One of his projects is writing up sample legislation that might alleviate noise and rodent concerns with chicken ownership and even allow roosters in situations where there's sufficient space between neighbors.

Not only does Nevins Farm have limited space for poultry, but overcrowding makes the birds unhappy and gives staff less time to take the birds' photos and write descriptions, all important parts of marketing roosters to the public. Often, overburdened rescues are doing all they can by posting a photo of a flock and saying "chickens [or roosters] available." MSPCA employees go out of their way to give each of the roosters a name and a description so charming that it makes me wish I could drive to Massachusetts and pick one up. *

"We want to do everything we can to remind people we do have roosters and that they need homes," Keiley says. But while there are a lot of farmers with backyard flocks that appreciate roosters, others take more convincing. It's why roosters looking for homes have such detailed descriptions on their adoption pages. "We know their personality and if we keep it a secret no one will adopt them," he says. "Whether they're adopting because they're a farm owner or want a pet rooster, they'll connect to the birds better this way."

In addition to his work for the shelter, Keiley has been advocating for the end of breed bans against dogs like Pit Bulls for over a decade. When he goes to public forums on the issue, he always finds a cohort of people who strongly believe Pit Bulls are dangerous and have no place as a pet. "That debate has people hotly contesting on both sides," he says.

This isn't the case for roosters.

Most cities that have decided to allow backyard chickens have done so

---

* One eleven-month-old rooster's page says, "If Captain had a high school superlative, it would be 'most likely to lead a rooster rebellion.' Captain is a young, Golden Sebright Bantam roo with a classic case of Napoleon syndrome. His small stature does not deter him from making his presence known! Despite his antics, we adore this spicy little roo and believe that he will absolutely thrive in a home with ladies to watch over. If you would appreciate a rooster with an undeniably strong sense of self, Captain has his bags packed and ready to go!"

thanks to advocacy from local poultry lovers (often after their illegal chickens were discovered by a grumpy neighbor), yet even they say that roosters have no place in urban life. "The advocates aren't advocating too strongly for it," Keiley says with a rueful laugh. He thinks the boys have a PR problem. "What's the first thing you think of when you hear the word 'rooster'? It's that crow. That's what defines roosters, and not just any crow but a 'wake you up early in the morning' crow."

Keiley adds, "Even if you get past the crow, the next thing people think is that roosters might be aggressive." If you've known more than a few people who grew up on a farm, you've heard a story about a mean rooster who chased kids around the yard and maybe even drew blood with a carefully placed spur or beak.

"People never get past start," Keiley says. "Roosters find themselves in this weird, 'nobody likes you' scenario that's really sad." It's his goal to make roosters loved again. It's hard to believe people used to not just like but *admire* male chickens. So what went wrong for the rooster?

～

It's possible we never would have domesticated the chicken at all if it weren't for roosters. Based on genetic sequencing of the chicken genome and ancient bones and artwork found at early civilization dig sites, many people now believe that the chicken was domesticated for its role in religious rituals and, particularly, cockfighting (one of the oldest sports in the world).[106] The most recent studies propose that the chicken was domesticated 3,500 years ago in Southeast Asia.[107] Traders, invaders, and voyagers brought chickens to new locations where the birds quickly took up residence.

Chickens were simply too easy to keep—and the rooster's natural fights for dominance too entertaining to watch—for it to appeal to only one human society. Once the rooster became part of everyday life, it didn't take long for people to become enamored.

In the Persian religion of Zoroastrianism, roosters were among the most sacred animals thanks to their crow, which announced that the day had come. It woke people up and got them to work.[108] Many ancient religions' sun gods and goddesses were associated with the rooster. They were also an early symbol of Christianity thanks to Peter being told that he would deny

Jesus "three times before the rooster crowed." In the ninth century, Pope Nicolas I ordered churches to put an emblem of a rooster on their highest point as a reminder of the biblical rooster, which eventually morphed into the tradition of putting up weathervanes with roosters on them. It seems that everywhere roosters went, they inspired some type of mythology or devotion. In Bali, people still claim a religious aspect to cockfights as part of an ancient Balinese Hindu ceremony that requires blood sacrifice. (While cockfighting has technically been illegal in Indonesia since 1981, it continues for religious purposes—even though many of the events often seem less about religion than gambling.) Of the twelve animals in the Chinese zodiac, the rooster is the only one that's always gendered in the West. Technically, the Chinese symbol used for the sign can mean a chicken of either sex, but the fact that it has come to be marketed as "rooster," with all the qualities people associate with male fowls, is telling.

Ancient Greeks held roosters up as symbols of courage. When General Themistocles was on his way to fight the Persians, he's said to have come across two cocks fighting. He pointed out to his troops that the roosters didn't need high-minded reasons like country or a desire to protect their families to fight, only the desire to not lose to each other.[109] (It's not the most rousing speech I've ever heard but apparently did the trick since the Greeks won the war.) After his victory, Athens apparently held public cockfights once a year so young men could go, watch, and learn how to be as courageous as a rooster. The laying hen is mostly ignored in Greek art and poetry, but references to fighting cocks are easy to find.[110]

It wasn't just the rooster's bravery that made him a worthy role model. People also respected the way he treated his hens—polygamous though he might be. There are many stories of Chinese weddings using a rooster as a proxy when the groom couldn't be present.[111] Wedding ceremonies in some European Jewish traditions included carrying a hen and rooster before the bride and groom.[112] Traditional Korean weddings wrap a hen and rooster in blue and red cloth—the same colors worn by the bride and groom—and set them on the wedding table. Together, the fowl were a symbol of fertility due to all the chicks a good hen can raise. But it was also a promise that the husband would protect and provide for his wife. The main reason people keep roosters today (other than for breeding) is because of their willingness to protect hens from danger—even at the expense of their own lives.

Chickens have two alarm calls they use to signal when a predator has been spotted. One indicates something in the sky—like a hawk—and another is for danger on the ground.[113] I've seen my own chickens do the alarm call for aerial predators on many occasions, worried about anything from the shadow of crows flashing overhead to a hummingbird who's gotten a little too close. They freeze like statues. Sometimes they'll be left standing on one leg for minutes, refusing to move even to get into a more comfortable position, while their eyes scan the sky. Usually, one will intermittently emit a small trill deep in her throat until the danger has passed. When they're really worried, they'll scatter under the cover of bushes and freeze in the greenery. I've lost one chicken to a hawk and saved another who was under attack just in the nick of time. After both occasions, I found the rest of the flock still frozen in their hiding spots—even after over an hour had gone by.

Alarm calling might give the rest of the flock enough warning for them to get to safety but does so at the risk of making the watchman the new target for a hawk's or fox's meal. Because of this, chickens (and roosters in particular) don't just alarm call as a dumb reflex, they actually make careful choices about what type of warnings to give and when. Carolynn L. Smith, a researcher at Macquarie University in Australia who has done in-depth investigations of chicken behavior, explored many of these alarm variations in a 2012 paper on chicken smarts.[114] One option is for a rooster to only do an alarm call when in the presence of a hen (or hens) he has previously mated with. Males that mate more frequently are more vigilant in their protection of the flock and, by extension, the continuation of their genes.[115] Roosters also vary their calls in a way that is more likely to keep themselves safe. When roosters are close to protective cover, they're more likely to make a longer alarm call; they give shorter, targeted calls when safety is farther away to make it harder for a predator to locate them. It's a bit like yelling "Help!" in the middle of a crowded street versus whispering to a 911 operator from under the bed. Roosters also are more likely to call loudly if there's a subordinate rooster nearby, knowing that a predator can only choose one target. Chickens have more practice being prey than humans do, but I'm not sure I would be so strategic in an emergency.

But roosters aren't just stoic defenders of the flock. They can also be quite sweet to their hens. Much like asking a date out to dinner, a rooster does something called "tidbitting," which isn't a courtship ritual so much as relationship maintenance with his hens. Rather than keeping it to himself, when a rooster finds a particularly delicious looking bit of food, he calls hens over and repeatedly picks up and drops the morsel as if to say, "Look what I found for you!" The hens appreciate this gesture. Even in a flock with multiple roosters, hens prefer to mate with whichever male brings females the most food.[116] Yet this isn't a purely transactional encounter. Mating rarely occurs right after a rooster presents a hen with a meal. She files that information away and keeps track of which roosters are the best providers when it comes time to think about romance.[117] Courting feels almost as complicated in the world of fowl as it does on Tinder.

Smith noticed that some males fake-tidbitted, going through the motions of picking up food without having any, and was curious whether hens held this kind of behavior against the roosters.[118] She set up a study where two spunky bantam Sebright roosters were put in two cages. Let's call them Goofus and Gallant. Whenever each of them was given food, they both tidbitted predictably for a nearby hen. But there was a twist. Every time Gallant got the food, the hen was given some too. When Goofus got the food, the hen got nothing. The researchers tried this with multiple hens and switched the role of each rooster to make sure the hens were choosing based on whether tidbitting led to food and not because one rooster was more handsome. The hens were much more interested in the rooster who always followed through on his promises and eventually stopped responding to the food calls of roosters who were all talk and no payoff.

Far from being bird-brained, these behaviors—just a small sampling of what researchers have discovered about the way chickens think—show chickens to be complex and strategic animals. Both tidbitting and alarm calls are types of communication usually associated with "smart" animals like primates or crows. But it's a common theme in animal behavior and intelligence studies that "dumb" animals get a lot more intelligent when we take the time to watch and understand them.

For centuries, the rooster had a good run as an animal who humans could learn a thing or two from. But when newly formed humane societies began campaigning against cockfighting, it was the beginning of the end for the rooster. In the 1800s, western and southern Africa were the only places where cockfighting *wasn't* taking place.[119] Throughout the world, rich and poor alike took part in the sport. In 1835, the Cruelty to Animals Act banned cockfighting in England, Wales, and some overseas territories, though it still continued openly if illegally. It wasn't until the U.K. passed the Protection of Animals Act in 1911 that a combination of strengthened regulation and public support for animal welfare laws drove the sport completely underground.[120] The United States took considerably longer. Only three states—Massachusetts, Delaware, and Vermont—had outlawed it by the beginning of the Civil War. It took until 2008 for all fifty states to ban cockfighting (New Mexico and Louisiana were the last holdouts), though it certainly hasn't been completely eradicated. Today it's still legal in many South American and Caribbean countries. Spain and France are among the countries that have made it illegal except for a few places with historic and cultural ties to cockfighting.

Without cockfighting, the rooster's only use was for food. Instead of being spoiled as potential champions (at which point, they'd fight to injury or death with another rooster), "extra roosters" were dispatched at a young age. On small farms and homesteads, a good rooster could still be useful, especially one who wouldn't try to spur humans. As people separated into cityfolk and countryfolk, chickens—and the rooster in particular—became emblematic of a certain romanticized way of life. (There's a reason why even today so many faux-farmhouse home goods have roosters on them. As more people moved to the city, they started emulating the idyllic countryside in their home decor.) There are few things that scream "you're in the country now" more than a rooster. But people had so many decorative roosters in their homes on dishes and hand towels that they neglected to notice the birds were disappearing from the landscape.

During the twentieth century, changes to farming practices meant that real live roosters were hardly needed by anyone anymore.

Until the last century, chicken meat was largely a byproduct of the egg industry. You needed hens to make eggs and you needed roosters to get more chickens. Chicken breeds like the Plymouth Rock or the Rhode Island Red are considered "dual purpose" or "heritage breeds" today. One hundred years ago, they were just the chickens everyone had. They laid eggs reliably and produced enough meat that farmers could sell a roast chicken dinner to people in town.

Since chickens were kept mostly for eggs, it's no surprise that the first changes to this model happened in the egg industry. Today, Petaluma, California, located about forty miles north of San Francisco, seems like a quaint town, but in the early 1900s, people called it "the richest little city in America."[121] Those riches were built on eggs. In the late 1870s, Petaluma residents Lyman C. Byce and Dr. Isaac Lopes Dias invented the first commercially viable incubator. It came in 460- or 650-egg sizes, a vast improvement over a hen's usual clutch of no more than a dozen chicks.[122] By the 1900s, Petaluma Incubator Company was even shipping its products as far as Australia.

Now that chicken farms could easily have flocks numbering in the thousands, people began to think about ways to make the business even more efficient by finding breeds that laid more eggs or ate less feed. Scientific research, like Darwin's theory of evolution and Mendel's experiments with pea plants, changed the way people thought about breeding. Offspring weren't an average of the parents, as had previously been theorized, but depended on dominant and nondominant genes. Instead of hoping for good or healthy animals overall, people now wanted to breed for specific traits like egg laying or meat production. And with more and more farms moving from selling diverse crops and animal products to specializing in one thing, chickens on an "egg farm" couldn't just lay some eggs and be healthy; they had to be hyper-productive.

Just as the industrial model of farming made it easy for people to specialize—building hatcheries to supply the burgeoning local egg farms with chicks year-round—we started expecting our animals to specialize too.

Petaluma farmers found what they were looking for in a new strain of the Single Comb White Leghorn chicken, bred to produce two hundred eggs per year at a time when few chickens could even lay half that. Unfortunately, breeding for one trait does have its downsides. The roosters from hyper-productive breeds were generally unpleasant to the hens, each other, and their keepers. They also didn't produce as much meat as dual-purpose breeds, bred as they were for egg laying and egg laying alone.[123] If a farmer could keep from losing money raising and selling the males for meat, he was lucky. The cockerels were sold as "squab broilers" (because their small size made them seem similar to pigeons, a popular meat at the time) when they were about a month old.[124] So when the practice of sexing chicks became popular in the 1930s, farmers stopped bothering to raise the males and started killing them after sexing instead. *

As large egg-laying operations became more popular, it created a space for poultry farms that raised and sold birds exclusively for meat. It seems fitting that if the egg industry began on the West Coast of the United States, the broiler industry began on the opposite side of the country. In 1910, chicken was considered a rare delicacy, and per capita consumption in the U.S. was only 15.5 pounds per person a year; in less than sixty years, per capita consumption would increase by over 140 percent, far more than any other meat.[125]

It all changed in the 1920s when a woman named Cecile Steele intended to order fifty chicks for a backyard poultry operation and wound up with five hundred instead. She raised them for eighteen weeks and sold them for sixty-two cents per pound. It was profitable enough that she kept doing it and eventually built a chicken shed that could house ten thousand birds at a time. Other people along the Delmarva (Delaware, Maryland, Virginia) Peninsula began opening large broiler farms of their own and breeding birds that would put on weight faster. In 1925, the average broiler was 2.5 pounds when it went to market at 112 days old. Today it's more like 6.4 pounds at 47 days. These broilers grow so quickly on so little feed, that it costs more to slaughter a laying hen than the egg-laying breeds are worth in meat. The system for both became so efficient that, accounting for inflation, the average cost of both chicken meat and eggs are now less than a third of what they would have been in the 1940s.

With the end of cockfighting, and as dual-purpose breeds became a spe-

---

* A man named James K. Hirst actually brought chick sexing to Petaluma from Japan over a decade before this, as Thea Lowry writes in her history of the Petaluma egg industry, *Empty Shells*. Hirst advertised "guaranteed day-old pullets," but when Petaluma's large hatchery operators got wind of this they shunned him and, eventually, shut his business down too. The hatcheries worried what would happen if customers started demanding only female chicks.

cialty rather than the norm, the need for roosters diminished to almost nothing (just a few per flock unless someone was raising show poultry). For most of the country, roosters were past tense. A rooster's crow stopped being part of the ambiance of the country and became a nuisance.

The fall of the rooster was complete.

We forgot all the good things a rooster could bring to a flock. We forgot that the rooster, once upon a time, was a gentleman.

Handsome Mr. Marple found a new home quickly. Only a week after my initial post, I left him in the hands of his new owner, a woman named Laurie, and said goodbye. Five months passed and I still thought about him often. Many people trying to rehome a rooster on backyard chicken groups looked for takers with notes like, "Please don't tell me if you're going to eat him. I'd like to believe he's going to a good home." But I wanted to know exactly where Mr. Marple was going and the type of person taking care of him.

It reminded me of when I was a child and my friend's parents told me their dog had been sent off to a farm. A decade or so later, I was visiting with them and wondered if they'd ever gone to visit the dog in his new home. "Surely he must have died by now," I said. They gave me a long look.

Many of you readers might have heard this common euphemism for euthanizing a pet. I had not. All these years, I'd been imagining their dog frolicking with sheep in front of a red barn when really he was long gone. It bothered me. I didn't want to imagine something just to make me feel better if there was a possibility it wasn't true.

When I'd been frantically trying to rehome Mr. Marple, a local friend mentioned that you could take unwanted roosters to the local farm store. Apparently, they had cages there filled with roosters looking for homes—though they might not find one. Anyone willing to pay a few bucks could take one. I hated the idea of leaving him there and never knowing where an animal I'd raised had ended up.

This was why I'd sheepishly texted Laurie a few times since I'd said goodbye to Mr. Marple, asking for an update. (I worried about being one of those former owners who was so bothersome she'd regret taking him in solely because it meant dealing with me.) When I asked her how he was settling in with the new flock and her resident rooster, she sent me pictures of them together. "He is becoming part of the flock," she texted. "No fighting with the older roo and that makes me happy."

A month later, wondering if he was crowing yet, I checked in again.

"I think he is. He sounds like a teenage boy going through puberty trying to crow," she wrote back with plenty of laughing emojis.

Finally, knowing Mr. Marple must be fully grown by now, I sent Laurie another message. This time I asked if it would ever be okay for me to come out and visit Mr. Marple at her farm. She responded with an enthusiastic yes.

～⌒

When I arrive on a Sunday around noon, Laurie is out doing farm chores in cut-off shorts, tall muck boots, and two sweatshirts.

"They got brussels sprouts and apples for a snack this morning," she says as she leads me to the run. Her farmhouse is on the edge of a large pond and small birds flit in and out of blackberry bushes in the misty rain. The run is next to a horse paddock, and the brown horse occasionally nudges the fence and jiggles raindrops off the tarp that offers the birds some shade in their open yard. It's a peaceful place.

Mr. Marple is the only rooster to twelve hens. "I wish you'd come a few weeks ago. We just lost Roo-bert, my other rooster, to a raccoon attack. He and Mr. Marple were best friends." She hadn't known how well the two boys would get along and had been amazed to see how nice they were to each other from the very beginning. "He's just so gentle," she says of Mr. Marple. "I don't think he really crows either. I've heard him a few times, but I realized after Roo-bert was gone that I wasn't waking up to crowing in the morning anymore. I miss it."

Mr. Marple is standoffish and, as I suspected, either doesn't remember me or doesn't care. He's happily dust bathing beside the ladies. I knew this was a strong possibility, but there's a twinge of disappointment all the same. At least Laurie has only good things to say about him. About all her chickens really. "People can laugh, but chickens are therapy," she says. She can talk to them about anything and they happily burble back. There have been many times when she needed that, when she needed a reason to get out of bed in the morning. "I'm a survivor of domestic violence and this time last year things were really bad," she says. The animals helped. She wants to start a farm for other women in similar situations and their kids. "They can build skills and confidence and get out in the world while also having a therapy farm for the children," Laurie tells me.

Her son doesn't really care for the chickens, but when her friendliest hen, Honey, walked up to him a few weeks ago, even he warmed to them. "He was like, 'Mom, they're not so bad.' I think he thinks if he likes them, he'll have to start doing chicken chores," she laughs. She doesn't mind doing it herself. Caring for chickens is more of an excuse to spend time with the birds than a chore.

She wants to give back—to people, to chickens. It's why she was always quick to step up when she worked at a farm store and someone came in asking if anyone knew anyone who could take an extra rooster. "I'm very blessed that I came across your post needing to rehome him," she says of Mr. Marple. "He is pretty awesome. He's such a sweet boy. It would be nice if all roosters were like that."

By the time I leave, Mr. Marple has come a little closer to me but has stayed out of arm's reach. He's busy being a chicken. He doesn't know how lucky he is to have found a place like this to spend his life. But I do. It was hard to say goodbye to him the first time, but today it's easy. And needing to rehome Mr. Marple had one silver lining: it made room for two new rescue hens that I might not have been able to adopt otherwise.

As I leave, I tell Laurie that my one regret is that I didn't get a chance to hear him crow. "As long as I have him, or even his babies, you're always welcome," she says. "If I get a good video of him crowing, I'll text it to you."

CHAPTER TWELVE:
THE CHICKEN WHO DIDN'T KNOW
HOW TO BE A CHICKEN

WHEN THE RED HENS FIRST CAME TO HEARTWOOD HAVEN, a farm animal sanctuary in Gig Harbor, Washington, they were scared of the sky. One hundred of them had just arrived from an egg farm where they'd lived the first year or two of their lives stuffed together in battery cages. They huddled together under the roof that first day. Then, slowly, a few brave ones peeked out into the chicken yard—scratched to dirt by the hundreds of hens and roosters that had come before them—and started to explore.

Compared to hens the sanctuary had gotten in the past, these ones were in good shape, the co-founder, Kate Tsyrklevich, told me over the phone. Heartwood Haven has gotten batches where the hens were almost naked—walking around for months like they'd already been plucked until their plumage grew back in. That didn't mean this crew looked normal. Nearly all of them had lost feathers from their necks or backs from stress or picking by other bored hens in too-close quarters. They'd all been debeaked to varying degrees. While some hens simply had a top beak that was roughly the same size as the lower, others had been debeaked so badly their top beak went back nearly to their nostrils.

It had been a joy to raise my flock of chickens from the time they were a day old, but I knew that for every chick I bought, there was a rooster like Mr. Marple or one of those hundreds of chicks I'd seen tumbled into a garbage can at the hatchery just because there were more of them than customers wanted. By buying and loving my own flock of chicks, I was contributing to a system in which many others were disposable. My chickens had given me so much. Rescuing was a way I could do something in return for their species.

So I'd come to take two of these little red hens home with me. Their names, I knew without hesitation, would be Thelma and Louise.

⤳

It took me nearly a year to find them. In the U.K. a group called the British Hen Welfare Trust has been rescuing and rehoming commercial laying hens since 2005. As of 2022, they've placed over 890,000 chickens in homes throughout the country. The United States doesn't have anything like it for one very good reason: the entire U.K. is roughly the size of the state of Oregon. Though most states have some commercial egg farms, rescuing and adopting these chickens across the entire U.S. would be a logistical nightmare. There wasn't a national organization handling rescues of "ex-bats," as the hens are commonly called, or even one associated with each region of the U.S.

Still, I'd seen a few Americans post on social media about their rescue hens; they were out there. I set up a news alert for the keyword "battery hens," hoping to hear about a large rescue from an egg farm or a sanctuary pleading for more adopters. No such luck. That's when I started emailing every farm animal sanctuary I could find that had ever mentioned having hens.

When I got a response at all, it often came months later. There were a lot of no's. Most places simply didn't have hens that needed homes, and, though all my chickens were very much pets, other organizations only adopted to vegans. One day in desperation, I emailed a large rescue headquartered in California. "We don't currently have any adoptable hens," their response began, "but Heartwood Haven does and they adopt to folks in Oregon!" The email included a link to this small Washington sanctuary's adoption form.

I filled it out as soon as I closed the email. We drove to pick the hens up two weeks later.

In the six weeks since Heartwood Haven rescued the hens from the farms they came from, the girls had gotten some of the color back in their once white-pale wattles and combs and were now happily exploring the yard, dust bathing and scratching in the dirt for tasty morsels. But there was still something strange about them. While my spoiled hens I'd raised from chicks always had a glint of mischief in their eyes, these ex-battery hens felt subdued. It was like they were sleepwalking through the motions of being a chicken.

When one of the sanctuary founders gave them watermelon in their first week there, the hens didn't know what to do with it. It took the resident rooster tidbitting pieces in front of them before they'd dig in. But the hens learned quickly. Once they understood that watermelons were food, they crowded around slices and pecked them down to the rind in a flash of reddish-orange feathers.

Out of the original one hundred hens, most had already gone to new homes. By the time we arrived, only thirty remained. (A few more would stay with the sanctuary permanently due to more severe health issues.)

When we got to the chicken yard, Tsyrklevich threw out questions at an auctioneer's pace. What kind of food did I use? Did I have chickens at home? How many? How many of these hens was I taking? Did I use a dish for the chickens' food, or would they be eating it off the ground? (I had no idea that this was still a common arrangement.) I felt dazed. She said she'd rather give the badly debeaked hens to people who had raised food dishes because the girls couldn't peck food off the ground like a normal chicken; they used their beaks like shovels. All the hens looked like they'd been caught in a particularly brutal windstorm.

Because the hens were Red Sex Links, an industrial hybrid that would lay nonstop even through the winter, they were likely to have issues with their reproductive systems. Tsyrklevich listed off a number of potential issues to look for: egg yolk peritonitis, an infection that can be caused by an egg breaking inside of a hen; egg binding from eggs getting stuck inside the repro-ductive tract; ovarian cancer; and so on and so on. Even with the best possible care, Thelma and Louise were unlikely to live more than a few years before these illnesses—or something else—caught up to them, she warned.

Tsyrklevich grabbed one with a particularly bad beak at random from the flock milling about my feet and put her in the wire cage I'd brought to take the girls back home. She would have chosen another at random but my eye had caught on a little red hen with a neck so bare of feathers she looked more like a Turken, a chicken breed known for having a naked neck, than any hen I'd seen before. There was just something about her. I watched the way she wandered around the yard, taking a quick peck at a chicken here, eating a bite of greens there, scooping a sip of water over here. Finally, she walked up to the debeaked chicken in the cage and peered somewhat haughtily at her. I loved her immediately. She went into the cage as well.

They wandered around their new cage, but the debeaked one stuck her head out between the bars over and over again. A *troublemaker*, I thought. That one would be Thelma. The other, my naked-neck hen with a certain *je ne sais quoi* that I simply couldn't leave behind, Louise.

~

The hens made a few sounds on the way out of the sanctuary, perhaps com-plaining about one of the rescued pigs who was trying to steal food out of a nearby chicken coop, but were silent the rest of the way home. I looked back at them a few times over the two-and-a-half-hour drive back to Portland and they were always either asleep or simply resting on the bottom of their trans-port cage. After the difficult life they'd had up until this point, maybe they didn't care what happened to them anymore. With so many chickens pushed together in battery cages, they'd never been able to form pecking orders or even bond with the other hens. Humans probably seemed like interchange-able, unintelligible sources of food.

Exhausted after the long day, I ran around putting the finishing touches on the small coop where Thelma and Louise would spend at least the next month. This was to make sure they weren't carrying any viruses or health issues that might pass to the rest of the flock. It would also give them space to heal. I opened the door and the girls walked right inside and began pecking at the food and dish of oyster shells, a calcium supplement commonly given to hens, like they hadn't eaten before in their lives. Every eggshell is formed with calcium and high-production breeds need a lot of it, often more than supplements can ever make up for. It was then that I noticed Thelma was missing one of her toenails. Whatever had caused it must have happened a while ago since it had scabbed over into a shortened nub.

Thelma and Louise put themselves to bed at seven that night even though, being late June, it stayed light until nine thirty. The next morning, I opened the door to their coop and they came out into the run right away. Other than a few happy trills at the oyster shells the day before, they were quiet. Watching them was like watching an animatron of a chicken, as though they were just going through the motions.

I'd been warned that Thelma and Louise might be too stressed out from their drive and new surroundings to lay for the first day or even week after their arrival, but when I checked the nest box there were two large brown eggs waiting for me. They hadn't made a peep.

Whenever the rest of my chickens lay an egg, their egg song ricochets around the yard. I know who has just laid an egg even when I'm inside the house because their songs are all a little different (though all of them are equally loud). It's like listening to an avant-garde symphony, each hen's calls filling in the spaces left by the others.

Yet Thelma and Louise were silent.

This, more than the debeaking or the feather loss, made me sad. Had they lost the egg song? Maybe battery hens are so surrounded by noise and other hens all day that they learn there's no point in singing it. While all my chickens came from hatcheries where they never had a mother hen to teach them anything, it felt like there were integral parts of being a chicken that they all knew—dust baths and pecking orders and, yes, the egg song. The first few rough years of Thelma's and Louise's lives hadn't just taken away their health, it had taken away some part of their chickenness too.

Heartwood Haven wouldn't tell me what farm Thelma and Louise came from or even what state it was in, only that it was a place that kept chickens in battery cages. Even if some farmers wanted to give the birds a chance by rehoming them, my guess is that they worried that the hens' poor condition could create bad PR for them and the egg industry. So I don't know exactly what Thelma's and Louise's lives were like before they were "spent," but I can guess.

Thelma and Louise would have started their lives at a commercial hatchery, fertilized eggs turned and warmed by a machine until they hatched. Freshly out of the shells and dried off, Thelma and Louise were downy puffballs the color of apple cider. But this wasn't a hatchery that supplied backyard farmers and separated chicks from their eggshells by hand. In the hatcheries that supply the commercial egg market, chicks leave the incubators on a series of conveyor belts.

The chicks are tossed from one belt to the other, peeping all the way, until they reach the sexing area, where males are separated from females. Female chicks continue on; males (as well as weak or deformed chicks) are typically sent to a macerator where they're killed.* If the pullets are debeaked at the hatchery on hatch day, it's done using infrared light. This newer technology is less prone to cutting the beak back too far, but many farms still use the old hot blades when the chicks are about five days old. (Judging by how far back Thelma's beak was removed, whoever debeaked her likely used the latter method.) The chicks are also vaccinated. Finally, not yet finished with their first long day, a downy Thelma and Louise would have been packed into plastic crates and transported to a pullet rearing facility, probably in the back of a climate-controlled truck.[126]

The young chicks are transferred from the crates into battery cages sized for younger birds. These cages use the same wire mesh floors that the birds will have in their adult housing. The hens get used to pecking at a nipple water feeder and sticking their heads between the bars for the food that goes past

---

* The egg industry in the United States and abroad has been trying to find a commercially viable way to sex chicks while still in their shells to eliminate the mass killing of male chicks—roughly six billion a year worldwide. While some grocery stores in Europe are already selling a limited number of no-cull eggs, the technology available isn't fast, cheap, and scalable enough (yet) to be adopted in the United States.

on a conveyor belt. The main difference between pullet and adult housing is that chicks need a heat source to keep them warm. At first, the chicks have a lot of room to run around. As they get older and bigger, their unchanged quarters start to seem smaller. Typically, at about sixteen weeks old, brighter lights are switched over to a long period of darkness. It's meant to mimic the short days of winter and get the birds ready to lay once they're brought to the egg farms. No matter what time of the year these hens hatch, the farms put them on a cycle that mimics a chick hatched in winter—coming into lay right at the height of spring and longer days.

At about sixteen weeks old, Thelma and Louise would have looked like gangly hens—fully feathered with reddening combs and wattles but without the heft and fluff of an adult. They were ready to go to a place that, for most hens, is their final destination.

Thelma and Louise would have been pulled out of their cages and crated for transport again. Sara Shields, a farm animal behavior and welfare specialist for Humane Society International, where she specializes in poultry production, says that some farmers prefer to hire women for the job because they're more gentle. It's a task where it's easy for the hens to get injured.[127] The birds are scared, there's a lot of wing flapping and trying to escape. Some people might grab the chickens one at a time, while others might take one pair of legs in each hand to yank the birds out of the cage.

The hens are packed tightly in transport crates tall enough that the birds can sit in them but not stand. It's actually better this way—less chance that the birds will slide around as the truck accelerates and decelerates along its route. The trip to the laying barn is a short drive for some pullets and a very long one for others.

At the laying barn, Thelma and Louise would have been put into cages again. There they meet their cagemates, the closest the hens will come to having a flock. In the United States, it's hard to know exactly how much room they're given in these cages. Unlike in other countries, there's no minimum space per bird legislated by any government agency.[128] The United Egg Producers, a large industry group, recommends a minimum of sixty-seven square inches of space—a little bigger than an iPad—for Leghorn hens and slightly more for chickens like Thelma and Louise. But this is simply a recommendation.

From the day the pullets arrive in the laying barn, the lights are stepped up to make the "days" longer, eventually reaching a peak of sixteen hours a day of light. Thanks to manipulation of the lights and feed, the pullets begin laying eggs soon after arriving at the farm. The floors of the cages have a gentle slope so eggs roll out to a conveyor belt that takes them to be washed, processed, and put into cartons. The lack of exercise combined with the fact that hens leech calcium from their bones to create eggshells makes the likelihood of osteoporosis and broken bones high. The hens can sometimes die suddenly from fatty liver hemorrhagic syndrome, essentially because they get overweight from inactivity and their high-energy layer feed. They can also develop something called Cage Layer Fatigue, which can cause their spines to fracture, leading to paralysis. Hens with CLF die because they can't reach food or water. Even with calcium and phosphorous supplements, there simply isn't enough to replace what they're losing by laying so many eggs. Because industrial barns are set up to minimize human labor, it can be a while before the dead hens are found.[129]

If the hens make it through this, they usually live each day like the last one—eating, drinking, laying eggs. Thelma and Louise, in their life as caged layers, never learned to perch, use their wings, or even scratch in the dirt. As I've seen in my own flock, hens are very particular about where they want to lay their eggs. They will wait to use a specific nest box or find a secluded spot in the yard. Hens in a battery cage never have privacy or nesting materials. Shields and others have seen battery hens climb under each other just before they're about to lay an egg, using their cagemate's body to create the feeling of a nest. There have been studies showing the need for a private nesting area is more important to hens than even food.[130]

Like many hens in battery cages, Thelma and Louise probably did something called "vacuum dust bathing," where they lay on the floor of their wire cage and fluffed their feathers, going through the motions of dust bathing without any dust to do it with. Dust bathing helps hens clean their feathers (instead of shower water washing our dirt away, the dust can get between their feathers, clearing out excess oil as well as mites and dead skin), but it also seems to be calming. All of these behaviors are deeply ingrained and instinctive; none of them can be expressed in a battery cage.

At a year and a half, the age that most chickens go through their first adult molt, one of two things happen to these hens: they molt or they're killed before they have the chance to. Left to their own devices, chickens slowly lose and regrow feathers over the course of roughly two months. But growing feathers takes so much energy that hens stop laying eggs in order to do it. A barn full of hens that stop laying for two months isn't worth much to a farmer. So some farms will simply consider their hens spent around this age, while others put their hens into what's often called a "forced molt" to squeeze a few extra months out of them.

Forcing hens to molt used to be done by removing food and even water completely for a few days. Egg farms in industrialized countries generally don't do that anymore (though in the United States it's technically legal). Instead, most producers change the lighting to make the "days" as short as eight hours and put the hens on a severe diet. The switch from high-energy food to low nutrients shocks their systems. Rather than having one hen and then another go through a long molt, forcing a molt condenses the process. Afterward, the hens can go back to laying for six to nine more months. It does allow the egg industry to need fewer hens—up to 50 percent fewer every year than without forced molting—but is hard on the birds, who can lose a significant amount of body weight in just those few weeks.[131]

When the hens are anywhere from a year and a half to a little more than two years old, the egg industry is done with them. Typically, the day they're taken out of the laying cages is the last day of their lives.

Someone rolls a cart down the aisles of the barn that looks more like part of a magic act than a killing machine. One model I found for sale has a metal box on one side next to a large metal canister that looks ready to blow up balloons.[132] The canister is full of carbon dioxide. The worker pulls hens out of the cage, puts them into the box, and closes the lid. The boxes are pumped full of CO_2 and the hens quickly suffocate and die. Workers open a side panel of the box so the dead hens can tumble out to be disposed of. The process repeats until the barn is silent.

Spent hens are worth so little money that their carcasses commonly end up composted or landfilled.

While some countries have higher animal welfare minimums for battery cages, this story isn't all that different for hens in countries like China or Mexico. In the last few years, a few countries have banned the practice of keeping hens in battery cages (Switzerland was the first country to phase out their use) or tried to promote the use of cage-free housing, but a majority of the world's eggs are still produced from hens who never even got to stretch their wings.[133]

But that isn't where Thelma's and Louise's story ended.

Like most of the world was doing in the summer of 2020 when I adopted them, Thelma and Louise quarantined in their small coop for a month without ever going into the world outside their run. Every day, I gave them fresh water and picked grasses, dandelion greens, and clover, then watched them wolf it down. But when I opened the door to set down treats or refresh their bowls, Thelma angled for a way to escape the run. I knew how she felt. We were both eager for our worlds to expand again.

Thelma and Louise never had a moment of drama between them, though they were also far from developing any deep fowl friendship. It occurred to me a few days after their arrival that while they'd come from the same farm, it was entirely possible that they'd never met before they were put into a truck to go to the sanctuary. Now they lived together in a two-by-seven-foot run. What a strange way to meet. But as we spent more time together, I noticed moments of sweetness between them.

Louise's bare neck started regrowing feathers toward the end of the first week. Long, quill-like pinfeathers poked out of her skin until feather tufts sprouted from the tips like small flowers. I started seeing Thelma gently lean over to nibble on the outside of the sheaths to help break them off and free the feathers. Louise always stood perfectly still, accepting her coopmate's ministrations while closing her eyes until it was over. Louise seemed to help Thelma too. Sometimes when I gave them fresh greens, I watched Thelma grab them right out of Louise's beak and gobble them down herself. Louise never seemed bothered by this behavior, she simply reached down to grab another mouthful for herself. Because of her beak, Thelma had trouble ripping plants out of the ground.

I spent a lot of time watching them. I pulled up a lawn chair and stared at them as they went about their business. They didn't seem to mind. Most of the time they were eating or taking naps in the sun. I was fascinated by the ways that Thelma had learned to compensate for her ruined top beak. She scooped her whole face down into the bowl of pellet food to spoon the pieces into her mouth, and when she drank, she brought her head up so quickly that a stream of water arced from her mouth like a girl doing a hair flip in the ocean. It was almost graceful.

After a week, they finally took food from my hand, eyeing me suspiciously the whole time. (If they saw me so much as make a move toward petting them, they bolted in the opposite direction.) It was an important step. By the time they were ready to come out of quarantine and join the rest of the flock, I knew I could coax them back into the coop with a few treats.

The ex-bats and the rest of the flock each knew the other was there. When my main flock free-ranged in the upper yard, they'd peer at Thelma and Louise—the wire run safely separating them from any potential fighting.

For the most part, Thelma's and Louise's move from their temporary accommodations into the main coop was seamless—except when it came to bedtime. They walked into the nest area without any problem, but night after night I found Thelma and Louise snuggled up, side by side in a nest box. The same nice, clean nest boxes that were supposed to be reserved for egg laying. I tried to lift the birds out and place them onto a perch one by one, but as soon as I grabbed the second hen, the first one would jump down and settle back in her preferred spot. They simply didn't understand the point of perching to go to sleep. I gave up. To this day they both sleep together on the straw blanketing the nest floor.

Now that their world had gotten even bigger, they were curious about everything. When I got the hose out one day to water some plants, Thelma trundled along next to the spray of water, cocking her head in interest and occasionally retreating to shake the droplets off of her feathers. Sometimes they walked to the storm door and stood there staring at their reflections in the glass. Thelma developed the habit of "pecking" me and Lyle with her blunt-tipped beak. It felt more like someone politely tapping me than the pinch I sometimes got from the other girls.

I noticed that while the flock I raised from chicks only made a purring noise when they were at their absolute peak happiness—a dust bath in the sun when the weather wasn't too hot or too cold—Thelma and Louise did it constantly. For them, every day was the best day they'd ever had.[134]

When it was time to close the chickens back in their run in the evening, Thelma bounded toward me with the rest of the chickens to get the treats I always threw on the ground. Not Louise. On particularly nice nights, Louise would get close enough to take a few treats, sure, but once she saw that I wanted her to go into the coop, she ran in the opposite direction. There was still daylight left and she'd spent enough of her life constrained.

I don't know if you've ever tried to catch a chicken who didn't want to be caught, but the birds can run up to nine miles an hour, a speed that's hard to match when you're bending down to grab them. Often I had to call Lyle down to the coop to help me catch her with a pincer move. Louise thrashed in my grip, making one last bid for freedom. I knew it probably didn't feel comfortable when I held them either. Thelma and Louise had gained a few more patches of feathers since their arrival, but when I picked either one up all I felt were the prickles of old broken feathers and the new ones in sharp sheaths trying to break through their skin.

Even as the ex-bats settled into the flock hierarchy, I kept being reminded that they weren't quite like the other girls. They could be grumpy at mealtimes, sharply pecking any others who got too close to them. Louise in particular made a sound when she was annoyed that sounded like a prehistoric yodel. Their behavior reminded me of rescued street dogs adopted into homes. The dogs were so used to fighting for every scrap of food that it was hard to break the habit of thinking starvation was just around the corner. Thelma and Louise had come from a chicken-peck-chicken world.

Then there were their eggs.

The first few times my husband and I cracked one of Thelma's and Louise's light brown eggs, they shattered all over the countertop. The shells were so much thinner than either of us were used to. The yolks were pale and broke easily. Lyle wondered if we should eat these eggs at all. "Aren't they, you know, not as good as the ones from our chickens?" he said, referring to the flock we'd raised.

"They're *literally* the same eggs as from the grocery store," I said.

"Still. . . ."

He must have come around because he started using Thelma's and Louise's eggs to make breakfast. But he never really sounded convinced.

～

Saving some spent hens here and there is the kind of practice that's likely been going on for a long time in a piecemeal fashion. While it's still not mainstream in the United States, that's not the case in the U.K. thanks to the British Hen Welfare Trust. When I started a Zoom to talk to Jane Howorth, founder of BHWT, it was nighttime in England. She had just come in out of the rain, doing the last check on the chickens for the night. Her brown hair was up and her bangs brushed over the top edge of her glasses. Chickens had consumed not just her daytime hours but her evening schedule as well.

When she was nineteen, she saw a television program about factory farming in Britain and was particularly struck by the plight of chickens who might go through their lives without ever setting foot outside. "I saw them as the underdog of the animal world," she said. There were more of them in cages than any other farm animal in the world. "They're out of sight, out of mind," she told me.

So, many years later, when Howorth moved to the countryside and could finally have chickens of her own, she didn't just want any chickens. She had to have rescued battery chickens, she recalled with a laugh. Those farms didn't generally advertise. She had to drive up and down country lanes until she stumbled across a battery farm and knocked on the door. She told the farmer that she wanted some chickens and wondered if she could have some when his would otherwise go to slaughter. "I went in planning to get twelve and came out with thirty-six." She had put enough boxes in her small car to carry twelve chickens but hadn't prepared for extras, hens who would have all been sent to slaughter the next day if she couldn't take them with her. She asked the farmer if he had anything she could put the hens in. He handed her some sacks.

This was how she wound up with thirty-six hens crammed into her car, some in boxes and sacks and some simply running loose in the backseat. "We'd never allow people to do that now," she told me. Howorth set the chickens up in her yard, the proud owner of three times as many hens as she'd planned on having.

One of the chickens, a pumpkin-colored hen named Vicky, clearly had something wrong with her; her stance was more like a penguin than a hen. The rest of the flock picked on her viciously. A veterinarian told Howorth to put the sick hen down, that there was nothing to be done. "I thought, I'm not going to cull her, she's just a funny shape." Howorth put Vicky in an area on her own and nursed her back to health. They developed a special relationship as Vicky healed. "She'd waddle toward me and crane her neck, asking to be picked up," Howorth recalled. Other times Vicky would claim the dog bed as her own, wanting to be closer to her human.

Vicky lived for a year and a half. "The relationship I built with her . . ." Howorth said, trailing off. "They're such grateful little creatures, really." The way she talked about Vicky made it seem like the red hen was still in the room with her—not a memory from 1995. Howorth's face softened when she talked about the hens. Even if I hadn't been able to see her, I would have still heard the smile in her voice. This was a woman who had been enchanted by chickens.

In the early 2000s, Howorth turned forty and both of her parents died within nine months of each other. "It was one of those moments that makes you realize life is short," Howorth said. "I decided I was going to do something in a much more structured way to help chickens." She wound up putting an ad in a local free paper. Howorth still remembered the text nearly verbatim:

> *We've never seen the sunshine and never tasted grass.*
> *Is there anyone out there who can offer us a second*
> *chance to enjoy a better life? We're spent battery hens*
> *due to go to slaughter. Please help us if you can.*
> *Call Jane.*

"That was it," Howorth said. "I don't know what the hell hit me." She thought she'd get a couple calls.

Her phone started ringing off the hook.

BHWT has only grown since then and while they've rescued truckloads of chickens, it's just a drop in the bucket. There are roughly forty-two million commercial laying hens in the U.K. Howorth can't think about how many of them don't get rehomed or she'd drive herself insane.

"We make a difference to the lucky few and we hope to have a halo effect on the birds we can't save from slaughter," she said. Until people rescue or have chickens of their own, they don't think much of them. "Every time we rehome a flock of three to four chickens, they're the most perfect educational tool," Howorth explained. Watching the hens transform from pale, skittish birds into friendly, fluffy pets can make more of a difference than any pamphlet on what the egg industry is like for hens. She was glad to see the U.K. ban battery cages in the years since the BHWT started, though she made it clear that her organization's intent wasn't to call out egg farmers as much as it was to educate consumers. "We as consumers are the ones buying the eggs," Howorth said. She considered herself a supporter of the egg industry; the only reason farmers were willing to keep giving hens to the BHWT was because of the relationships she'd built with them, though she was pushing for all eggs to become as close to free-range as possible. It was up to consumers to demand better conditions for hens—and be willing to pay more for it.

Slowly but surely, it was happening. The European Union banned battery cages in 2012,* and nearly 60 percent of eggs produced in the U.K. are now free-range.[135] In the United States, only about 30 percent of laying hens are even raised cage-free.[136] What I would call truly free-range eggs—commonly referred to as "pasture-raised," from hens that live their entire lives pecking on grass—are hardly more than a rounding error in the overall egg market.**

"There's still a lot of work to be done but I think we've made a big impact," Howorth said. Chickens still can't compete with dogs and cats in pet popularity, but, at least in the U.K., they're almost as popular as caged birds like parakeets or canaries (and definitely more popular than rabbits or hamsters).[137]

The market for pet chickens is far from saturated in countries where

---

* "Enriched Colony Cages" are still allowed, though they're considered only a step up from battery cages. The hens are caged but have perches as well as dust bathing and nesting areas.

** Egg labeling can be confusing. In the United States, eggs with a "free-range" label only require hens have "access" to the outdoors without requirement for the amount or quality of outdoor space or that the hens even use it, according to USDA guidelines. There is no USDA oversight for the term "pasture-raised," though it is understood to mean the hens spend some part of their lives actually enjoying the outdoors and have a coop or barn to use as shelter or to lay eggs in.

they're popular. "You get more and more people wanting chickens. We have roughly twelve thousand adopters a year and about 50 percent of those are people new to hen keeping," Howorth said. "I thought I was doing this to help chickens, and actually, I'm not just helping chickens, I'm helping people. It's spreading so much joy." These adopters never knew what their lives were missing until they took a couple scraggly, rescued hens into their backyards.

⌒∘

By early November, Louise's bare neck started to fill in with feathers. Her once naked, red rump was covered with a layer of fluff. Poor Thelma was still naked under her wings, on her back, and on her behind. On cold days, Thelma tried to puff up her remaining feathers to keep herself warm, but it could only do so much. I put the radiant heater in the coop earlier than usual for our Pacific Northwest winters; Thelma snuggled next to it while she slept.

Louise began perching on first the lowest rung of the chicken ladder in the chicken run, then the taller one, which she had to flutter up to. Soon after, I watched Thelma get a running start and flap her wings as hard as she could to lift herself a few inches off the ground. Flying hadn't even been on my list of things I thought the two might be able to learn, but it seemed that over the months they'd been in my care, they'd been strengthening those muscles too.

Thelma and Louise still didn't like to be petted—too shy or too prickly for it to be comfortable—but they followed me eagerly around the yard once they learned that human yardwork meant bugs for chickens. While the rest of the flock might putter about in my general vicinity, Thelma and Louise were always directly underfoot. If I disturbed the ground to plant a bulb, Louise was there kicking through the small pile of loose dirt. When I tore up a strip of sod, Thelma hoovered up the worms and larvae that thought they'd found a safe place to spend the winter. Weeding was never-ending and cold and muddy and a lot less fun than buying and placing new plants. I'd always hated it. But I soon found myself happily making time for the chore as long as the chickens were out with me. I even found myself enjoying it. The once lonely task was transformed into a source of entertainment (though I had to look down at my feet when carrying weeds to the yard waste bin for fear of stepping on a chicken's toes). On more than one occasion, Thelma managed to get tangled in a pile of ivy vines and stood there patiently until I rescued her.

It had been months since they'd changed from the silent chicken automatons I'd brought home into these funny, quirky birds. They were becoming more chicken-like every day. When they started talking more often, gossiping in the way that chickens do as they go about their days, it was with a low growl that had an eerie similarity to my tenth-grade English teacher, who'd smoked her entire life and had the low-pitched rasp to prove it. Theirs were the voices of someone with a past.

One afternoon, we were sitting with the chickens in the yard when Lyle looked over at the girls. Thelma had cuddled up to Loretta, our Easter Egger, and the two were napping in the sun. "They're really just like normal chickens now. It's pretty amazing," he said. "You'd never know that they'd spent most of their lives in a terrible place."

On the inside, it was a different story.

In December, Thelma's and Louise's eggs started to change colors. They'd both started off the same thin-shelled beige, but while Louise's eggs had gotten so dark I could almost mistake them for my Black Copper Marans Olivia's eggs, Thelma's were almost white. Every hen actually starts out with white eggs in her oviduct and the pigment is added little by little as the egg forms. It's not uncommon for a hen's eggs to get lighter as the season goes on, like a printer running out of toner. But Thelma's eggs weren't just getting paler; they were getting so thin that sometimes they came out feeling more like a rubber balloon than an egg. The eggs actually popped when other hens nested on them, leaving sticky, eggy residue all over the coop. I worried. There were too many ways a hen—and a rescue hen in particular—could die from reproductive issues.

I took Thelma to a vet, where she got antibiotics in case the problem was an infection in her oviduct. This, apparently, wasn't uncommon. But the vet sounded worried when I mentioned that neither girl had ever taken a break from laying over the winter. I don't use supplemental light, but Thelma's and Louise's output only went down from nearly an egg a day to an egg every two or three days. It was no surprise Thelma's body was still covered in bare spots;

she was spending so much energy laying misshapen eggs, she didn't have any left to regrow feathers.

A few weeks later, it was clear the antibiotics hadn't done what they were supposed to. Now I didn't even see Thelma's eggs, only the smears of yolky liquid matted into the nest box straw. Luckily there was something else we could try, an implant that I like to refer to as chicken birth control.

If having pet chickens is a growing phenomenon, spending money to have those chickens *not* lay eggs is still mostly unheard of. The implant is so tiny that it comes preloaded into a needle. All the vet has to do is inject it under the bird's skin.

Every chicken reacts to the drug differently, but Thelma stopped laying eggs almost immediately. Just a few short weeks later, all her formerly bald spots began sprouting new purple pinfeathers. She looked like someone mixed a chicken with a porcupine. Thelma started following me around the yard. If I sat, she'd lay down beneath my chair or peck at the sides of my shoes. She'd always been curious about me and what I was doing, but now she was like my shadow. Maybe she wasn't feeling well—having new feathers push out from their skin isn't the most comfortable for birds—or maybe something had changed between the car rides to and from the vet's office.

The rest of the flock often walked up to me, checked whether I had treats or not, then left when they determined I wasn't handing out anything interesting. Not Thelma. She just liked being wherever I was. Sometimes I'd get wrapped up in a book and startle when I heard a chicken beneath my chair. She snuck next to me so quietly that I rarely knew she was there until I heard the rustle of her feathers. It wasn't out of the ordinary for us to sit like that for over half an hour. I wondered if she was this friendly because of the life she'd had before or whether this was just who she'd always been, a chicken who liked to be around humans, only she'd never been given the chance until now.

Some of Thelma's and Louise's natural behaviors came back as soon as they were given the chance to express them—dust bathing, foraging, laying in the sun—but their bodies and minds took longer to heal. A year after they were rescued, the hens' feathers were almost completely regrown with the exception of their still sparse tail feathers. Some things won't change. They will probably always sleep on the floor of the coop. Their beaks will never grow back. But they've found a place for themselves in the flock and with me. It's not uncommon for them to walk up to the front door and peer inside the glass. They knock politely until they see me. Their world has already expanded so much, maybe they think the house is an obvious next step.

➤

One day, after Thelma's feathers were almost all regrown, I was sitting outside with the flock when Peggy started singing the egg song. She began while coming out of the nest box like she was announcing the beginning of a New Orleans second line and continued as she walked up the hill toward the flock. One by one, the others joined in. I heard Emmylou with her squeaky, high-pitched bantam voice and the two other large-breed girls chiming in between Peggy's notes. The song came in waves, ricocheting throughout the yard. As I stood to walk toward the girls, I heard two new voices. They were low-pitched and awkward, like they didn't quite know where to join in. I walked closer to the sound and saw Thelma and Louise, one on either side of the driveway. They stretched their necks upward with every loud note.

I've jokingly referred to hens belting the egg song as them "singing the song of their people." But perhaps it's less of a joke than I'd thought. We may never know what it's really for, if it means anything, or why hens do it after laying some eggs but not others. But it's undoubtedly something they do together. Once you know what it sounds like, you can't mistake it for any other sound in the animal kingdom. That was the first day Thelma and Louise sang the egg song. It hasn't been the last.

I wonder how much time I'll have left with Thelma and Louise—with all the hens really—since chickens are simultaneously so resilient and yet so fragile. I wonder what new stories I'll gather about the flock and their antics. They always seem to be up to something. There is so much more to know about all of them.

As it turns out, my grandma was right on that phone call so many years ago. Three wasn't enough chickens. Not at all.

EPILOGUE:
COMING HOME TO ROOST

"People have forgotten this truth," the fox said. "But
you mustn't forget it. You become responsible forever
for what you've tamed."
- The Little Prince

I WENT OUTSIDE TO CHECK ON THE LADIES AROUND NINE O'CLOCK at night. The sky was purple with the last of sunset. It was still over ninety degrees. I had to leave the coop door open to the run for extra ventilation.

The chickens were standing tall on their perches, wings stretched out from their sides, beaks open, breathing furiously. Thelma and Louise had left their confined nest boxes to stand on the floor of the coop, looking for any wisp of fresh air. I hated seeing them this way. It had already broken the record for the hottest temperature ever recorded in Portland, Oregon—108 degrees. The next two days, I knew, were going to be even hotter.

The average temperature for this time of year was a balmy seventy-six. Now it was hotter in the Pacific Northwest than in Dubai.

I'd fretted about the chickens all day. They were adept at cooling themselves by digging down into the colder layers of dirt in the shade but there was only so much they could do when the temperature climbed above one hundred. I had pages for "how to prevent heat stress in chickens" open on both my phone and my computer. The problem was that there wasn't much of a line between their normal responses to heat and dangerous ones like seizures, lethargy, and death. The birds could cool themselves down until they couldn't.

I watched the eight hens in my flock breathing for a little while longer and made a decision. Tomorrow I would bring them into the house.

Every time I'd walked to the coop earlier that day, I'd worried there would be a dead hen lying too still on her side. I'll admit that some hens were more beloved than others, tiny Emmylou with her constant mischief or Peggy, the only hen left from my original three chicks, but I couldn't think of a single hen in the flock without a flood of stories coming to mind. They weren't just any chickens—they were individuals with a place in both the flock and in my life that would be irreplaceable. We had more eggs than my husband and I could ever hope to eat. (I gave a lot of them away.) It was easy enough to get more chickens. But I was responsible for these hens and I knew them all well. I discovered that there was no amount of loss that was acceptable to me anymore.

The next day when the temperature creeped toward one hundred degrees, I grabbed each hen from the yard—Peggy, Loretta, Emmylou, Thelma, Louise, Olivia, Phryne, and Scully—and brought them to the shower stall in our basement bathroom. It got up to 116 degrees before the so-called "heat dome" dissolved, freeing the Pacific Northwest from being trapped inside of the hot-weather equivalent of a snow globe. The chickens didn't seem to mind their new accommodations too much. Their heavy breathing stopped after half an hour. They laid three eggs in the shower. My flock made it through the heatwave. Many people had animals who weren't so lucky.

⁓

Years ago, when I was still living in New York City, I spent hours transfixed by a livestream of a Brahman steer who had been on the run in Brooklyn all morning. He'd likely escaped from one of the many live markets that supplied fresh meat to a wide section of New York. He charged past pedestrians on busy sidewalks. People looked out of their windows and did double takes as they saw a cow sprinting by. He wound up in a field in Prospect Park where the NYPD tried to use soccer nets (and a lot of reinforcements) to corral the steer, who'd made a break for freedom. After a lot of near misses, the police trapped him in the dugout, between a fence and a police vehicle. The steer mooed. He was shot with a tranquilizer dart and tried, but failed, to jump over the police cars before the drugs knocked him off his feet. As the police moved in, the livestream I was watching zoomed out and over to New York Harbor, ending on a video of the Statue of Liberty.[138]

But rather than being taken back to a live market for slaughter, the steer was named Shankar and brought to live at an animal sanctuary that already housed another bull, Freddie, who'd gone on the run in Queens.[139] Freddie was only spared after public pressure coaxed the slaughterhouse into saving him.[140] This is a common outcome for animals who escape, whether cow or goat or chicken. Even proud carnivores seem bothered by the idea of *this particular animal* winding up as a hamburger or nugget even though millions of others like them die without notice every year. And this isn't just a phenomenon in the United States. In 1998, two pigs known as the Tamworth Two escaped from a slaughterhouse in England, were rehomed to a sanctuary, and had a family movie made about them. After a cow in Poland evaded capture for four weeks by swimming between islands, there was public outcry to save her. "She fled heroically," wrote a local politician, saying that the country would prosper if all citizens were as determined as this cow.[141] The politician helped rally public support to save her. Sadly, the efforts to catch her and send her to a sanctuary stressed the cow (who'd become emaciated from all the swimming and running and life on the islands) so much that she died of a heart attack. News coverage of these animals is always fawning; the outcry against sending them to slaughter is universal. By doing something unusual and daring, they seem better or more worthy than other animals like them. It allows us to rally around saving them while condemning the rest.

We love our pets but seem to look down on domestic animals, farm animals in particular, for being so biddable as to be domesticated in the first place. We yearn for the "untamed" wilderness, leaving unspoken our feelings about what we've tamed. Wild birds have millions of fans all over the world in the form of bird-watchers. Bird lovers buy expensive binoculars and travel to see new species but would hardly give a second glance to the birds in a backyard coop. The fact that chickens are so numerous has certainly led us to value their eggs and meat less than we did in the past. Their commonness has made most of us value them less as animals too.

As you're reading this, there are as many as twenty-six billion chickens alive on farms throughout the world. The only difference between them and the chickens in my backyard or living feral in tropical climates is that the latter were given the chance to be a chicken. And I was given the chance to get to know them.

~

We tend to think that the animals we raise for food are somehow different from the ones in our homes, that they need less stimulation and care than our dogs or cats, that it's not a problem to treat them like machines because that's what they've been bred for. And that's if we think about what their lives are like at all. In the early 2000s, news came out about researchers in Israel who bred featherless broiler chickens who could put all their energy into putting on weight and not have to be plucked after their deaths.[142] Nothing seems to have come of the project—yet—but it speaks to the fact that we breed chickens as though they're robots with useful features we can add on or take away.

Some scientists have started referring to the time we're living in as the Anthropocene, a proposed geologic epoch marked by visible human impacts on the planet and atmosphere. Imagine an alien civilization digging up our ruins thousands of years in the future. They would find remnants in the soil like microplastics, nuclear residue, and all the stuff we left behind in land-fills all over the world. A few years ago, I stumbled across an article in *Royal Society Open Science* that proposed the presence of broiler chicken carcasses, a species so distinct from chickens that they can't survive without human intervention, could be another marker of the Anthropocene.[143] Bird skeletons are usually too thin (and their bodies too prone to predation) for them to last intact in the wild. But there are countless billions of chicken carcasses mummifying in trash bags from our kitchens. We reshaped the chicken, and now the chicken could be a defining feature of what humans leave behind on this planet. There's a certain poetry in the thought.

Now maybe you're going to finish this book and have chicken for dinner. But everyone should know what these animals would live like in an ideal world and what we're making them live through in order to produce cheap food. Maybe knowing more will change the choices you make or the standards you demand for these animals. Maybe not. That's for you to say.

I often hear from people who have cut back on meat that they don't eat red meat anymore because of its impact on the environment but do eat chicken. And it's true that chickens have a smaller environmental footprint than giant beef cattle, but there's no cruelty footprint that's higher. The way we raise the majority of animals for food today, there are simply no guilt-free options. Since I stopped eating chicken, I notice it everywhere: chicken stock in soups, chicken meatballs at the deli, multiple restaurants that specialize in only selling products made from chicken. It's no wonder that chickens are not just the most numerous bird, but also the most numerous terrestrial vertebrate species on the planet. We kill more than sixty-five billion of them every year. In wild birds, the most popular species in human history was likely the passenger pigeon, which had a population of as many as five billion in the 1800s.[144] People say that the sky used to turn black when flocks of passenger pigeons flew overhead. The last one died in a zoo in 1914. We hunted the species to extinction. Today there are more house sparrows than any other wild bird in the world. With a global population of approximately 1.6 billion, they pale in comparison to chickens.[145]

⤙

At the very least, we are responsible for what we have created, and the domestic chicken—laying hens, broilers, and fancy breeds—is a thoroughly human invention. One thing I've always loved about having a flock with breeds of different shapes and sizes is that it surprises people, and surprise leads to questions. When people think of a chicken, they do not think of one that looks like Emmylou, my speckled bantam. She only weighs a few pounds and is small enough that I can comfortably carry her in one hand. She has a beard of orangish feathers around her face that lighten each year. Like all speckled breeds, her new feathers come in flecked with more white after every molt. Her feathered feet *should* look like bell-bottoms, but, due to a quirk of genetics, her foot feathers are nearly two inches long on either side. It's ridiculous. If I don't trim them, Emmylou walks like someone wearing oversized snowshoes. She's everyone's favorite.

Once, when I was sitting with the chickens in the yard, someone working on the house noticed her. "Look at her feet!" he said. He looked away then looked at her again. "Oh, wow. I can't believe it. I just can't believe it." He asked me what her breed was and where I got her from, not seeming to believe she could come from the same place as the other hens. "Just wow," he said, shaking his head in awe. His entire life, he'd assumed chickens were one way, and yet, here they were, something different entirely.

Over the years, Emmylou has gotten into more trouble, or just troubling situations, than any other hen in the flock. There was the time she flew up on the roof and refused to come down until it started raining. Sometimes she gets into all-out brawls with other hens who try to use the nest box when she's laying an egg. Then there was the hawk attack, when I found the rest of the flock in their usual hiding places but only a small tuft of Emmylou's feathers. I was sure she'd been carried away. My husband and I searched the yard for hours without luck. Every time I was ready to give up, I heard her squeaky voice calling. I figured that grief was playing tricks on me. Finally, Lyle thought to pick up the compost bin and check the tiny space between it and the garage. Sure enough, Emmylou had wedged herself in there and was hiding. She didn't have any injuries. The hawk had taken some of her tail feathers but nothing else.

Recently, she's decided to start hanging back from the rest of the flock when I put everybody inside for the night. Emmylou won't come in (or close enough for me to catch her) until she sees me grab a handful of treats and hold them out to her. Then she comes running. Even the chicken sitter knows that the only way to get Emmylou inside is to hand-feed her treats. That bird has us all trained.

The pleasure of having animals has always been in building a relationship like this: one where you know all their quirks and can tell stories about them like any other close friend. Domestic animals let us get close enough that we don't just get to witness and record them like a scientist in the bushes. We become part of their story as well.

ACKNOWLEDGMENTS

THIS BOOK SIMPLY WOULD NOT EXIST WITHOUT PEGGY, BETTY, Joan, Dolly, Emmylou, Loretta, Wanda, Harriet, Phryne, Scully, Olivia, Thelma, Louise, and Mr. (né Miss) Marple. Thank you for introducing me to the world of chickens and for sometimes sitting on my lap or shoulder so I can give you a pet. A related thanks to my dogs, Mesa and Bandit, for not minding (too much) that they have to trade outside time with the ladies.

It seems to be the convention of acknowledgment sections to save significant others for last, but I absolutely could not have written this book without the unwavering support of my husband, Lyle, who has been waiting for me to publish a book since our first date. Thank you for listening to me talk about chickens ad nauseam for years and still offering to build a bigger coop so I can have more of them. You are the best one.

I also want to thank my friends Christina Lane, Katie Lee, and Liz Unger for thinking a book about chickens was a great idea. Special thanks to Ella Hall, Rae Swon, and Anastasia Lugo Mendez for reading early drafts of the book and for being a sounding board when I needed to troubleshoot a tricky section. Your comments and perspective were invaluable. I'm lucky to have you all as friends.

According to family lore, the first word I ever spoke was "woof" while trying to communicate with a dog who took his walks past our apartment window. Thank you to my mom (my second word) for letting me grow up around a menagerie of animals and not getting too mad when I read at the dinner table. Thanks to my dad for writing me stories when I was little and to Joseph for encouraging me to write some of my own. I also want to thank my grandma, who might have scoffed at my modern chicken-keeping methods but who always asks how the chickens are doing when I call.

I first fell in love with journalism in college when I realized it meant whenever I had a question, I could just call up an expert and they would answer it for me. I've never stopped being grateful and amazed by the knowledge, passion, and so much time people have been willing to share with me. Thank you so much to everyone who let me interview them (and pet their chickens) while I researched this book. I'm honored that you trusted me with your stories. Thank you also to my wonderful chicken sitter Renée, who might love the ladies (almost) as much as I do.

As a journalist with only so many bookshelves in her home, I would have been crushed by paper if it weren't for the existence of the Multnomah Public Library system and their generous policy of letting patrons have up to one hundred and fifty physical and fifty digital books out at any time. I'm lucky to live here. Thank you also to the many digital services like Internet Archive and Google Books that have scanned copies of books and poultry journals that haven't been in print for a century.

Writing sometimes feels like a solitary process but this book wouldn't exist without a team of people who believed it should be in the world. Thank you to my agent, Zoe Sandler of ICM, for thinking I had a book in me before I was ready to admit it to the world and for making this whole "publishing my first book" process as painless as possible. Thank you to the whole team at Agate, especially Doug Seibold, Jane Seibold, and Amanda Gibson for being such champions of the book and answering my one million questions. Thank you also to Hazel Eriksson at William Collins for wanting to bring this book across the pond.

This book was made so much better by Clara Chaisson, who fact-checked certain sections. Thank you also to Maryn McKenna for generously lending me your expertise. Any remaining errors or oversights are mine and mine alone.

I'd also like to thank editors from my life as a freelance journalist who have not just let me write my heart out about chickens but made the work better and made me a better writer: Maria Godoy, Jesse Hirsch, Choire Sicha, Nicole Clark, and Serena Golden.

A few weeks after I started keeping chickens, I realized I was taking enough photos of them that I should probably get them their own social media account. Little did I knew that thousands of people would wind up getting to know and love my backyard flock. I've come to truly love my online chicken community, a rare and diverse place on the internet where everyone is welcome (as long as you love chickens). Thank you to all my fellow chicken people for your heartfelt comments and *especially* to everyone who ever told me they couldn't wait to buy a copy of this book when it came out. Your words always came exactly when I needed a boost to keep going during the four years it took me to write it.

Thank you, dear reader, for deciding to spend time with me and my flock.

WORKS CITED

1. Lu Ann Jones, *Mama Learned Us to Work: Farm Women in the New South* (University of North Carolina Press, 2003), 70–76.
2. Deborah Fink, *Open Country, Iowa: Rural Women, Tradition, and Change* (SUNY Press, 1986), 125.
3. "Per Capita Consumption of Poultry and Livestock, 1965 to Forecast 2022, in Pounds," National Chicken Council, 2021, https://www.nationalchickencouncil.org/about-the-industry/statistics/per-capita-consumption-of-poultry-and-livestock-1965-to-estimated-2012-in-pounds/.
4. USDA, *Poultry - Production and Value 2020 Summary*, April 2021, https://www.nass.usda.gov/Publications/Todays_Reports/reports/plva0421.pdf.
5. Yinon M. Bar-On et al., "The Biomass Distribution on Earth," *Proceedings of the National Academy of Sciences* 115, no. 25 (June 2018): 6506–11, https://doi.org/10.1073/pnas.1711842115.
6. Tove Danovich, "America Stress-Bought All the Baby Chickens," *New York Times*, March 28, 2020, https://www.nytimes.com/2020/03/28/style/chicken-eggs-coronavirus.html.
7. "Baby Chicks," *My Pet Chicken*, accessed January 29, 2020, https://www.mypetchicken.com/catalog/Baby-Chicks-c36.aspx.
8. "526 Mailable Live Animal," USPS, accessed March 1, 2022, https://pe.usps.com/text/pub52/pub52c5_008.htm.
9. Keith Strunk, *Prallsville Mills and Stockton* (Arcadia Publishing, 2008), 83–85.
10. Winifred Gallagher, *How the Post Office Created America* (Penguin Books, 2017), 206–7.
11. Tove Danovich, "The U.S. Postal Service Will Mail You Baby Chickens in a Cardboard Box. Yes, Live Chickens," *The Counter*, May 17, 2018, https://thecounter.org/united-states-postal-service-mail-order-chickens/.
12. Rebecca Dean et al., "The Risk and Intensity of Sperm Ejection in Female Birds," *The American Naturalist* 178, no. 3 (September 2011): 343–54, https://doi.org/10.1086/661244.
13. James McWilliams, "The Lucrative Art of Chicken Sexing," *Pacific Standard*, December 14, 2017, https://psmag.com/magazine/the-lucrative-art-of-chicken-sexing.
14. "Do Poultry Mourn Over the Loss of a Flock Mate?" *BackYard Chickens*, January 14, 2015, https://www.backyardchickens.com/articles/do-poultry-mourn-over-the-loss-of-a-flock-mate.67429/.
15. John Price, "A Remembrance of Thorleif Schjelderup-Ebbe," *Human Ethology Bulletin* 10, no. 1 (March 1995).

16. Gervase Markham, *A Way to Get Wealth, Containing Six Principall Vocations, Or Callings, in Which Every Good Husband Or House-Wife May Lawfully Imploy Themselves* (John Streater, 1668), 113.

17. F. C. Elford, *Farm Poultry* (Macdonald College, 1912), 58.

18. J. H. Postlethwait, "Cleanliness Is Essential," *Reliable Poultry Journal* 16, no. 4 (June 1909): 502–3.

19. CDC, *Antibiotic Resistance Threats in the United States*, 2019.

20. Christopher J. L. Murray et al., "Global Burden of Bacterial Antimicrobial Resistance in 2019: A Systematic Analysis," *The Lancet* 399, no. 10325 (February 2022): 629–55, https://doi.org/10.1016/S0140-6736(21)02724-0.

21. Laura J. Shallcross and Dame Sally C. Davies, "Antibiotic Overuse: A Key Driver of Antimicrobial Resistance," *British Journal of General Practice* 64, no. 629 (December 2014): 604–5, https://doi.org/10.3399/bjgp14X682561.

22. National Research Council (US) Committee to Study the Human Health Effects of Subtherapeutic Antibiotic Use in Animal Feeds, *Antibiotics in Animal Feeds* (National Academies Press US, 1980), https://www.ncbi.nlm.nih.gov/books/NBK216502/.

23. Maryn McKenna, *Big Chicken: The Incredible Story of How Antibiotics Created Modern Agriculture and Changed the Way the World Eats* (National Geographic, 2017), 504.

24. David Pierson, "FDA to Phase Out Non-Medical Antibiotic Use by Farms," *Los Angeles Times*, December 12, 2013, https://www.latimes.com/business/la-fi-fda-antibiotics-20131212-story.html.

25. FDA, personal communication, February 2021.

26. Maryn McKenna, "Antibiotic Use in US Farm Animals Was Falling. Now It's Not," *Wired*, December 14, 2021, https://www.wired.com/story/antibiotic-use-in-us-farm-animals-was-falling-now-its-not/.

27. "Over the Counter Antibiotic for Turkeys (and Other Poultry)," *BackYard Chickens*, May 4, 2018, https://www.backyardchickens.com/threads/over-the-counter-antibiotic-for-turkeys-and-other-poultry.1241745/#post-19926642.

28. Michael San Filippo (AVMA), personal communication, October 2020.

29. Tove Danovich, originally published as "The House Chicken," *Under the Henfluence* (blog), August 20, 2020, https://underthehenfluence.substack.com/p/the-house-chicken.

30. Nathan J. Emery and Nicola S. Clayton, "Do Birds Have the Capacity for Fun?" *Current Biology* 25, no. 1 (January 2015): R16–20, https://doi.org/10.1016/j.cub.2014.09.020.

31. Kelly Kazek, "The Battle for the World's Oldest Chicken," *Al*, April 11, 2018, https://www.al.com/living/2018/04/the_battle_for_the_worlds_olde.html.

32. Tove Danovich, originally published as "The House Chicken," *Under the Henfluence* (blog), August 20, 2020, https://underthehenfluence.substack.com/p/the-house-chicken.

33. David Segal, "Hype, Money and Cornstarch: What It Takes to Win at Westminster," *New York Times*, February 13, 2010, https://www.nytimes.com/2010/02/14/business/14kennel.html.

34. Peter Holley, "The Silicon Valley Elite's Latest Status Symbol: Chickens," *Washington Post*, March 2, 2018, https://www.washingtonpost.com/news/business/wp/2018/03/02/feature/the-silicon-valley-elites-latest-status-symbol-chickens/.

35. James Joseph Nolan, *Ornamental, Aquatic, and Domestic Fowl, and Game Birds: Their Importation, Breeding, Rearing, and General Management* (Published by author, 1850), 180–82.

36. Andrew Lawler, "Giants Upon the Scene," *Why Did the Chicken Cross the World?* (Atria Books, 2014).

37. A. F. Hunter, *The Asiatics* (Reliable Poultry Journal Publishing Company, 1904).

38. W. Wingfield and C. W. Johnson, *The Poultry Book* (W. S. Orr & Company, 1853), 2.

39. Samuel Orchart Beeton, *Beeton's Book of Poultry and Domestic Animals* (Ward, Lock, and Tyler, 1870), 426.

40. John Henry Robinson, *The First Poultry Show in America: Held at the Public Gardens, Boston, Mass., Nov. 15-16, 1849. An Account of the Show Comp. from Original Sources*, (Farm-Poultry Publishing Company, 1913), 3.

41. Robinson, *The First Poultry Show in America*, 8.

42. George P. Burnham, *The History of the Hen Fever* (James French and Company, 1855).

43. Robinson, *The First Poultry Show in America*, 13.

44. Tove Danovich, originally published as "There's, Like, a Lot of Chickens in Here," *Under the Henfluence* (blog), November 17, 2019. https://underthehenfluence.substack.com/p/3712137_there-s-like-a-lot-of-chickens-in-here.

45. Gabriel N. Rosenberg, *The 4-H Harvest* (University of Pennsylvania Press, 2016), 26.

46. Rosenberg, *The 4-H Harvest*, 34.

47. Rosenberg, *The 4-H Harvest*, 37.

48. Rosenberg, *The 4-H Harvest*, 43.

49. David Hudson et al., *The Biographical Dictionary of Iowa* (University of Iowa Press, 2008), 453–54.

50. Thomas Wessel and Marilyn Wessel, *4-H: An American Idea: 1900-1980* (National 4-H Council, 1982), 25.

51. Rosenberg, *The 4-H Harvest*, 51.

52. Rosenberg, *The 4-H Harvest*, 68.

53. Susan Jo Keller, "4-H Clubs Move Beyond 'Cows and Cooking' Image," *New York Times*, August 18, 1996, https://www.nytimes.com/1996/08/18/nyregion/4-h-clubs-move-beyond-cows-and-cooking-image.html.

54. Kiera Butler, *Raise: What 4-H Teaches Seven Million Kids and How Its Lessons Could Change Food and Farming Forever* (University of California Press, 2013), 20.

55. Cary J. Trexler et al., "Urban Elementary Students' Conceptions of Learning Goals for Agricultural Science and Technology," *Natural Sciences Education* 42, no. 1 (December 2013): 49–56, https://doi.org/10.4195/nse.2013.0001.

56. Katherine C. Grier, *Pets in America* (University of North Carolina Press, 2006), 197.

57. May Syme, "My Pet Bantam," *The Daily Colonist*, October 22, 1922.

58. Flannery O'Connor, "Living with a Peacock," *Holiday Magazine*, September 1961.

59. Iben Meyer and Björn Forkman, "Dog and Owner Characteristics Affecting the Dog–Owner Relationship," *Journal of Veterinary Behavior* 9, no. 4 (July 2014): 143–50, https://doi.org/10.1016/j.jveb.2014.03.002.

60. Christine J. Nicol, *The Behavioral Biology of Chickens* (CABI, 2015), 104.

61. Tove Danovich, "Chickens vs. Neighbors," *Backyard Poultry Magazine*, August/September 2020.

62. Glenda Cook et al., *An Evaluation of 'HENPOWER:' Improving Wellbeing & Social Capital in Care Settings*, September 2013, https://www.equalarts.org.uk/media/HENPOWERfinalreport.pdf.

63. Melissa Caughey, *How to Speak Chicken* (Storey Publishing, 2017), 44–45.

64. B. F. Skinner, *The Shaping of a Behaviorist* (Knopf, 1979), 241.

65. Keith Martin, "The Saga of the Bird-Brained Bombers," *NIST*, August 29, 2017, https://www.nist.gov/blogs/taking-measure/saga-bird-brained-bombers.

66. B. F. Skinner, "Pigeons in a Pelican," *American Psychologist* 15, no. 1 (1960): 28–29, https://doi.org/10.1037/h0045345.

67. James H. Capshew, "Engineering Behavior: Project Pigeon, World War II, and the Conditioning of B. F. Skinner," *Technology and Culture* 34, no. 4 (October 1993): 835–42, https://doi.org/10.2307/3106417.

68. John N. Marr, "Marian Breland Bailey: The Mouse Who Reinforced," *The Arkansas Historical Quarterly* 61, no. 1 (2002): 59, https://doi.org/10.2307/40031038.

69. Skinner, The Shaping of a Behaviorist, 266.

70. Marian Bailey and Bob Bailey, *The Best Animal Trainers in History: Interview with Bob and Marian Bailey, Part 1*, interview by Dr. Sophia Yin, August 13, 2012, https://drsophiayin.com/blog/entry/the-best-animal-trainers-in-history-interview-with-bob-and-marian-bailey/.

71. Marr, "Marian Breland Bailey: The Mouse Who Reinforced," 59.

72. Bailey and Bailey, *The Best Animal Trainers in History*.

73. "General Mills Contract," received by Keller Breland, *University of Central Arkansas IQ Zoo and ABE Archives*, September 17, 1947, https://www3.uca.edu/iqzoo/Media/PDF/Originals/091747_barnes.pdf.

74. Keller Breland and Marian Breland, "A Field of Applied Animal Psychology," *American Psychologist* 6, no. 6 (1951): 202–4, https://doi.org/10.1037/h0063451.

75. "General Mills Contract."

76. Breland and Breland, "A Field of Applied Animal Psychology," 202–4.

77. Animal Behavior Enterprises, Inc., *I.Q. Zoo*, June 19, 1974, https://www3.uca.edu/iqzoo/Media/PDF/061974iqzoo.pdf.

78. Michael T. Kaufman, "ABOUT NEW YORK; Cross Out a Landmark on the Chinatown Tour," *New York Times*, August 14, 1993, https://www.nytimes.com/1993/08/14/nyregion/about-new-york-cross-out-a-landmark-on-the-chinatown-tour.html.

79. Tom Vanderbilt, "The CIA's Most Highly Trained Spies Weren't Human at All," *Smithsonian Magazine*, October 2013, https://www.smithsonianmag.com/history/the-cias-most-highly-trained-spies-werent-even-human-20149/.

80. Marr, "Marian Breland Bailey: The Mouse Who Reinforced," 59.

81. Susan Hazel et al., "'Chickens Are a Lot Smarter Than I Originally Thought': Changes in Student Attitudes to Chickens Following a Chicken Training Class," *Animals* 5, no. 3 (August 2015): 821–37, https://doi.org/10.3390/ani5030386.

82. Humane Society of the United States, *An HSUS Report: The Welfare of Animals in the Chicken Industry* (December 2013), 6, https://www.humanesociety.org/sites/default/files/docs/hsus-report-welfare-chicken-industry.pdf.

83. "About Chickens," Humane Society International, May 2014, https://www.hsi.org/wp-content/uploads/assets/pdfs/about_chickens.pdf.

84. Christine Nicol, *The Behavioral Biology of Chickens* (CABI, 2015), 133.

85. Sraboni Chaudhury et al., "Role of Sound Stimulation in Reprogramming Brain Connectivity," *Journal of Biosciences* 38, no. 3 (September 2013): 605–14, https://doi.org/10.1007/s12038-013-9341-8.

86. Tsuyoshi Shimmura et al., "Persistent Effect of Broody Hens on Behaviour of Chickens: Persistent Effect of Broody Hens," *Animal Science Journal* 86, no. 2 (February 2015): 214–20, https://doi.org/10.1111/asj.12253.

87. Yvan Perré et al., "Influence of Mothering on Emotional and Social Reactivity of Domestic Pullets," *Applied Animal Behaviour Science* 75, no. 2 (January 2002): 133–46, https://doi.org/10.1016/S0168-1591(01)00189-7.

88. Nicol, The Behavioral Biology of Chickens, 139.

89. Christine Nicol, "How Animals Learn from Each Other," *Applied Animal Behaviour Science* 100, no. 1–2 (October 2006): 58–63, https://doi.org/10.1016/j.applanim.2006.04.004.

90. Tove K. Danovich, "I Have 9 Chickens. This Time of Year I Buy Eggs at the Store," *Heated*, October 27, 2020, https://heated.medium.com/i-have-9-chickens-this-time-of-year-i-buy-eggs-at-the-store-b1b43879ec91.

91. "ISA Brown," *ISA Poultry*, https://www.isa-poultry.com/en/product/isa-brown/.

92. Lori Marino, "Thinking Chickens: A Review of Cognition, Emotion, and Behavior in the Domestic Chicken," *Animal Cognition* 20, no. 2 (March 2017): 127–47, https://doi.org/10.1007/s10071-016-1064-4.

93. Andrew Lawler, *Why Did the Chicken Cross the World?* (Atria, 2014), 15–16.

94. Lawler, *Why Did the Chicken Cross the World?* 17–18.

95. Lawler, *Why Did the Chicken Cross the World?* 18.

96. Brian Brown, "The Wild Chickens of Fitzgerald," *Vanishing Georgia*, November 27, 2020, https://vanishinggeorgia.com/2020/11/27/the-wild-chickens-of-fitzgerald/.

97. Juliane Kaminski et al., "Evolution of Facial Muscle Anatomy in Dogs," *Proceedings of the National Academy of Sciences* 116, no. 29 (July 2019): 14677–81, https://doi.org/10.1073/pnas.1820653116.

98. Márta Gácsi et al., "Species-Specific Differences and Similarities in the Behavior of Hand-Raised Dog and Wolf Pups in Social Situations with Humans," *Developmental Psychobiology* 47, no. 2 (September 2005): 111–22, https://doi.org/10.1002/dev.20082.

99. Beatrix Agnvall et al., "Brain Size Is Reduced by Selection for Tameness in Red Junglefowl– Correlated Effects in Vital Organs," *Scientific Reports* 7, no. 1 (December 2017): 3306, https://doi.org/10.1038/s41598-017-03236-4.

100. Lori Marino, "Thinking Chickens: A Review of Cognition, Emotion, and Behavior in the Domestic Chicken," *Animal Cognition* 20, no. 2 (March 2017): 127–47, https://doi.org/10.1007/s10071-016-1064-4.

101. E. Gering et al., "Mixed Ancestry and Admixture in Kauai's Feral Chickens: Invasion of Domestic Genes into Ancient Red Junglefowl Reservoirs," *Molecular Ecology* 24, no. 9 (May 2015): 2112–24, https://doi.org/10.1111/mec.13096.

102. M. Johnsson et al., "Feralisation Targets Different Genomic Loci to Domestication in the Chicken," *Nature Communications* 7, no. 1 (December 2016): 12950, https://doi.org/10.1038/ncomms12950.

103. Paul Guzzo, "Ybor City's Free-Roaming Chickens May Have a Jamaican Grandpa," *Tampa Bay Times*, February 15, 2018.

104. Guzzo, "Ybor City's Free-Roaming Chickens."

105. Tove Danovich, originally published as "The Marvelous Mr. Marple," *Under the Henfluence* (blog), June 6, 2020.

106. Yi-Ping Liu et al., "Multiple Maternal Origins of Chickens: Out of the Asian Jungles," *Molecular Phylogenetics and Evolution* 38, no. 1 (January 2006): 12–19, https://doi.org/10.1016/j.ympev.2005.09.014.

107. James Gorman, "Before Chickens Were Nuggets, They Were Revered," *New York Times*, June 7, 2022, https://www.nytimes.com/2022/06/07/science/chicken-domestication-origin.html.

108. Maneckji Nusservanji Dhalla, *Zoroastrian Civilization from the Earliest Times to the Downfall of the Last Zoroastrian Empire, 651 A.D.* (Oxford University Press, 1922), 185.

109. Stephanie Lynn Budin, *Intimate Lives of the Ancient Greeks* (Praeger, 2013), 126.

110. Eric Csapo, "Cockfights, Contradictions, and the Mythopoetics of Ancient Greek Culture," *Arts: The Journal of the Sydney University Arts Association* 28 (2006): 18.

111. Selina Ching Chan, "Love and Jewelry," in *Modern Loves: The Anthropology of Romantic Courtship & Companionate Marriage*, ed. Jennifer S. Hirsch and Holly Wardlow (University of Michigan Press, 2006), 37.

112. Ivan G. Marcus, *The Jewish Life Cycle: Rites of Passage from Biblical to Modern Times* (University of Washington Press, 2004), 149–50.

113. Carolynn L. Smith and Jane Johnson, "The Chicken Challenge – What Contemporary Studies of Fowl Mean for Science and Ethics," *Between the Species: An Online Journal for the Study of Philosophy and Animals* 15, no. 1 (February 2012): 78, https://doi.org/10.15368/bts.2012v15n1.4.

114. Smith and Johnson, "The Chicken Challenge," 78.

115. David R. Wilson and Christopher S. Evans, "Mating Success Increases Alarm-Calling Effort in Male Fowl, Gallus Gallus," *Animal Behaviour* 76, no. 6 (December 2008): 2029–35, https://doi.org/10.1016/j.anbehav.2008.08.021.

116. T. Pizzari, "Food, Vigilance, and Sperm: The Role of Male Direct Benefits in the Evolution of Female Preference in a Polygamous Bird," *Behavioral Ecology* 14, no. 5 (September 2003): 593–601, https://doi.org/10.1093/beheco/arg048.

117. Carolynn L. Smith and Christopher S. Evans, "Multimodal Signaling in Fowl, Gallus Gallus," *Journal of Experimental Biology* 211, no. 1 (July 2008): 2052–57, https://doi.org/10.1242/jeb.017194.

118. Carolynn L. Smith et al., "Individual Recognition Based on Communication Behaviour of Male Fowl," *Behavioural Processes* 125 (April 2016): 101–5, https://doi.org/10.1016/j.beproc.2016.02.012.

119. Lawler, *Why Did the Chicken Cross the World?*, 101.

120. Jordan Curnutt, *Animals and the Law: A Sourcebook* (ABC-CLIO, 2001), 279.

121. Thea Lowry, *Empty Shells* (Manifold Press, 2000), 1.

122. Lowry, *Empty Shells*, 35.

123. Lowry, *Empty Shells*, 134.

124. Michael K. Boyer, *The Curtiss Poultry Book* (Wilmer Atkinson Co., 1911), 14.

125. Jerry Dennis Lord, "The Growth and Localization of the United States Broiler Chicken Industry," *Southeastern Geographer* 11, no. 1 (1971): 29–42, https://doi.org/10.1353/sgo.1971.0000.

126. Sara Shields (Humane Society International), in discussion with the author, April 2021.

127. Shields, in discussion with the author, April 2021.

128. USDA, in discussion with the author, May 3, 2021.

129. Sonia Faruqi, *Project Animal Farm* (Pegasus Books, 2016): 52–95.

130. C. A. Weeks and C. J. Nicol, "Behavioural Needs, Priorities and Preferences of Laying Hens," *World's Poultry Science Journal* 62, no. 2 (2006): 296–307.

131. United Egg Producers, *Guidelines for Cage Housing* (2017), https://uepcertified.com/wp-content/uploads/2020/02/Caged-UEP-Guidelines_17.pdf.

132. "Depopulation Cart," *FPM Inc.*, http://www.fpmne.com/depopulation-mak-cart/.

133. Clive Phillips, "Proposed Poultry Standards Leave Australia Trailing behind Other Industrialised Countries," *The Conversation*, December 1, 2017, http://theconversation.com/proposed-poultry-standards-leave-australia-trailing-behind-other-industrialised-countries-88302.

134. Tove Danovich, originally published as "Still Life with Thelma and Louise, My 'Ex-Batt' Chickens," *Catapult*, November 3, 2020.

135. "Industry Data," *Egg Info*, 2020, https://www.egginfo.co.uk/egg-facts-and-figures/industry-information/data.

136. "Facts & Stats," *United Egg Producers*, 2021, https://unitedegg.com/facts-stats/.

137. "PFMA's Tip Top Research Details Top Ten Pets," *Pet Food Manufacturers' Association*, 2021, https://www.pfma.org.uk/news/pfma-releases-latest-pet-population-data.

138. Tove Danovich, originally published as "Hooked on the Taste of Freedom!" *Topic*, 2018.

139. "'Brooklyn Bull' Died Shortly after Arriving at Sanctuary," *AP News*, May 3, 2018, https://apnews.com/article/07c80ef1d3fa43199aa50eefa5cecd44.

140. Ewa Kern-Jedrychowska, "How Freddie the Cow Managed to Save His Own Life," *DNAinfo New York*, January 22, 2016, https://www.dnainfo.com/new-york/20160122/jamaica/timeline-how-freddie-cow-managed-save-his-own-life.

141. Avi Selk, "The Briefly Inspirational and Ultimately Depressing Story of the Most Heroic Cow in Poland," Washington Post, February 25, 2018, https://www.washingtonpost.com/news/animalia/wp/2018/02/25/the-briefly-inspirational-and-ultimately-depressing-story-of-the-most-heroic-cow-in-poland/.

142. "Featherless Chicken Keeps Cool," *AgBiotech Net*, May 21, 2002, https://www.cabi.org/agbiotechnet/news/1365.

143. Carys E. Bennett et al., "The Broiler Chicken as a Signal of a Human Reconfigured Biosphere," *Royal Society Open Science* 5, no. 12 (December 2018): 180325, https://doi.org/10.1098/rsos.180325.

144. Bennett et al., "The Broiler Chicken as a Signal."

145. Corey T. Callaghan et al., "Global Abundance Estimates for 9,700 Bird Species," *Proceedings of the National Academy of Sciences* 118, no. 21 (May 2021): e2023170118, https://doi.org/10.1073/pnas.2023170118.

INDEX

C